MICHAEL
COLLINS
AND THE CIVIL WAR

MICHAEL COLLINS

AND THE CIVIL WAR

T. Ryle Dwyer

MERCIER PRESS
IRISH PUBLISHER – IRISH STORY

TO FIONA, DAVE, NORA AND FINN DEENEY

MERCIER PRESS

Cork

www.mercierpress.ie

© T. Ryle Dwyer, 2012

ISBN: 978 1 78117 032 8

10 9 8 7 6 5 4 3 2 1

A CIP record for this title is available from the British Library

Printed and bound in the EU.

CONTENTS

PREFACE

Although I grew up and received all of my primary and secondary school education in Ireland, I do not remember hearing anything about Michael Collins until I went to university in Texas in the mid-1960s. It was not so much that he was written out of Irish history, but rather the fact that twentieth-century Irish history was not taught in school at the time. It was still less than forty years since the Civil War of 1922–3 and it seemed that the wounds were still too raw to cover the period in school. That was understandable enough, considering that in Texas the wounds of the American Civil War, which had ended a century earlier, were still apparent.

My first introduction to this period of Irish history was while taking a course on European history between the two world wars. I wrote a term paper on the causes of the Irish Civil War. I had thought it was fought primarily over the partition question and was stunned to learn that the conflict had essentially nothing to do with partition. I went on to write a master's thesis on the Anglo-Irish Treaty, and a revision of that was published in the *Capuchin Annual* 1971, marking the fiftieth anniversary of the Treaty.

Since then I have written over twenty books on Irish history, and this book is the final part of a trilogy covering the life of Michael Collins. *Michael Collins: The Man Who Won the War* dealt with his early years and his part in the War of Independence, *'I Signed My Death Warrant': Michael Collins & the Treaty* covered his involvement in the Treaty negotiations of 1921, and this book deals with the final eight months of his life leading up to the Civil War and his untimely death.

In 1990, I was invited to take part in an RTÉ discussion programme. Other panel members were Tim Pat Coogan, Mary Banotti and the late Brendan O'Reilly. As a historian I felt distinctly uncomfortable when the programme began to sound like a case for the canonisation of Collins and, to some extent, the demonisation of Éamon de Valera. When I remarked that Collins was no saint, Joe Duffy, who was chairing the programme, joked that Mary Banotti – a grandniece of Michael Collins – had just fallen off her stool.

Some weeks later I received a letter from Liam Collins – who had given me access to the papers of his uncle Michael Collins – mentioning that he had heard the programme. 'I was very taken aback at the time by your contribution,' he wrote. 'Since then I have decided to read your publication *The Man Who Won the War*. And quite frankly I am very glad I did so. As I see your book, it recognises in quite a fair and honest way the pluses and minuses of the man.'

Having written and read so much about Collins, I did not expect any surprise findings while researching this study, especially as so much has been written about him in recent years, but I was to be proven wrong. Collins has become an iconic figure of twentieth-century Irish history. Like President John F. Kennedy, he was assassinated at the height of his career and the similarities do not end there. There have been many conspiracy theories surrounding both men's deaths and their love lives. For decades it seemed that nobody could suggest anything critical of Collins. However, his triumphs and failures should be kept in perspective.

What I found most surprising during my research was not that Collins was involved in the taking or holding of human hostages for political purposes, but that this has essentially been ignored by history. What was even more surprising was that history has also ignored the fact that Winston Churchill retaliated against Collins by sponsoring the same kind of hostage-taking.

My aim in my three books on Collins has been neither to deify nor to demonise the man, but to present a balanced picture of an individual who lived in exciting times, his many contradictions and the phenomenal range of responsibilities that he undertook during his relatively short life.

T. RYLE DWYER
Tralee

1

'WE WILL NOW CALL ON THE IRISH PEOPLE TO RALLY TO US'

After a protracted debate stretching over five weeks, with a break for Christmas, Dáil Éireann formally approved the Anglo-Irish Treaty on Saturday 7 January 1922. This was the first major step in the settlement of the Irish question and it marked a milestone in Irish history.[1] 'I do not regard the passing of this thing as being any kind of triumph over the other side,' Michael Collins told the Dáil immediately following the vote. 'I will do my best in the future, as I have done in the past, for the nation. What I have to say now is, whether there is something contentious about the Republic – about the government in being – or not, that we should unite on this: that we will all do our best to preserve the public safety.'

'Hear, hear,' said Éamon de Valera, among others.

'When countries are passing from peace to war or war to peace,' Collins said, 'they have had their most trying times on an occasion like this. Whether we are right or whether we are wrong in the view of future generations there is this: that we now are entitled to a chance; all the responsibility will fall upon us of taking over the machinery of government from the enemy. In times of change like that,' Collins continued, 'there are always elements that make for disorder and that make for chaos. That is as true of Ireland as of any other country; for in that respect all countries are the same.'

He called for 'some kind of joint committee' to preserve peace during the forthcoming transition, in which a democratically elected government would quickly take over the full reins from the British-appointed administration that had run Ireland from Dublin Castle for over a century. 'Now, I only want to say this to the people who are against us – and there are good people against us – so far as I am concerned this is not a question of politics, nor never has been. I make the promise publicly to the Irish nation that I will do my best,' Collins said. 'The president knows how I tried to do my best for him.'

'Hear, hear,' de Valera said.

'Well, he has exactly the same position in my heart now as he always had,' Collins added.

'I claim my right, before matters go any further, to register my protest,' Mary MacSwiney interjected, 'because I look upon this act tonight worse than I look upon the Act of Castlereagh. I, for one, will have neither hand, act, nor part in helping the Irish Free State to carry this nation of ours, this glorious nation that has been betrayed here tonight, into the British Empire – either with or without your hands up. I maintain here now that this is the grossest act of betrayal that Ireland ever endured.'

Some deputies later said that they thought de Valera was about to agree with Collins before the interjection of Mary Mac-Swiney. He responded instead by calling on those who voted against the Treaty to meet at the Mansion House the following afternoon.

'Some kind of an arrangement could be fixed between the two

sides,' Collins maintained. 'Some kind of understanding ought to be reached to preserve the present order in the country.'

'I would like my last word here to be this,' de Valera said. 'We have had a glorious record for four years; it has been four years of magnificent discipline in our nation. The world is looking at us now … ' At that point he burst into tears and sobbed uncontrollably. Others were also in tears.[2]

When the talks first began with the British back in July 1921, President Éamon de Valera had promised British Prime Minister David Lloyd George that he would submit British proposals to the Dáil and formally respond. Then, in early August, he wrote to Lloyd George that, as he had predicted, the Dáil had rejected the British proposals; but he sent this letter before the Dáil had even met, much less considered the document. When it did meet the following week, de Valera presented it with a *fait accompli* and simply asked it to endorse his letter of rejection.

After the Anglo-Irish Treaty was signed, de Valera issued a statement to the press: 'In view of the nature of the proposed Treaty with Great Britain, President de Valera has sent an urgent summons to the members of cabinet in London to report at once, so that a full Cabinet decision may be taken.'[3] He was essentially stating that it was a matter for the Dáil cabinet to consider. If the cabinet had opposed the Treaty, would the Dáil have been given any more say than it had with the July proposals? But the cabinet did accept the Treaty by four votes to three, and de Valera then announced it was a matter for the whole Dáil. 'There is a definite constitutional way of resolving our political differences – let us not depart from it, and let the conduct of the cabinet in this matter be an example to the whole nation,' he said. Once the Dáil had approved of the Treaty by sixty-four votes to fifty-seven, however, he said that only the Irish people could ratify it.[4] 'The resolution recommending the ratification of a certain treaty is not a legal action,' de Valera told a meeting of anti-Treaty deputies at the Mansion House on the day after the Dáil vote. 'That will not be completed until the Irish people have disestablished the Republic which they set up of their own free will.'[5] He kept moving the goal line.

Opponents of the Treaty established a committee consisting of de Valera, Austin Stack, Cathal Brugha, Harry Boland, Liam Mellows, Mary MacSwiney and Erskine Childers. They decided that de Valera should formally resign as president and would then run for re-election and that there 'should be no co-operation with the pro-Treaty leaders' in implementing the Treaty. They also decided that 'no action should be taken likely to lead to violence or civil war.'[6] De Valera told the Mansion House gathering that he would run for re-election on a platform of 'no co-operation with pro-Treaty leaders' on matters relating to the implementation of the Treaty.[7] If re-elected, he would not include any Treaty supporters in his cabinet.

When the Dáil reconvened on Monday 9 January 1922, de Valera formally announced his resignation. Collins suggested that de Valera continue as president with a joint committee to preserve peace, while the pro-Treaty side would set up the Provisional Government in accordance with the London agreement. 'No one here in this assembly or in Ireland wants to be put in the position of opposing President de Valera,' Collins explained. 'The practical step in my estimation is to form a committee, if necessary on both sides for some kind of public safety.'[8]

When the British parliament had called elections to select members for the northern and the southern parliaments in line with the Partition Act in May 1921, Dáil Éireann had used the elections to elect a second Dáil. Anyone elected to either parliament was entitled to sit in the Dáil. Of all those elected to the southern parliament, only the four deputies elected for Trinity College failed to take their seats in the Dáil. Six Sinn Féin deputies were elected to the northern parliament, but five of those – de Valera, Collins, Arthur Griffith, Eoin MacNeill and Seán Milroy – had also been elected to the southern parliament; Seán O'Mahony was the only Dáil deputy elected exclusively to the northern parliament. As a result he was the only Dáil deputy who was not entitled to sit in the southern parliament that was supposed to implement the Treaty.

Members of the Dáil had had no problems using the British machinery in the past, and Collins essentially wished to adopt the same approach in having the Second Dáil call itself the southern parliament to secure the implementation of the Treaty. He called for a new executive to be formed from the two sides of the Dáil to preserve public safety and to facilitate a British withdrawal as soon as possible, which was the essence of what they had been fighting for. 'We are faced with the problems of taking Ireland over from the English, and they are faced with the problem of handing Ireland over to us, and the difficulties on both sides will be pretty big,' Collins said. 'It does not matter what happens so long as we are assured that we are taking over Ireland and that the English are going out of Ireland.'[9]

'We will have to proceed constitutionally in this matter,' de Valera replied. 'I have tendered my resignation and I cannot, in any way, take divided responsibility. You have got here a sovereign assembly which is the government of the nation. This assembly must choose its executive according to its constitution and go ahead.'[10]

If de Valera was re-elected in those circumstances, Collins warned, 'everybody will regard us as being simply a laughing stock'.[11]

De Valera said he would 'carry on as before and forget that this Treaty has come' if he was re-elected. 'I do not believe that the Irish people, if they thoroughly understood it, would stand for it,' he added.[12]

'Remember,' he continued, 'I am only putting myself at your disposal and at the disposal of the nation. I do not want office at all.'[13] He was essentially saying that he wished to go back to private life but, because he was more intelligent and perceptive than most Irish people and could see things that they could not understand, he would therefore agree to serve them. 'I do not ask you to elect me,' he said. 'I am not seeking to get any power whatever in this nation. I am quite glad and anxious to get back to private life.'[14] It would be more than fifty years before he would actually retire from public life.

Arthur Griffith saw the president's tactics as a 'political manoeuvre to get round the Treaty' by exploiting the emotions of the deputies. 'There was no necessity for him to resign today,' Griffith said. 'His resignation and going up again for re-election is simply an attempt to wreck this Treaty.'[15]

The Treaty provided for a Provisional Government to take over the administration of the country from the British regime at Dublin Castle, and de Valera now argued that the pro-Treaty side should form a Provisional Government while he would remain on as president of Dáil Éireann to maintain the integrity of the Republic, at least until it had been formally disestablished by the Irish people. 'If the Provisional Government goes to Dublin Castle and takes on the functioning we will not interfere with them,' he said. 'Let them deal with their government as they please.'[16]

Collins tried to propose that Griffith 'form a Provisional Executive', but Eoin MacNeill, the speaker, ruled the Dáil had to vote on de Valera's nomination first. A roll call vote was then taken. When de Valera's name was called he declined to vote. It was his way of showing that he was not seeking the office but was just making himself available. He lost – but only by two votes – sixty to fifty-eight. Even if he had voted in his own favour he would not have won, but he would have lost by only the closest of margins.

The problems of implementing the Treaty in the face of obstructionist opposition soon became apparent. Article 17 of the Treaty stipulated that 'a meeting of members of parliament elected for constituencies in southern Ireland' should select a Provisional Government – all the members of which had to signify in writing their acceptance of the Treaty. But de Valera balked when Collins tried to have the Dáil set up the Provisional Government. It made no practical difference if the British said its authority was derived from Westminster, or if the Irish claimed the authority derived from Dáil Éireann. 'There must be a president elected,' de Valera insisted. He would not agree to the simultaneous election of the chairman of a provisional government. 'Try to proceed constitutionally,' he said.[17]

De Valera was adamant that the Dáil could not transfer any of its authority, or do anything to implement the Treaty until the Irish people had formally ratified it. He was contending, in effect, that there would have to be two Irish governments – the Dáil executive, which would be recognised under Irish law, and the Provisional Government, which would take over from the administration at Dublin Castle and would thus be recognised only under British law. However, the Dáil had adopted its constitution without ever submitting it to the people, so it had the power to change its set-up if it so wished.

In April 1919 de Valera had been elected *príomh-aire* (prime minister) of Dáil Éireann, but he subsequently changed the title without even consulting the Dáil, or any of his cabinet colleagues in Ireland. During a visit to the United States in June 1919 he had proclaimed himself 'president of the Irish Republic', because this would obviously have more appeal to the Americans. Before standing for re-election as 'president' in the Second Dáil on 26 August 1921, he had admitted that 'no such office had been created'. He rectified the situation by obliquely slipping the title 'president' into the constitution with an amendment limiting the size of the cabinet to seven specified officers – 'the president who shall also be prime minister' and the ministers for foreign affairs, home affairs, defence, finance, local government and economic affairs.[18] Now he was essentially insisting that members of the Dáil had to elect a president and that they could not call him chairman of the Provisional Government without the formal approval of the Irish people. Griffith resolved the wrangle the next day by giving in to de Valera's demands and agreeing that he would only act as president. 'If I am elected,' Griffith told the Dáil, 'I will occupy whatever position President de Valera occupied.'

'Hear, hear,' exclaimed de Valera. He had won his point. 'I feel that I can sit down in this assembly while such an election is going on.'[19] Minutes later, however, he changed his mind and announced that he was walking out of the Dáil 'as a protest against the election as president of the Irish Republic of the chairman of the delegation who is bound by the Treaty'.[20] He then walked out of the chamber followed by his supporters, in what could only be described as a contemptuous gesture towards what he insisted was the sovereign assembly of the nation. His actions seemed all the worse in the face of the conciliatory attitude adopted by his opponents.

Collins was indignant. 'Deserters all!' he shouted at those leaving. 'We will now call on the Irish people to rally to us. Deserters all!'[21]

Griffith was duly elected president without any further opposition.

2

'YOU ARE A TRAITOR'

Following his election as president, Arthur Griffith proceeded to call a meeting of the southern parliament. Only pro-Treaty deputies and the four unionists elected at Trinity College turned up at the Mansion House on Saturday 14 January. A speaker was elected and Piaras Béaslaí proposed a motion approving the Treaty, which was promptly agreed without a division. A further motion was then approved ratifying the appointment of an eight-man Provisional Government. Collins accepted the title of chairman of the Provisional Government. The Dáil cabinet had agreed to all of this in advance, so the members were just going through the motions – duplicating everything to satisfy both de Valera and the British. With the exception of Griffith and Richard Mulcahy, members of the Dáil cabinet were appointed to the same portfolios in the Provisional Government, so the two administrations were effectively being combined under the dual leadership of Griffith and Collins.

As part of the transitional process, Collins and his team of ministers went to Dublin Castle on 16 January 1922. He formally handed the resolution approving of the Treaty to the lord lieutenant, who then officially passed authority over a great many government buildings to the Provisional Government. In the process, Collins received his commission from the crown, but he obscured this with an exquisite piece of audacity. He issued a statement to the press immediately afterwards, announcing that the Provisional Government had 'received the surrender of Dublin Castle at 1.45 p.m. today. It is now in the hands of the Irish nation.' Thereafter, even historians have referred to what happened that day as 'the surrender of Dublin Castle', despite the fact that much of Dublin Castle was retained for the convenience of the outgoing British administration. Moreover, a garrison of Royal Corps of Engineers remained at the castle until August, when the whole place was finally handed over. The Provisional Government established Collins' office in the room previously occupied by the town clerk in City Hall.

The task confronting the Provisional Government was formidable. There they were, 'eight young men in the City Hall standing amidst the ruins of one administration, with the foundations of another not yet laid, and with wild men screaming through the keyhole,' according to Kevin O'Higgins, who quickly established himself as probably the most dynamic of the younger ministers following his appointment as minister for justice in the Provisional Government. 'No police force was functioning through the country, no system of justice was operating, the wheels of administration hung idle, battered out of recognition by the clash of rival jurisdictions.'[1]

There was a serious crime situation developing due to this power vacuum. Hamar Greenwood, the chief secretary for Ireland, had already reported to the British cabinet that there was an 'alarming increase in the amount of ordinary crime, particularly highway robberies and house breaking'.[2]

On 20 January Collins left for London, where he joined Kevin O'Higgins and Éamonn Duggan, the minister for home affairs.

They had been engaged in discussions to speed up the exchange of powers. The Provisional Government was authorised to raise money by overprinting British postage stamps with *Rialtas Sealadach na hÉireann* (Provisional Government of Ireland). The British also authorised the Provisional Government to collect the land annuity payments due to the crown as a result of the loan of money around the turn of the century to tenant farmers for the purchase of the land they were renting. The British were insisting that this money would ultimately have to be repaid to Britain, but Collins insisted on reserving that issue for further consideration.

Collins was taking on mammoth responsibilities as chairman of the Provisional Government, especially as he was also minister for finance for both the Dáil and the Provisional Government, which meant that he was in charge of fourteen different offices or departments, including the treasury, internal revenue, board of works, customs and excise and others of the old Dublin Castle regime. These would normally be taxing enough for any politician, but as chairman of the Provisional Government he also had to oversee the transition of the overall structures of government, which necessitated frequent visits to London. He was stepping down as director of intelligence of the IRA, but he continued as president of the Supreme Council of the Irish Republican Brotherhood (IRB). On top of all these he was required to play an arduous political role in defending his new regime against the constant sniping of political opponents, as well as overseeing the drafting of a new constitution, the establishment of a new army and a new police force, and preparations for a general election, or a possible referendum, to secure the ratification of the Treaty. In the circumstances he had to delegate a considerable amount of authority in the daily work on such matters, for example to Eoin O'Duffy in the formation of the new army, Michael Staines in setting up a new police force and James Douglas in drafting the new constitution.

***

Nine of the thirteen members of the headquarters staff of the IRA supported the Treaty, but a majority of divisional commanders were anti-Treaty. They met on 10 January 1922 to formulate their policy. Next day the four anti-Treaty members of the IRA headquarters staff – Rory O'Connor, Liam Mellows, Seán Russell and Jim O'Donovan – served notice on Richard Mulcahy, minister for defence in the Dáil, demanding that he call an army convention, or they would call it themselves. In response to their demands, Mulcahy summoned a meeting of the headquarters staff and divisional commandants to discuss the situation on 18 January 1922.

Many of those who had been most active in the IRA during the War of Independence had naturally kept a low profile during the struggle. They would have been known locally and within the higher echelons of the IRA, but they burst onto the national scene during the growing unrest generated by the Treaty controversy. The anti-Treaty officers demanded a full convention on 5 February to select an executive that would take over supreme control of the army from the minister for defence. Ernie O'Malley, who had been one of the more active IRA fighters, explained that he would not recognise the authority of either the new minister for defence, Mulcahy, or Eoin O'Duffy, who succeeded Mulcahy as chief of staff. O'Malley's remarks were a blatant repudiation of de Valera's statement a few weeks earlier that the army owed full allegiance to the Dáil through the minister for defence.

De Valera was opposed to the holding of the army convention and conveyed this to Rory O'Connor personally, but O'Connor made it clear at the army meeting on 18 January that he had no time for the Long Fellow.[3] 'It doesn't matter to me what he said,' O'Connor explained. 'Some of us are no more prepared to stand for de Valera than for the Treaty.'[4]

Collins appealed to the anti-Treaty officers to hold the line for the time being, because the British could not be expected to hand over facilities to the IRA if the latter withdrew its allegiance to the Dáil. For the next six months Collins played a double game. Publicly he supported the Treaty, while privately he tried to convince republican militants that he was as determined as ever to rid the country of the British, only now he was attempting to do so by peaceful means. Once the British had withdrawn, he indicated to his militant friends, it would be a lot easier to change the obnoxious aspects of the Treaty unilaterally. 'My idea is that if we can get our own army we can tell the British to go to hell.'[5]

In reality he was acting in much the same way he had conducted himself throughout the Black and Tan period. When in a tight situation in the past he would go up to the enemy and talk with them as if he were a sympathiser. Playing this double game came quite naturally to him, but now he seemed to be playing it with everyone – at times possibly even with himself. He wanted republicans to trust him, but Jim O'Donovan, the director of chemicals, sparked an unseemly row at the meeting of IRA leaders on 18 January.

'You are a traitor,' O'Donovan snapped at Collins, 'and you should have been court-martialled long since for treason.'

Collins jumped up in indignation. Even many of the anti-Treaty people present were incensed. There were shouts of 'apologise' and 'withdraw'.

'I will not withdraw the word,' O'Donovan insisted. 'It is true.'[6]

Most of the anti-Treaty people present wished to set up their own independent headquarters, but Liam Lynch, the commander of the 1st Southern Division of the IRA and a member of the Supreme Council of the IRB, would not hear of this, and Frank Aiken, the commander of the 4th Northern Division of the IRA, supported Lynch. Eventually it was decided that a full convention of the IRA would be held in two months' time. The meeting agreed that in the interim four men, two from each side of the Treaty divide, would 'act as a watchdog committee' under the chief of staff with a power of veto in order to 'guarantee that republican aims shall not be prejudiced'.[7] Mulcahy, who was to preside over the committee, did not like the arrangement, but he agreed to it in order to buy time. The committee, which was to meet the headquarters staff every Tuesday afternoon, never really amounted to much anyway, because Ernie O'Malley, one of the pair selected to represent the anti-Treaty side, was so determined to break away from the Dáil that he did not attend any of the meetings.

3

CHAIRMAN OF THE PROVISIONAL GOVERNMENT

At thirty-one years of age Michael Collins was confronted with the mammoth task of essentially reorganising the whole system of government. To make matters worse, he was obviously troubled by the growing rift between himself and his former colleagues.

'I am more sorry than you are that the president and Harry are on the other side from myself,' he wrote to a friend of Harry Boland. 'I believe they have missed the tide, for, were it not for taking the bold course I am certain this country would have been split by contending factions, whether we liked it or not. If there be but good will on all sides I am convinced we may still bring the whole thing to final success. In any case, we are going forward, the English are evacuating this country, and surely no one will claim that we can possibly be worse off when that evacuation is complete.'[1]

The Big Fellow was playing his double game on both the political and military fronts. He met General Sir Nevil Macready for forty-five minutes in his office at City Hall on 30 January 1922. The general came in mufti. Macready was already urging the British government to withdraw the troops as quickly as possible. Collins, for his part, was trying to get the British to believe that he was only stringing along the more militant republican elements until he could get the people to ratify the Treaty.

'Among the various Sinn Féiners with whom from time to time I came in touch, Michael Collins struck me as the easiest to deal with,' Macready later wrote. 'He had what few of his countrymen possess, a sense of humour, and, above all, the gift during a conversation of sticking to essentials. On several occasions, after the creation of the Provisional Government during discussion with him and his colleagues, he would call one of his friends who had wandered into the realms quite foreign to the matter under discussion to order, and complete the discussion with the least possible waste of time.'[2]

Macready added that Collins was, 'Tall, dark, strong but loosely built, with an apparent indifference to personal appearance, a *bon vivant*, an admirer of the other sex, and from all accounts a cheery companion when free from the cares of office.'[3]

One of the Big Fellow's tasks was to draw up a new constitution. He established a committee to do the work and wanted to appoint James Douglas as chairman. Although a Quaker from County Tyrone, Douglas was an ardent nationalist who had managed the Irish White Cross, established in February 1921 to distribute funds raised by the American Committee for Relief in Ireland for victims of the War of Independence. 'I said I would be glad to serve on the committee,' Douglas recalled, 'but I was quite unfitted to be chairman.'

Arthur Griffith tried to insist on the appointment as chairman of his writer friend Darrell Figgis, who had been national secretary of Sinn Féin. But Collins, who had been instrumental in ousting Figgis as national secretary in April 1919, balked at this idea. The Big Fellow appointed himself as chairman, instead, with Figgis as vice-chairman and the sole paid member of the drafting committee. Douglas reported that Collins told him 'that he might not be able to attend very often and wished me to report to him regularly what occurred at meetings when he was absent'.[4]

Collins did preside at the committee's first meeting at the Shelbourne Hotel. 'You are not to be bound by legal formalities but to put up a constitution of a Free State and then bring it to the Provisional Government who will fight for the carrying of it through,' Collins told them. 'It is a question of status and we want definitely to define and produce a true democratic constitution. You are to bear in mind not the legalities of the past but the practicalities of the future.'[5] In addition to Figgis and Douglas, the committee included lawyers Hugh Kennedy, James Murnahan, Kevin O'Shiel and John O'Byrne, along with the academic Professor Alfred O'Rahilly and the former civil servant James MacNeill, a brother of Eoin MacNeill, the initial leader of the Irish Volunteers. Collins delivered 'a short speech in which he said he would attend as often as possible,' Douglas recalled. 'In fact, he did not attend again as far as I can recollect, but I saw him once or twice a week for the purpose of consideration.'[6]

The committee undertook the detailed drafting of a constitution. In notes to Douglas, Collins indicated that he wanted one that would be short, simple and easy to alter as the final stages of complete freedom were achieved. He desired that it contain only what was necessary to establish a constitutional machinery to govern Ireland, and he suggested the committee omit everything already covered in the Treaty, such as the oath and the clauses dealing with the governor-general. He also asked that the authority of the constitution should be derived solely from the Irish people, and that no phrase was to appear which vested executive powers in the British monarch. In short, he was asking the committee to draw up a republican document that would be acceptable to the British, but this was essentially an impossible task.

Although Collins did not intend that the actual constitution should be ready before June, he asked that a rough draft be prepared by the end of February. He apparently intended to use this draft constitution to placate the republican opponents of the Treaty and then, once the people ratified the Treaty at the polls in April, the constitution would be completed. 'If they did not have an election till after the constitution was drafted,' Collins told the British on 5 February, 'the Treaty would be beaten in Ireland.'[7]

Collins was aiming to have an election in mid-April and follow this with the constitution in June, but he ran into difficulties when de Valera and the anti-Treaty side demanded that the electoral registers should be updated. W. T. Cosgrave was given the task of arranging the update, but he found that this could not be done before May, so it was decided to let the old registers stand.[8]

In late January Collins also set out to establish the new police force. Following the transfer of power to the Provisional Government, the British had promptly agreed to demobilise the Royal Irish Constabulary (RIC) and to transfer the Dublin Metropolitan Police (DMP) to the control of the Provisional Government. The Auxiliaries, the force of former army officers set up to assist the RIC, began withdrawing immediately after the handover. The last of the force were gone by 1 February, when their former headquarters at Beggars Bush Barracks, Dublin, was handed over to the forces of the Provisional Government.

At the first meeting of the Provisional Government it had been decided that the force would be put in the hands of a 'trained police or military officer'. Collins informed his colleagues on 28 January that a police organising committee was being formed. A meeting was called for the Gresham Hotel on 9 February. Collins attended and nominated Richard Mulcahy, minister for defence, to chair the meeting and Michael Staines to chair the police organising committee, with Patrick Walsh, a district inspector of the disbanding RIC, as its vice-chairman. Walsh was clearly the 'trained police … officer' who was being asked to organise the force. He had served in the RIC throughout the country – from Cork to Donegal.

The following day Staines was able to announce sub-committees to supervise organisation, recruiting, training and conditions of service. These included former policemen such as District Inspector John A. Kearney of Boyle, Sergeant Matthias McCarthy of Belfast, Constable Thomas Neary of Dublin and Sergeant Éamonn Broy of the DMP. All these had provided invaluable service to the IRA intelligence service run by Collins during the War of Independence. The following week the organising committee reported with a blueprint for the 'People's Guard', which would comprise 4,300 policemen. The nascent force set up a recruiting and training base at the Royal Dublin Society, which would provide its facilities at Ballsbridge until the Spring Show in May. The Provisional Government decided on 27 February that the new force would be called the Civic Guard, which was loosely translated as *Garda Síochána*.

The anti-Treaty republicans sought to frustrate the formation of the new force. Austin Stack was bitterly critical of the role of former District Inspector John A. Kearney, who had been head constable in Tralee at the time of the arrest of Roger Casement. The same day the RIC had arrested Stack. 'This man Kearney was, from my experience of him, one of the most vigilant servants the enemy had in this country, and he did his best – by open means and underhand – to beat us,' Stack said.[9]

This was grossly unfair. There was no doubt that Kearney had been helpful to Casement. He had called a local doctor, Mikey Shanahan, to treat him and left him alone with the doctor, who was known to have Sinn Féin sympathies. Afterwards Kearney showed Shanahan a newspaper photograph of Casement with a beard and identified him as the clean-shaven prisoner. He was not looking for information from Shanahan but informing him that the RIC already suspected the identity of the prisoner, so it was necessary to rescue him from the police station. Kearney warned his wife to keep the children upstairs as he felt the barracks would be raided. When Shanahan told Stack that Casement was being held, Stack pretended to believe the prisoner was a Norwegian sailor, but he already knew it was Casement, because he had talked to Robert Monteith, who had landed with Casement from the submarine that morning. Monteith actually told him that Casement was anxious to get word to Dublin to call off the Rising, which was planned for Sunday, because they were not going to get sufficient German help.

Kearney also sent a message to Stack to visit Con Collins, who had been arrested earlier in the day. Was this an invitation to Stack to come and rescue Casement? Patrick Pearse had informed Stack of the plans for the Rising some weeks earlier, and instructed him to do nothing that would rouse suspicions before the day. In the circumstances his decision not to rescue Casement might have been understandable, but when he went to the RIC station, he was carrying 'a large number of letters, i.e. fully 20 or 30 letters I imagine', according to Stack himself. These included letters from James Connolly, Bulmer Hobson and Patrick Pearse. The Hobson letter included a circular from Eoin MacNeill urging the Volunteers to resist forcefully any attempt by the crown authorities to suppress or disarm them. One must ask why Stack went to the barracks carrying such letters. When he was searched the letters were found. With the plans for the Rising so obviously going wrong, was he carrying the letters so that he would be arrested?[10]

Stack should have been explaining his own erratic behaviour rather than snidely questioning the conduct of Kearney, who had tried to help Casement and subsequently helped the IRA while he was a district inspector of the RIC in Roscommon. But in the aftermath of Stack's scurrilous allegation, Kearney, who had a large young family, found it necessary to emigrate to England for all their sakes in April 1922.

Collins resented efforts to depict as Black and Tans those policemen who had helped his intelligence service. 'The "Black and Tans" we have organising our civic guard are the men who remained in the RIC and DMP at the daily risk of their lives,' he told a dinner in Naas at the height of the controversy. 'Many of the greatest successes we gained were gained entirely by true men who stood for us in the enemy service.' The men who were helping to organise the Civic Guard were 'those men who stood with us always,' he said. 'We are not one bit ashamed of it. Not only are we not going to apologise, but we are very proud to have them, and very glad to have them.'[11]

4

'COERCION-OF-ULSTER
IS UNTHINKABLE'

Back in 1917 and 1918, when the various Irish parties met in the Irish Convention to try to address the changed political conditions in Ireland after 1916, growing nationalism and the call for independence, Sinn Féin refused to take part. De Valera accused the British of undermining the process by assuring Ulster unionists that they would not be coerced into a republic. Bolstered by the assurance, unionists insisted on having their own way and, when the nationalists balked, the convention inevitably ended in failure. 'It was evident to us,' de Valera wrote before the convention reported, that 'with the "coercion-of-Ulster is unthinkable" guarantee, the unionists would solidly maintain their original position.'[1]

Thus de Valera must have known that partition would form part of any Anglo-Irish settlement when he gave a similar guarantee in writing to Lloyd George on 10 August 1921. 'We agree with you,' de Valera wrote, 'that no common action can be secured by force.' If the British stood aside, the Irish factions would settle partition among themselves without resorting to force.[2] 'The minority in Ulster had a right to have their sentiments considered to the utmost limit,' de Valera explained to a private session of the Dáil on 22 August 1921, according to the official record. If the Republic were recognised he would be in favour of giving each county power to vote itself out of it if it so wished. Everyone knew what he meant: Counties Fermanagh and Tyrone, which had Catholic nationalist majorities, should have the right to opt out of Northern Ireland. If this were agreed, nationalist Ireland would have to accept partition or coerce the remainder of Northern Ireland. He was opposed to such coercion.[3]

The Treaty was concluded with the Irish delegation on behalf of the thirty-two counties of Ireland, even though the majority in Northern Ireland were not even consulted, but provisions were included in the Treaty to protect their interests. They were given the right to withdraw from the united Ireland within a month of the ratification of the Treaty, but in that event a boundary commission would be set up to redraw the border 'in accordance with the wishes of the inhabitants, so far as may be compatible with economic and geographic conditions'.[4]

The Treaty's provisions in relation to partition had the potential to be even more favourable than the county-option that de Valera had advocated the previous August, because in addition to Counties Fermanagh and Tyrone, the boundary commission could also transfer other contiguous areas such as the city of Derry, and considerable territory in southern parts of Counties Armagh and Down. Shorn of so much territory, Collins argued, the remainder of Northern Ireland would become an unviable economic entity, and hence he believed that the Treaty contained the means to end partition.

Lloyd George sent one of his secretaries, Geoffrey Shakespeare, to Belfast with a copy of the Treaty and instructions to tell Sir James Craig, the prime minister of Northern Ireland, that 'the boundary commission is for the whole nine counties [of Ulster] and not for the six counties, if option is exercised'.[5] Shakespeare understood this to mean that parts of Counties Cavan, Monaghan and Donegal could be transferred to Northern Ireland as well as parts of the other six counties of Ulster being transferred to the Irish Free State.

'We protest against the declared intention of your government to place Northern Ireland automatically in the Irish Free State,' Craig wrote to Lloyd George. 'It is true that Ulster is given the right to contract out, but she can only do so after automatic inclusion in the Irish Free State.'[6] On 9 December 1921, three days after the Treaty was signed, Lloyd George had told Craig that the boundary commission was little more than a technical matter. 'You explained that it was intended only to make a slight readjustment of our boundary line, so as to bring into Northern Ireland loyalists who are now just outside our area, and to transfer, correspondingly, an equivalent number of those having Sinn Féin sympathies to the area of the Irish Free State,' Craig reminded Lloyd George the following week.[7]

During the Treaty debate in the House of Commons on 14 December, however, Lloyd George indicated that the boundary commission would likely transfer Fermanagh and Tyrone to the Irish Free State. The British, in trying to convince Craig, said privately that the boundary commission would merely re-draw the border to provide for pockets of Protestants in Counties Monaghan and Donegal to be included in the north, in return for similarly sized pockets of Roman Catholics in the six counties, so that the overall size of Northern Ireland would remain essentially the same. It was hardly surprising that Craig could 'place no reliance on the personal assurance' that only minor adjustments were contemplated. 'The Ulster cabinet will refuse to take part in the boundary commission and will proceed to any lengths necessary.'[8]

'For the unionists the language of treason and confrontation had become a habit,' according to historian Paul Canning. 'They found it difficult to speak otherwise.'[9] Craig had ironically been a vocal proponent of a boundary commission before partition was introduced in 1920. The British cabinet was told in December 1919, for instance, that he strongly favoured 'a boundary commission to examine the distribution of population along the borders of the whole of the six counties, and to take a vote in those districts on either side of and immediately adjoining that boundary in which there was a doubt as to whether they would prefer to be included in the northern or the southern parliamentary area'.[10]

The northern unionists were more bitterly opposed to the Treaty than de Valera. They saw it as a betrayal. As a result the unionist press seemed to be more favourable to the Long Fellow than to Collins, who was variously described in the Orange press as a 'gun man', a 'dishonourable politician', as well as a 'conjuror', who was 'bereft of all honour', and was prepared 'to break his oath on the slightest pretext'. By contrast de Valera was described as honest and sincere in his ideals. 'One can admire the attitude of Mr de Valera, who is out for an Irish Republic or nothing,' one Orange journal noted. 'These Orange journals are keenly desirous of seeing Mr de Valera's policy prevailing,' *The Freeman's Journal* noted. 'If Ireland would only reject Mick Collins along with the Treaty, Carsonia [a derogatory republican term for the six counties] would rejoice.'[11]

This attitude was somewhat surprising. Collins had challenged de Valera to present his alternative to the Treaty during the Dáil debate and de Valera proposed what became known as Document No. 2. This included the six partition clauses of the Treaty verbatim. The only difference was a declaration to the effect that 'the right of any part of Ireland to be excluded from the supreme authority of the national parliament and government' was not being recognised, but for the sake of internal peace and in order to divorce the Ulster question from the overall Anglo-Irish dispute, de Valera said he was ready to accept the partition clauses of the Treaty, even though they provided 'an explicit recognition of the right on the part of Irishmen to secede from Ireland'. In other words, the unionists of Northern Ireland did not have a right to partition, but the rest of the island was willing to accept partition anyway. 'We will take the same things as agreed on there,' de Valera told the Dáil. 'Let us not start to fight with Ulster.'[12]

Although Craig stated publicly that he suspected that Lloyd George had given Collins a secret assurance in relation to the boundary commission, the Big Fellow publicly denied receiving any kind of guarantee from the British prime minister. Nevertheless he intimated privately that he had received assurances from members of the British delegation. Seán MacEoin, who had seconded Griffith's motion proposing the Treaty in the Dáil, stated that Collins did actually get a commitment in writing from Lord Birkenhead. 'If the six counties opted out of the all-Ireland parliament, the British government agreed that instead of one representative on the boundary commission they would accept Collins' nomination of their man and this gave the Free State two members instead of one,' Birkenhead wrote to Collins, according to MacEoin. 'This would rectify the situation in Ireland's favour.'

'Collins gave me that letter to read,' MacEoin explained. But the letter vanished after Collins' death.[13] It seems strange that nobody else ever mentioned seeing it.

Ernest Blythe rather contemptuously dismissed MacEoin's story. As a northern Protestant and a member of both Griffith's cabinet and the Provisional Government, Blythe had a deep personal interest in the Ulster situation, but he dismissed the suggestion that Griffith and Collins had ever been given such an assurance. Blythe later wrote:

> If you knew Seán MacEoin even fairly well, you would know that he inclines to give play to his imagination and his sense of the dramatic when he is talking about other people and wants to make his story sound a little sensational. I venture to say that no one knowing him even fairly well would attach any importance to testimony from him which on a matter not directly concerning himself, was intrinsically unlikely. Birkenhead may, like all men, have been foolish in some respects, but he certainly was not enough of a blithering idiot to write a letter of the kind suggested. Whatever he may have done during negotiations by way of innuendo or private hint to suggest vaguely the possibility of substantial transfers to the Free State we can be sure that he did not speak as suggested by MacEoin.[14]

Birkenhead was actually one of the British ministers who privately assured the unionists that the boundary commission would not transfer large areas. 'The real truth is,' he wrote to Arthur J. Balfour, 'that Collins, very likely pressed by his own people and anxious to appraise at their highest value the benefits which he had brought to them in a moment of excitement, committed himself unguardedly to this doctrine, and that it had no foundation whatever except in his overheated imagination.'[15]

Had Griffith and Collins ever been given such an assurance, Blythe believed that they would undoubtedly have mentioned it in cabinet. 'I was present at a good many cabinet meetings with both in the early months of 1922, and I never heard either of them say anything of the kind,' he explained. 'Of course both believed in making our maximum claim and both hoped for the best, and people may have confused what they said we should claim with what they believed we might get.'[16]

Blythe was present when Kevin O'Higgins actually asked Lloyd George what the twenty-six counties were likely to get from the boundary commission. 'He could not possibly forecast the decision of a judicial commission,' the prime minister replied.[17]

In his own account of a private meeting with Lloyd George just hours before the Treaty was signed, Collins indicated that the prime minister had referred to his predictions: 'He remarked that I myself pointed out on a previous occasion that the north would be forced economically to come in.'[18] Lloyd George had not disagreed with the assessment, but that is vastly different from guaranteeing that the territory would actually be transferred.

The following day, less than twelve hours after the Treaty was signed, Lloyd George actually told his cabinet that 'a boundary commission would possibly give Ulster more than she would lose'.[19]

If the British did give any such assurance to Collins, surely he should have insisted on getting something in writing. Moreover he should have insisted on a proper explanation for the qualifying phrase stipulating that the transfer of territory would be compatible with 'economic and geographic conditions'.

In the circumstances, stories about secret assurances must be treated circumspectly. There was no doubt, however, that such stories were circulating, and they help to explain both the confidence on the southern side that the boundary commission would transfer considerable territory and the anxiety among unionists.

5

'THERE WAS NO ULSTER QUESTION'

Both the nationalist and unionist communities of Northern Ireland saw the Treaty as a betrayal, though the nationalists would have been somewhat placated by the squealing of the unionists. Eoin O'Duffy, who succeeded as chief of staff of the IRA following the elevation of Richard Mulcahy to minister for defence, told the officers of the northern IRA when they met in Clones in January 1922 that Collins had only agreed the Treaty with the British as 'a trick' in order to obtain arms and supplies to continue the fight with the British.[1]

The War of Independence had developed very slowly in the north, because, unlike other parts of the country, the IRA in the six counties had to fight the Protestant population as well as the British. In fact, there was more hostility towards Irish nationalism in Northern Ireland than in any British city. There was a massive backlash, for instance, when the IRA avenged the killing of Tomás MacCurtain, the lord mayor of Cork, by killing the chief suspect, RIC District Inspector Oswald Swanzy, in Lisburn as he was coming from church with his father on 22 August 1920.[2]

Collins had sent two men from Cork – Dick Murphy and Seán Culhane – but the assassination had disastrous consequences for the Catholic population in Lisburn, as most of them were burned out of the area. Over 300 Catholic homes were destroyed there and the violence spread to Belfast, where violent mobs rampaged until the imposition of a curfew at the end of August. Over thirty people died in the violence, which was to have a profound influence on subsequent events. When GHQ sought to have the IRA burn Belfast in March 1921 – in retaliation for the burning of Cork in December 1920 – the IRA in Belfast balked at 'what they felt was a reckless and dangerously counter-productive policy'.[3]

There was little appreciation in Dublin of the difference and handicaps under which the northern IRA had to fight, and there was a distinct tendency on the part of GHQ to expect them to wage the type of war that suited the twenty-six counties. Questions must be asked about the extent to which Collins understood the reality of what was happening in the six counties. He visited Armagh, one of his constituencies, in September 1921, during the Truce. Eoin O'Duffy, who was at this time assistant chief of staff of the IRA and the IRA's liaison officer in Northern Ireland, preceded Collins onto the platform. While O'Duffy's remarks were largely ignored in the twenty-six counties, they did attract international attention. De Valera had been talking about settling differences amicably with the unionists, but if they did not go along, O'Duffy said, it would be necessary take appropriate action and put the screw on them by boycotting Belfast businesses. 'Sinn Féin would have to tighten that screw ... and if necessary, would have to use lead against the Ulsterites,' he told the gathering of some 10,000 people, according to a report in *The New York Times*. 'He did not make that statement as a threat,' he reportedly explained next day. 'He did not want to threaten them at all, but as he had said before those people must not be allowed to stand in the way of the march of a nation. The Ulster question, he asserted, would settle itself in a month's time without the shedding of a drop of blood if the crown forces cleared out of Ulster.'[4]

'In Ireland today there is peace everywhere except in the domain of this parliament,' Collins told the Armagh gathering. 'There is violence, disorder, bloodshed, intolerance.' If Ulster was entitled to self-determination, he insisted that Counties Fermanagh and Tyrone were also entitled to it. 'In those counties the majorities are with us,' he said. 'Are these counties to be coerced into remaining within a union which they do not wish for? Are the 300,000 Catholics in the remaining part of the area to be coerced into obedience to an authority to which, morally, they owe no allegiance?'[5]

Religious intolerance was 'the product solely and entirely of British policy' and it would 'quickly disappear when English force and fraud which buttress it up are removed,' Collins told the crowd. 'The Orangemen have been used as a tool in preventing what is now inevitable. The moment is near when they will no longer be of use as a tool, when they will, in fact, stand in the way of an agreement with Ireland which has now become essential to British interests,' he continued. 'Then they will be thrown aside, and they will find their eyes turned to an England which no longer wants them.'[6]

In Ulster there were five divisions of the IRA, three of which were centred primarily in the six counties of Northern Ireland. The 1st Northern Division primarily covered Donegal, while the 5th Division covered Monaghan and Cavan. The 2nd Division covered Derry and Tyrone, and the 3rd Division covered all of Antrim and the north-eastern half of Down, while the 4th Division covered the other half of Down and all of Armagh. That left most of Fermanagh in the Midland Division, under Commandant Seán MacEoin.

'Prior to the Truce in July 1921, the percentage of the Catholic population in the 3rd Northern Division that was in sympathy with the IRA was roughly 25%,' according to James McCoy, the adjutant of that division, which was centred in Belfast. 'Taking into consideration the proportion of the Catholic population to the whole, our support in the Division would have been something less than 10% of the entire civil population.' There were only 1,639 volunteers in the IRA divisions within the six counties before the Truce. With de Valera promising that Sinn Féin could settle problems with the unionists if the British would stand aside, a kind of power vacuum developed on the nationalist side during the Treaty negotiations, when there was a great influx of volunteers into the IRA. By October 1921 the strength had nearly doubled to over 3,000 IRA and violence became more pronounced after the Truce. According to McCoy, between two-thirds and three-quarters of these so-called 'Trucileers' joined the IRA for sectarian reasons – to fight the Orange gangs.[7]

More people were killed during the first five months of the Truce than had been killed in the last seven months of the War of Independence. During November 1921 there had been considerable unrest in the area surrounding St Matthew's Catholic church and a nearby convent in East Belfast. Despite a week of sectarian violence, the British had handed over security to the Northern Ireland regime on 22 November 1921 and one of the worst sectarian outrages occurred in Belfast that day. A bomb was thrown into a tramcar as it passed through Corporation Street carrying about seventy workmen from the shipyards home from work. Eight men were killed and nine others wounded. There was provocation on both sides, but each seemed to have a selective memory about the sectarian outrages.

It was 'Collins who more than any other politician would take on the role as unofficial leader of the Northern Catholic minority.'[8] He sought to impress the unionists by openly adopting a conciliatory approach, but behind the scenes he supported an aggressive hardline policy, seeking to convince the Catholic minority in the north of his sincere commitment to their cause and at the same time seeking to unite the IRA within the island as a whole to minimise the split in the south. If Collins or MacEoin really believed that the British were committed to handing over so much of Northern Ireland that partition could not survive, it seemed strange that both of them became deeply involved in a policy that heightened tensions in Northern Ireland during the following weeks and months.

While Collins was in London to discuss the transfer of power to the Provisional Government on 21 January 1922, Churchill arranged for him to meet privately with the Northern Irish prime minister, Sir James Craig, to discuss the possibility of developing relations between their respective governments. 'Can we come to some agreement – some agreement which will allay the horrors of the past, calm down the people, try to encourage the best elements throughout the whole of Ireland, and then leave the road open in some future time for the Ulster people whether they will come into your Free State or whether they will not?' Craig began. 'It is for you to decide on your future policy.'[9]

'Sir James Craig is not a brilliant man,' wrote Bertie Smyllie of *The Irish Times*, 'but he has the great advantage over so many of our present day politicians of knowing what he wants, and, moreover, having the courage of his convictions.' He had come to public prominence during the Boer War, when he formed a special force out of the South Down Militia to fight in South Africa. 'Craig may be right or he may be wrong, but he always is sincere, and forces you by his very sincerity to agree with him,' Smyllie added.[10] He had the facility to convince people that he was a moderate and conciliatory individual, and he was able to persuade British politicians that he was 'all that stood between them and the really intractable body of Protestant extremists in Northern Ireland'.[11]

Craig and Collins apparently got on well together. For three hours they discussed various issues affecting the future of the island. 'We were able to put our joint names to a document,' Craig explained. By so doing, he contended, the Free State effectively recognised Northern Ireland and established a precedent for talks between 'Irishmen who wished well to their common country'. They decided to try to settle the boundary issue by mutual agreement, instead of relying on the boundary commission. Convinced that large areas of Northern Ireland would be handed over to the Free State, Collins was hoping that Craig would come to an all-Irish agreement with safeguards to protect the interests of northern Protestants. He argued that it would be impossible to have two governments in Ireland.

They discussed the Council of Ireland that was supposed to be set up to co-ordinate matters of common concern between the Dublin and Belfast governments under the Government of Ireland Act 1920, which had partitioned the island. Craig suggested that it should be scrapped and replaced by joint meetings of the two cabinets. Collins proposed instead that joint meetings of the two parliaments be held, and he also advocated 'a meeting of all Irish representatives to draft an Irish constitution'.[12]

'The time was not ripe for this,' Craig had replied.[13]

In the end they agreed to try 'to devise a more suitable system than the Council of Ireland for dealing with problems affecting all Ireland'. They also agreed to meet in Ireland 'at a subsequent date' to discuss the issue of prisoners taken by either side since the beginning of the Truce. Collins appeared to make another big concession by agreeing 'that the Belfast boycott is to be discontinued immediately', though this was 'without prejudice to the future consideration by his Government on the question of tariffs'.[14]

Seán MacEntee, a Roman Catholic from Belfast, had first proposed a boycott in the Dáil during August 1920. 'The most effective action' that the Dáil could take against the 'war of extermination' being waged on Belfast republicans, MacEntee argued, was to forbid citizens of the Irish Republic to engage in any trade or commerce with Belfast firms. Ernest Blythe, a Belfast Protestant, responded that 'an economic blockade of Belfast would be the worst possible step to take'. He suggested that there should just be 'a commercial embargo against individuals responsible for inciting the recent pogroms in Belfast'. Collins opposed the boycott at that time. He protested 'against the attempt which had been made by two deputies from the north of Ireland to inflame the passions of members. There was no Ulster question.'[15] Collins would seem to have been justified in opposing the boycott, but he had only a very superficial knowledge of the depth of sectarian bitterness in the north. 'There is really only one small question in Ulster and it has its pivot in the Belfast shipyards,' he wrote to Art O'Brien.[16] During the economic downturn following the end of the First World War, thousands of Roman Catholics had been dismissed from the shipyards where ships such as the *Titanic*, *Olympic* and *Britannic* had been built. Collins seemed to think the sectarianism was largely confined to the Belfast shipyards. Arthur Griffith suggested that the Dáil just prohibit the imposition of 'political or religious tests as a condition of Industrial Employment in Ireland'.[17] This was initially accepted, but the embargo was also implemented within a matter of days. Although essentially designed to undermine partition, the boycott actually enhanced it in the long term because it weakened commercial links between the north and the rest of the island.

Following the agreement with Craig, Collins received the approval of his colleagues in the Provisional Government for the pact, subject to a couple of reservations. The Big Fellow might have thought those reservations were realistic, but Craig was never likely to believe so. For instance, the Provisional Government 'decided that a peace policy should be adopted towards Ulster pending their action in regard to inclusion within Ireland, [and] provided Sir James Craig agreed to reprieve condemned prisoners and to release men like Dan Hogan'.[18] Hogan, commandant of the 5th Northern Division of the IRA, had been arrested along with nine other Monaghan men in Dromore, County Tyrone, while supposedly on their way to play a football game in Derry on 14 January 1922. They were caught with documents betraying their real intent to spring three men under sentence of death in Derry Jail – Patrick Leonard, Thomas McShea and Patrick Johnstone – who were to be executed on 9 February for their part in the killing of two Special Constables in the jail during an escape attempt on 2 December 1921.

Pending Northern Ireland's acceptance of some form of unity with the rest of the island, the Provisional Government also emphasised that it was necessary to implement 'a policy of non-recognition'. Local councils in Northern Ireland were to be encouraged to refuse to recognise the authority of the Stormont administration, and the Provisional Government decided 'in every way' to support those councils. If the Northern Ireland parliament refused funding to those councils, it was decided that the Provisional Government would provide 'the necessary funds' and then seek a refund from the British government.[19] Having concluded the pact with Craig, Collins told colleagues that the boycott of goods from Belfast had been 'comparatively ineffective'. If it became necessary they could set up an effective tariff-barrier instead. They might still have to fight the north, but they should first try to settle their differences peacefully. 'A peace had been started and should get a fair chance,' Collins argued.[20] In return for ending the boycott, Craig promised 'to facilitate in every possible way the return of Catholic workmen – without tests – to the ship yards as and when trade revival enables the firms concerned to absorb the present unemployed'.[21] This was so vague as to fall distinctly short of assuring that the dismissed Catholic workers would get their jobs back.

On just about every issue Collins appeared to concede. He betrayed his own uneasiness, however, in a letter he wrote to a friend: 'They will have me for what I am not,' he wrote. 'The more the rigmarole of my life continues to encompass politics the more uneasy I feel. I am a soldier.'[22]

6

THE COLLINS–CRAIG PACT

The agreement between Collins and Craig was initially welcomed from Belfast to Cork. 'Its reception by the unionist press of Belfast and by both the unionist and national press of Dublin, was equally favourable,' Hamar Greenwood reported.[1] 'The prospects of a really united Ireland were never brighter than they are at the present moment,' *The Cork Examiner* declared in an editorial. 'Though the process may be gradual, it decidedly looks as if friendship and goodwill will displace prejudice and feuds in the better times coming.'[2] The agreement had a distinct impact on Belfast, which 'practically returned to its normal state', according to General Sir Nevil Macready, the commander-in-chief of British forces in Ireland. 'There has been a great diminution of both political and ordinary crime.'[3]

While Collins appeared to concede on most issues, he was happy enough with the agreement, as was Craig. It quickly became apparent, however, that each was engaging in some wishful thinking about the other's position. 'With regard to the boundary commission I think I have satisfied him, and he has satisfied me, that it is far better that the two controlling interests should meet together and work out a boundary which will be agreeable to those who are living on that boundary rather than have an artificial line, which may leave behind it constant irritation and a great deal of trouble with which we have been afflicted in the past,' Craig told a unionist gathering at the Ulster Hall. 'I can promise you here today that there will be agreement on the matter,' Craig added. 'He and I will be faithful to the bargain we have entered into, and there will be no disturbance of those people who would desire to go from under our flag to the Free State.'[4]

The Northern Ireland prime minister's use of terms such as 'our land' and 'common country' certainly looked hopeful, as did his acceptance that there would be no hindrance of those wishing to give allegiance to the Free State. When Craig said that, Collins thought it meant people in the border areas would stay where they were while their area was simply transferred to the jurisdiction of the Dublin government, whereas Craig envisaged those people moving themselves physically to the twenty-six counties. 'I will never give in to any re-arrangement of the boundary that leaves our Ulster area less than it is under the Government of Ireland Act,' Craig told a cheering unionist throng at the Ulster Hall on 27 January 1922.[5]

Collins later explained that it would be best if the border were readjusted by agreement:

> We had repeatedly said that the north-east had nothing to fear from us – that we would not coerce them or place them under disabilities. We also stated that the question was an Irish one, and given freedom from British interference, the good sense of Irishmen would soon find a means of adjusting it. The agreed removal of the British appointed chairman naturally tended to this end. It would obviously be better for us to agree to a boundary than to have a boundary imposed by the casting vote of a chairman.

A boundary so imposed would leave local bitterness, which would never even arise in the case of an agreed boundary.[6]

As the nationalists of Northern Ireland were not consulted before Collins concluded the pact with Craig, this led to an amount of uneasiness within that community. Bishop Joseph MacRory of Down and Conor was clearly worried about the pact, as people in the north thought it would be difficult to agree mutually on a boundary. Various deputations were sent to Dublin to express their uneasiness. 'A peace policy has been started and should get a fair chance,' Collins told Bishop MacRory. Although he had essentially recognised Northern Ireland by concluding the pact, Collins was determined to go no further. In essence he still pursued a policy of non-recognition of Northern Ireland, even though the bishop clearly had reservations about this. 'If the policy of non-recognition was adopted, the people in the north would have to fight alone,' the bishop warned.

'Non-recognition of the northern parliament was essential – otherwise they would have nothing to bargain on with Sir James Craig,' Collins contended.[7]

On 30 January the Provisional Government decided it would support local bodies in Northern Ireland that refused to recognise the authority of Stormont and that it would also 'so far as its resources permitted, finance schools in the six counties where the teachers and managers do not recognise the Northern Government'.[8] The Provisional Government was effectively offering to fund the Catholic schools of Northern Ireland, if they refused to recognise the Belfast regime. Some 270 schools and 800 teachers took up the offer.

Next day, Collins discussed the Northern Ireland situation with Joe Devlin, the nationalist member of the British parliament from Belfast, when they met at the Gresham Hotel. On the following day, 1 February 1922, President Griffith and Collins consulted with a deputation of over two dozen nationalist representatives from the public boards of Newry, South and East Down, and South Armagh at City Hall. Patrick Lavery, chairman of Newry Urban Council, warned that they were prepared to fight rather than be included under Stormont. J. M. McQuillan of Armagh County Council said that South Armagh had made the biggest stand by electing the greatest outlaw in Ireland at the time – Collins. If an attempt was made to place them under the Stormont parliament, he said, they would set up a little Republic of their own.

Griffith said he could not understand why those people felt they were being 'let down' either by the Treaty, or by Collins meeting with Craig. Under the boundary commission, Dublin and Belfast would each appoint a representative and the British would appoint the third member of the commission. To the northern nationalists this meant that the Orange element and their British allies would have a built-in majority on the commission. It seemed ironic to Griffith and Collins that those people who had complained that an English appointee would effectively hold the balance under the boundary commission, were now objecting that Collins had agreed to try to settle the issue directly with Craig. 'If Sir James Craig and Mr Collins do not come to an agreement,' Griffith said, 'the boundary commission comes into operation.'[9]

Collins reportedly told the visitors that in their desire to be part of the Free State 'they were only trying to force an open door'.

There were two ways of resolving the partition issue – by peace or war – and he and his colleagues wanted to try the peaceful approach first. They had prepared detailed maps reflecting the political views of the people by the counties, by parliamentary constituencies, by Poor Law areas and even by different parishes. If they could come to agreement with Craig on behalf of the northern government it would be so much better, but Collins stressed that members of the Provisional Government were not going to sacrifice democracy. 'They would give way to nobody who was not a democrat,' he reportedly emphasised. 'They could afford to be generous and he would give more for one Orangeman converted to national principles than for a hundred English Liberal or Labour converts.'[10]

Craig came to Dublin on 2 February to meet Collins at City Hall, where they were closeted together for over two and a half hours. They discussed the release of prisoners. Collins thought that Craig would release the nationalist prisoners and not execute the three under sentence of death in Derry, but Craig gave no assurances. When Dan Hogan and 'the footballers' had still not been released on 26 January, Collins had written a letter of complaint to Craig. 'I left you on the understanding that these cases would certainly be dealt with promptly with a view to release.'[11] Craig's reply had been moderate and conciliatory in tone: 'If the prisoners will at once apply for bail, I will direct the attorney general not to oppose.'[12] But Collins did not want anyone recognising a Northern Ireland court. Craig had welcomed the signing of the pact as an indication of recognition, but Collins was privately insisting that his new policy 'must be coupled with a strict campaign of "non recognition"'.[13]

The main focus of the discussion between Craig and Collins on 2 February was on the proposed boundary commission. Collins was convinced the commission would transfer substantial areas of Northern Ireland to the control of the Dáil. During the Treaty negotiations the Irish side had indicated that the northern parliament could retain its existing powers, provided the powers reserved by the Westminster parliament were transferred to Dublin. In effect, Collins was using the boundary commission as a threat to mutilate the six counties of Northern Ireland if Stormont did not agree to an accommodation with the Dáil. But this threat had little chance of working because 'Craig was given to understand privately by several British ministers' that the boundary commission would just alter the boundary line rather than transfer large areas.[14] It seemed extraordinary that the two men did not realise at their first meeting that their interpretations of the purpose of the boundary commission were so different. 'The astonishing thing is that the two Irish leaders could have met for five minutes in London without discovering that someone had blundered,' *The Irish Times* noted.[15]

Following their meeting in Dublin, both Collins and Craig gave interviews to the Press Association explaining their positions. 'We were dealing merely with a ratification of our border line,' Craig explained. 'It appears to me to be fair and reasonable that any part of the boundary under discussion in regard to which we could not come to an agreement would remain as drafted in the Government of Ireland Act of 1920.' In other words, the boundary would remain the same unless the two Irish sides agreed otherwise. From maps produced at this latest meeting, however, Craig concluded that Collins had been promised 'almost half of

Northern Ireland, including the counties of Fermanagh, Tyrone, large parts of the counties of Armagh and Down, Derry City, Enniskillen and Newry'.[16]

Craig continued, 'After my conference with Mr Collins yesterday, the difficulties in regard to the boundary commission have been revived in an acute and serious form.'[17]

'Everybody on the British and Irish delegation perfectly understood that the boundary commission would mean the loss of Tyrone and Fermanagh to the north-east parliament,' Collins explained in his interview. 'Sir James Craig made it clear to me at the termination of the interview on Thursday that he regarded himself as having been tricked by British statesmen.'[18]

Craig's brother, Captain Charles C. Craig, a unionist member of parliament for South Antrim, told members of his local unionist association that Lloyd George and his colleagues 'had been guilty of the most horrible deception and double faced conduct towards them'. He said that Northern Ireland had already given up three counties of Ulster. 'If any attempt were made by the people in the south to take away large portions of the six counties, there would be no other result than a renewal of Civil War,' he warned.[19]

Churchill's wife, Clementine, on the other hand, suspected that Lloyd George had deceived Collins, but she realised that Craig had grounds for uneasiness. 'Surely the PM must have misled Collins over the Ulster boundary?' she wrote to her husband. 'I do hope Craig will not think he has been treated in a slippery way.'[20]

Churchill was clearly uncomfortable himself. 'Ireland is sure to bring us every form of difficulty and embarrassment,' he replied to his wife. 'I expect I shall have to bear the brunt of it in the House of Commons.'[21]

'At no time was there any question of being misled by Mr Lloyd George. I never went on any opinion of his on the subject. It was a matter for the inhabitants of the area involved and for them only,' Collins insisted. [22]

'It was on the plain interpretation of these words that I had taken my stand,' Collins explained.[23] But there was the added qualification stipulating that the transfer of territory would be 'so far as may be compatible with economic and geographic conditions'. This qualification was supposedly added to ensure that isolated nationalist areas like the Glens of Antrim or West Belfast, or Protestant areas of Dublin would not be transferred, but the danger that the phrase could be interpreted differently should have been apparent.

Before very long T. M. Healy, a seasoned political activist going back to the era of Charles Stewart Parnell in the 1880s, recognised that Lloyd George could be ousted from Downing Street and that his most likely successor, Andrew Bonar Law, would have very little sympathy with Dublin on the boundary issue. Bonar Law had resigned as Conservative leader for health reasons in 1920, but had since recovered his health and was an obvious alternative to Lloyd George, especially when the Conservatives were in a unique position of having a comfortable overall majority of their own in parliament. They were supporting the Liberal Lloyd George as prime minister because they had fought the 1918 election as a coalition, but they could bring him down at will. During the Treaty negotiations there was considerable uneasiness in Lloyd George's circles when Bonar Law became politically active again. Before the end of 1922, he would replace Lloyd George as prime minister.

'I met Bonar Law yesterday, and I could see he is bitter against any change being made in the Ulster boundary,' Healy wrote on 20 March 1922. 'If Lloyd George resigns, Bonar will be prime minister, and will hardly appoint a friendly umpire of the boundary commission.'[24]

It was naïve of Griffith and Collins to put such faith in the boundary proposals. Most members of the Dáil accepted Collins' interpretation, which explains why there had been so little opposition to the partition clauses of the Treaty. Why did people so readily accept this interpretation?

7

Taking Hostages

On 4 February 1922, President Griffith, Michael Collins, Kevin O'Higgins and Eoin MacNeill met at City Hall with a nine-person delegation from Derry, headed by the mayor of the city, Hugh C. O'Doherty. The deputation was lobbying for the city of Derry to be transferred to the Irish Free State. Collins suggested that a committee of people representing a wide section of nationalist opinion in Ulster be set up to advise the Provisional Government. Anti-partition, he said, 'was one common platform on which all nationalists in the area could stand'. When Mayor O'Doherty raised the issue of the three men due to be executed in Derry on 9 February, Collins assured the delegation that 'this matter had been engaging the constant attention of the Provisional Government'. He added that 'every effort was being made on their behalf'.[1]

Part of the loyalty that Collins attracted was prompted by the sense of caring that he projected. Men believed that he really cared about them as individuals and would go to extraordinary lengths to try to rescue them. Indeed, he seemed ready to go to such lengths to rescue the three – Leonard, McShea and Johnstone – in Derry, but publicly he tried to project a reasonable approach to affairs.

'We are determined on a peace policy in the north-east,' Collins declared publicly on 3 February.[2] 'Our attitude has been made perfectly clear, and it is that we will not coerce any part of

Ulster which is desirous of remaining in the area controlled by the northern parliament,' he told a Press Association reporter in London three days later. 'But neither will we allow the coercion of any part of Ulster which votes itself into the Irish Free State.'[3]

When asked if the Belfast boycott would be reintroduced, Collins prevaricated. 'I cannot say what our policy would be in the event of certain eventualities,' he replied. 'We are a reasonable people, and if the other people prove reasonable there will be no difficulty.'[4]

Having joined Griffith for talks with Lloyd George, Collins then went to the colonial office to meet Churchill and later met with Lord Birkenhead, the lord chancellor. Collins complained about the way the British essentially lynched Roger Casement and also blackened his moral character with his alleged diaries to prejudice his cause. With Collins professing absolute faith in Casement, Birkenhead invited him to see the diaries at the archives of the House of Lords where they were being stored. The Big Fellow and Éamonn Duggan took Birkenhead up on his offer and afterwards Collins told a friend that he was 'very familiar with Casement's handwriting' and if the diary that he saw 'was not authentic, it was a devilishly clever forgery'.[5]

Collins left Griffith in London and returned to Dublin on 6 February. He was, of course, extremely busy establishing the Provisional Government, but he was also involved in a very dangerous plot both to prevent the executions of the three men in Derry and to obtain the release of the 'footballers' being held on suspicion of trying to rescue them.

Eoin O'Duffy, put in charge of Beggars Bush Barracks on 1 February 1922 and organising a new army on behalf of the

Provisional Government, warned Collins that there was 'grave consternation' in Counties Monaghan, Cavan, Fermanagh and Tyrone over the continued detention by the northern authorities of Commandant Dan Hogan and members of the 5th Northern Division. Hogan was a brother of Michael Hogan, the Tipperary footballer killed on the field in Croke Park on Bloody Sunday. The IRA in border areas was demanding O'Duffy's authority 'to take immediate action to bring public opinion to bear on the situation'. Being from Monaghan, O'Duffy knew the local scene well and felt the whole thing had serious political implications for the forthcoming Sinn Féin Ard-Fheis. 'There are 54 affiliated clubs in Co. Monaghan and each of them are sending two delegates to the Ard-Fheis,' he wrote. 'This means 108 votes for Monaghan for the Treaty.'[6]

Collins had been instrumental in establishing a unified force called the Ulster Council, Northern Command or Northern Military Council to deal with the partition issue. It was created to co-ordinate activities within the six counties. Frank Aiken, from the anti-Treaty side north of the border, was selected to head the command, with Seán MacEoin, the pro-Treaty TD from the southern side of the border, as deputy leader. They arranged the kidnapping of prominent northern unionists to be held as hostages to block the three executions in Derry and to secure the release of the 'Monaghan footballers'. Eoin O'Duffy took a leading part with the Northern Command: 'I have arranged for the kidnapping of 100 prominent Orangemen in Counties Fermanagh and Tyrone,' O'Duffy wrote to Collins on 30 January. 'This was to take place last Tuesday, the 24 inst., but on account of the agreement arrived at between Sir James Craig and yourself I postponed action until tomorrow, Tuesday 31st inst. And failing to hear from you to the contrary the kidnapping will commence at 7 o'clock tomorrow evening.'[7]

The kidnappings were postponed, not because of any reservations on the part of Collins, but because he was due to go to London for further talks that week. In December 1918 he had actually advocated kidnapping President Woodrow Wilson of the United States. Collins was part of a four-man delegation sent to London – along with George Gavan Duffy, Seán T. O'Kelly, and Robert Barton – to try to explain the Irish situation to the American president during a stopover in London on his way to the Paris Peace Talks. 'We never got any nearer to him than a second secretary in the American Embassy,' Barton recalled. 'We had no success at all.' Collins was so annoyed at being given the cold shoulder that he suggested seizing Wilson to make him listen. 'If necessary,' he said, 'we can buccaneer him.' Maybe the Big Fellow was just letting off steam, but it provides insight into why some friends thought he was inclined to allow his enthusiasm for action to get the better of his judgement. This was essentially why they chose Richard Mulcahy as chief of staff of the IRA over Collins in early 1919.[8]

The hundred kidnappings proposed by O'Duffy were delayed until the Big Fellow's return from London on 6 February 1922. Units of the IRA crossed the border the next day, kidnapped forty-three unionists in Counties Fermanagh, Tyrone and Armagh, and then brought them south of the border. They were held hostage even though the three death sentences had already been commuted by the British government to prison terms. The IRA managed to take less than half of the targets because some of the units ran into stout resistance. After James Cooper, a member of the Stormont parliament, fended off the would-be kidnappers with a shotgun, the RIC and Special Constabulary were roused, and they arrested fifteen of the IRA volunteers involved in the raids in the Enniskillen area. Eleven of these were from Leitrim and Longford, and the other four were local volunteers who were acting as guides. The Ulster Special Constables (USC) were auxiliary policemen, who were generally recruited from the Ulster Volunteer Force, which was initially established in 1912 to resist Home Rule. The Special Constables were divided into three categories – the A Specials were a full-time force, while the B Specials were part-time members and the C Specials were reserves. They were overwhelmingly northern Protestants, as any Catholic who joined was ostracised within his own community.

The panic aroused by the kidnappings in the Orange community led to fears that as many as twice the intended number had actually been kidnapped. *The Irish Times* reported 'that 200 prisoners were taken in all at various points on the border'.[9] Captain Charles Craig, a brother of Sir James Craig, asked in the House of Commons if 200 had been taken hostage by the Free State.[10] The following day *The Irish Times* reported that 'some 70 "B Specials" and Unionists' were being held by the IRA in Ballybay Barracks.[11]

Hamar Greenwood informed the cabinet that the raids 'appear to have been carried out by local units of the IRA acting without the authority or prior knowledge of the Dublin headquarters of the organisation'. He added that 'the prompt action of the Provisional Government in dissociating themselves from these IRA activities and in promising that vigorous action would be taken to effect the early release of the kidnapped persons undoubtedly saved a very awkward situation, which at one time seemed not unlikely to develop on lines which might have ended in the complete frustration of all hopes of Irish peace'.[12]

Alfred (Andy) Cope, one of the assistant under-secretaries in what was left of the British administration at Dublin Castle, assured London that members of the Provisional Government 'are doing their best' in difficult circumstances. 'Collins has had great difficulty in holding in certain sections of the IRA who were out for hostages,' Cope wrote.[13]

Collins acted as if the whole thing was predictable behaviour on the part of disgruntled elements of the IRA over whom he had no control. It was essentially the British who had introduced the practice of hostage-taking during the War of Independence, when the Black and Tans and Auxiliaries seized people off the streets and took them on their trucks in an attempt to ensure that they would not be attacked or bombed. This was done with the full knowledge and, thus, the approval of the British cabinet. A year earlier, almost to the very day, for instance, General Sir Nevil Macready reported to the cabinet that a raid on the office of IRA Chief of Staff Richard Mulcahy had uncovered evidence suggesting that the British hostage-taking was successful. 'It is of interest to know from some of the documents captured in Mulcahy's office,' Macready wrote on 8 February 1921, 'that a Battalion Commander reported he had found some difficulty in overcoming the objections of his men to fire on lorries carrying hostages.'[14] Collins depicted members of the IRA as naturally outraged by the impending executions in Derry, but in denying any involvement in the seizing of loyalist hostages on 7 February 1922, he was not only misleading the British but also shamelessly deceiving some of his own colleagues.

President Griffith, who was still engaged in talks with the British in London at the time of the raids, reported that diehards in Britain were depicting the hostage-taking operation 'as an invasion of Ulster'.[15] He came under pressure from the British. 'If your people are going to pop into Ulster and take off hostages every time the Northern Government enforces the law in a way you dislike,' Churchill warned, 'there will be reprisals and we will have a fortified frontier and we will have to put there Imperial troops because they would be more impartial than Northern Ireland troops.'[16] Griffith asked Collins to issue an immediate repudiation of the supposed 'invasion' and provide an assurance that 'every possible step will be taken to have these hostages released and to prevent the malign influence at work in England against the Treaty from scoring a success'.[17]

Collins essentially blamed the procrastination in reprieving the three prisoners under sentence of death in Derry for generating the anxiety that led to the kidnappings in Northern Ireland. 'Throughout yesterday I was extremely anxious as to what might happen in view of pending executions of the three men in Derry prison,' Collins wrote to Lloyd George. 'I made special efforts to prevent acts of violence on the part of my people and as soon as I heard of reprieve last night I took steps to have information conveyed without delay to leading men on border in order to allay anxiety and to ensure against any untoward incident.' He assured the British prime minister that the members of the Provisional Government 'are making every effort to get the situation under control'.[18]

It was a volatile situation. Northern Irish Prime Minister Sir James Craig asked Churchill if there was 'any legal obstacle to our sending a flying column of 5,000 constabulary to recover the kidnapped loyalists'. He also suggested that British troops should occupy certain border areas in the twenty-six counties and retain those areas pending the safe return of those kidnapped.[19]

'Violent measures would do more harm than good and might entail the resignation of the Irish Provisional Government, thus creating chaos and leaving the extremists in control,' Churchill replied.[20] But he did promptly suspend the withdrawal of British troops from Ireland, because he obviously felt that they might have to occupy the border area to keep the contesting Irish sides apart. He did not suspect members of the Provisional Government, as they were 'taking vigorous measures to secure the release of the persons who were illegally captured,' Churchill assured the House of Commons. 'Some allowance must be made for Ministers who have only just assumed the responsibility of office, who are not in full possession of lawful and duly constituted power, and who have only partial control of the forces for the maintenance of law and order. We have every reason to be believe that they are doing their best in the very difficult circumstances in which they find themselves.'[21]

De Valera had no involvement in the kidnappings, but some newspapers mistakenly thought that he was behind them. 'As has been stated in the papers these were engineered by de Valera and his party who got hold of local sections of the IRA,' the British cabinet secretary, Tom Jones, noted. 'It is hoped that Collins is re-establishing his authority.'[22] Jones and other British officials allowed themselves to be deluded by press reports and by their own wishful thinking that Collins was acting in a strictly honourable way.

In a perceptive editorial, *The Irish Times* denounced the kidnappings as 'atrocious stupidity'. 'Morally, the raids were utterly indefensible and, politically, their effects may be calamitous. There is grave danger that they may provoke outbreaks of violence along the whole northern frontier and may disturb the always precarious quiet of Belfast. Already party passions run high and this reckless foray may bring them to the point of explosion.'[23]

'Telegrams arrive constantly from both the northern and southern governments,' Churchill wrote to his wife, who was holidaying in France. 'These theatrical Irishmen are enjoying themselves enormously, and apart from a few cruel things very little blood is shed … We must not get back into that hideous bog of reprisals from which we have saved ourselves,' he wrote.[24]

8

THE CLONES AFFRAY

Tensions were raised considerably on 11 February when the IRA in Clones, County Monaghan, tried to arrest a group of nineteen Ulster Special Constabulary men who were travelling from Belfast to Enniskillen by rail. Part of their journey was through County Monaghan. They had to change trains, with a half-hour layover, in Clones. They had already boarded the second train when Commander Matt Fitzpatrick of the IRA approached with his revolver drawn and called on them to surrender. One of the men responded by shooting Fitzpatrick in the head and he died instantly. Some of the Special Constables claimed the IRA fired first. Both sides were apparently convinced that the other side was responsible for the extended gun battle that became known as the Clones Affray. A sergeant and three Ulster Special Constables were killed on the train, eight others were wounded and the IRA took five as prisoners.

'It is possible that the tragedy was the result of a genuine misunderstanding on both sides,' Hamar Greenwood reported. 'Its real origin is to be found in the unfortunate error of judgment of the person responsible for sending a body of armed Special Constabulary into southern Ireland at a time when their presence was almost certain to arouse the suspicion that a reprisal was being attempted for the recent raids into northern territory.' He added that the 'deplorable political consequences' had 'their inevitable sequel' in the outbreak of further violence in Belfast, where thirty-nine people were murdered over the next three days.[1]

On 13 February a bomb was thrown among some twenty Catholic children playing in the Weaver Street area, killing two instantly and fatally wounding four others. 'In my opinion,' Churchill wrote to Collins, 'it is the worst thing that has happened in Ireland in the last three years.'[2] When the funerals of the four Ulster Special Constabulary officers killed in Clones were held, passions in Belfast were further inflamed.

'The difficulty is that the so-called Irish Republican Army organisation in County Monaghan are incensed at the arrest and detention in prison of certain Monaghan men who were arrested in the territory of the northern government, a month ago,' Churchill told the House of Commons. They were 'proceeding to play in a football match at Derry, but they were arrested because they were recognised "as the commander and headquarters staff of the Monaghan division of the so-called Irish Republican Army"'.[3]

General Macready was deeply uneasy about Churchill's decision to delay the further withdrawal of British soldiers. 'The suspension of the evacuation of troops from southern Ireland was no doubt ordered for good reasons,' Macready reported. 'I have not been informed what those reasons were. I hope, however, that when the evacuation is allowed to proceed it will be continued without interruption and with all reasonable expedition.' He added, 'Our continued presence in southern Ireland only acts as an irritant.'[4]

Some in Britain were clearly suspicious that the Provisional Government was involved in the hostage-taking. 'The latest raids, in which responsible Irish officers have taken part, speak ill for the effectiveness of the Provisional Government, and they have done much to imperil the Irish settlement,' the *Daily Telegraph* noted. 'The first question which occurs to us in considering the attack upon Ulster is – Who did it?' the *Morning Post* asked. 'Was it, as the Lord Chancellor suggests, merely some wild men not yet under the control of the Provisional Government, or was it done with the cognisance, or even at the direction of that Government.'[5]

Robert Lynn, a unionist MP from Belfast, told the House of Commons that Eoin O'Duffy was behind the raids and that some of the captured raiders were in the uniform of the army of the Provisional Government. This was undoubtedly correct, but Churchill did not assume that the Provisional Government was actually implicated just because some of those arrested were in the uniform of the new army. O'Duffy was officially chief of staff of not only the new army being formed, but also the whole IRA. Yet he and Collins were obviously not in control of its anti-Treaty elements. Churchill clearly did not suspect that Collins was implicated in taking the hostages. 'I am satisfied,' he told parliament, 'that the Provisional Government are using the whole of their influence and authority, as far as it goes, to procure their [the hostages'] release.'[6]

Churchill was also reported as saying, 'We have been in constant communication with the Irish Provisional Government, and they have assured me that they are doing, and will do everything in their power to secure the liberation of the persons kidnapped in the raids of last Thursday. We believe that such is their sincere wish and intention. The extent of their powers at the present time is much more doubtful.' At this point he exhibited uncharacteristic patience towards Irish nationalism. 'We are passing through a very difficult interim period, and until the Irish Provisional Government are properly equipped with properly constituted powers we cannot expect that they can have the control which is necessary, and which every civilised government has over its agents and forces,' he added. 'Therefore, we should not judge them at this stage by exactly the same rules as those by which we should judge an established government.'[7] Lord Birkenhead assured the House of Lords that 'Collins is in an extremely trying and anxious position; and I believe that he is doing his best to carry out the letter and spirit of his obligation.'[8]

'It was inevitable that the arrest and detention by the Belfast authorities of prominent IRA officers, who were proceeding to a football match, and the failure to notify in time the reprieve of the Derry prisoners, should be met locally by the seizure of prominent unionists,' Collins explained in a further telegram to Churchill on 16 February. 'I and those who work with me in the teeth of many difficulties are ready to settle all this matter in a spirit of peace and goodwill. In fact, we have already given proof of our sincerity by the – some say premature – withdrawal of the Belfast boycott. There can, however, be no real peace until the other side meet us in the same spirit and until the British government ceases to support the aggression of the dissenting population in East Ulster.'[9]

Under pressure from London, Craig was prepared to agree to release 'the Monaghan footballers', after the Provisional Government was credited with arranging the release of twenty-six of the forty-three hostages on 16 February. The British cabinet was informed, however, that Craig only agreed to the release 'on condition that the Provisional Government would recognise the validity of the decisions of the Ulster courts and would give a solemn undertaking not to ask in future for the release of any more prisoners on political grounds'.[10]

That day Churchill announced the setting up of a border commission to act as a peace-keeping agency to mediate in any future border disputes. 'I suggested this Commission in the first instance only as an alternative to drastic steps which Parliament would otherwise expect me to take for securing the area of Northern Ireland,' Churchill telegraphed Collins two days before the announcement was made.[11] The commission achieved very little and soon faded away. 'To those who knew anything of the two component parts of the Commission, the IRA and Ulster representatives,' General Macready wrote, 'the scheme was foredoomed to failure, though no doubt it looked very attractive in Whitehall … From the first, in spite of the loyal efforts of the British officers [to make the border commission work], the whole affair was a farce.'[12]

Collins sent Churchill a telegram on 16 February arguing for a resumption of the withdrawal of British soldiers:

> I have seen it suggested in the English Press that the suspension of the evacuation of the British troops from Ireland is for the purpose of helping the Provisional Government of Ireland. The best way in which the British government could help us at the present time is not by suspending the carrying out of the Treaty, but by so adhering to its spirit and letter that Ireland will be convinced that Britain is really delivering the goods this time. Many people in Ireland believe that even at this late hour England will again trick us, and this belief is used as much as possible to our disadvantage by those who oppose us.

> The people and government of England should understand
> that Ireland has just emerged from the Black and Tan era, and
> that it is inevitable that feeling should continue for a time to be
> suspicious, not only of England's good faith, but of the good sense
> of any Irishmen who would trust England.[13]

The frequent killing of nationalists in the north had the potential
to undermine the Treaty settlement by weakening support for
the Provisional Government within nationalist Ireland. Collins
sought to exploit this in his relations with the colonial secretary.
Some 2,000 ordinary police, Ulster Special Constabulary and
British soldiers occupied the small nationalist town of Newry
and were throwing their weight around, 'tracking every person
suspected of having nationalist sympathies and in general
doing their best to make trouble,' Collins complained. This was
'only possible under the protection of British troops' who were
'apparently part of a determined plan to exasperate nationalist
feeling beyond endurance, and therefore stir up strife between
neighbours,' he continued. 'I have already pointed out to you the
inevitable result of their policy.'[14]

However, Collins had not just gone along with O'Duffy's
dangerous kidnapping scheme; he had actually added a reckless
touch of his own by sending two members of his old Squad – Joe
Dolan and Charlie Byrne – to England to kill the hangman John
Ellis and his assistant William Willis. 'Mick Collins told us to get
them at all cost, but if we were captured we could not expect any
help from him, as we could not identify ourselves as part of the
newly formed National Army,' Dolan later recalled.[15]

'We were told to get in touch with a man named Paddy Daly,

who was one of the Liverpool Irish Volunteers,' Dolan continued. 'He would show us where to go to find the men who we were to shoot, and that he would give us the assistance of whatever number of Liverpool Irish Volunteers as we might consider necessary.' They met Daly and arrangements were made. 'I undertook the shooting of Ellis, and six or seven of the Liverpool men came along with me,' Dolan explained. 'We went by train to Rochdale where Ellis lives, and some of the Liverpool Volunteers conducted me to the house and pointed it out to me. I walked up to the door alone and knocked at the door, which was opened by Mrs Ellis.' She said her husband was not there. 'I did not believe her at the time,' Dolan continued. 'I forced my way into the house and looked around. There was no one there and I had to accept her assurance that he had left already for Ireland. Our boats had probably crossed.'[16]

Willis was from the Manchester area, so Charlie Byrne went after him with some Manchester Volunteers. Their motorcar broke down on the way. 'Charlie wanted to hold up the first car that came along and commandeer it to carry out the job, but the others would not hear of this,' according to Dolan.[17] The mission was therefore aborted, but Willis had probably left for Ireland by that time anyway.

The Provisional Government was deliberately trying to de-stabilise conditions in Northern Ireland. Richard Mulcahy, the minister for defence, noted that 'the general aim underlying all operations in Carsonia is to disorganise the economic structure of the territory and to make the hostile inhabitants realise that aiding and abetting the activities of the Enemy does not pay'.[18] On 24 February, Mulcahy, on Collins' instructions, commanded

O'Duffy to pay sixty IRA volunteers £3 a week to form the Belfast Guard to protect nationalists in the city.

While Collins may not have masterminded the taking of the unionist hostages, he certainly approved of the whole thing and must share responsibility for the tragic sequence of events sparked by these kidnappings. His aggressive IRA policy in Northern Ireland proved counterproductive in the existing volatile sectarian mix. Although he seemed to get away with the reckless gamble personally, the only gain was the release of the so-called 'Monaghan footballers'. In the process, however, uncontrollable passions were roused and many people lost their lives in Belfast and Clones.

Griffith feared that the explosive violence in Northern Ireland could well prompt a re-think on the attitude of British politicians in relation to the boundary commission. 'If the British government stands firmly on this situation we'll be saved,' he wrote to Collins on 15 February. 'Otherwise disaster.'[19]

9

'THE RATS LEAVING THE SHIP'

The Sinn Féin Ard-Fheis was supposed to be held at the Mansion House, Dublin, on 7 February 1922, but two days before it was due to take place the convention was postponed for a fortnight as Collins and Griffith were busy in talks with the British. The big issue was whether Sinn Féin would go along with de Valera's suggestion that the party should insist that its main aim would be to secure international recognition 'as an independent Republic'.[1] In contrast, Collins wished the Ard-Fheis to call on the Provisional Government 'to take an immediate opportunity' of submitting the Treaty to the electorate for ratification.[2]

Even though Collins was anxious to go to the electorate, de Valera brought his campaign to the public with the first of a series of political rallies around the country before the postponed Ard-Fheis. He allowed himself to be introduced to the crowd from a platform under the Parnell monument in O'Connell Street as 'President de Valera – head of the Irish Republic'.[3] The huge crowd, which welcomed him, was largely made up of 'what railway people call "novelty traffic",' according to Tim Healy. 'There was a great curiosity and no enthusiasm.'[4]

The Irish people would not accept the Treaty because it was signed under duress, de Valera told the crowd. 'We, Irish republicans feel no more bound by that agreement signed in that fashion than the nationalists of the generations that have passed felt themselves bound by the equally infamous Act of Union,' he said. 'The independence and unity of Ireland have been hopelessly compromised unless you prevent it.'[5]

De Valera gradually began to emphasise his opposition to the partition issue, even though he had indicated a willingness to accept a county option solution on 22 August 1921. Now, almost six months later he seemed to be adopting a very different attitude. 'As far as I was concerned,' he said, 'I would rather have taken the old Council of Ireland Bill for the whole of Ireland than the fullest measure of Home Rule for twenty-six counties. I have made my position as regards partition clear in the Ard-Fheis speech of October 26. It was clear to the chairman of the delegation when he went to London, because in the draft treaty there was a proposal with regard to the six counties.'[6] In fact, there was no Ulster clause in the draft treaty provided to the delegation as a guide before they went to London.

At a public rally in Cork on 19 February, de Valera raised the political temperature. 'If the Treaty was signed under duress the men who went to London broke faith with the Irish people,' he declared. 'If it was signed without duress they were traitors to the cause.'[7] It was particularly volatile stuff. The country was 'in greater danger' than at any time in the last 750 years, he said, because 'for the first time in that period a suggestion was being made to give Britain democratic title in Ireland'. In other words, the Irish people were being asked to endorse a treaty which meant that the British would henceforth have democratic rights to Ireland. He therefore challenged the Provisional Government to fulfil its promise to provide a constitution that would give the Irish people complete freedom. 'Let them make the boast good,' de Valera said, 'frame it, and then come before the people and they would know what they were voting on.'[8]

Over 3,000 delegates gathered at the Mansion House for the postponed Ard-Fheis on 21 February. The proceedings were dominated by the personalities of de Valera and Collins. Even though Griffith had been elected president of the Dáil, de Valera was still president of Sinn Féin.

'As long as I have been working in the Sinn Féin movement,' de Valera said in his opening presidential address, 'I have never had a partisan idea in my mind and I hope I will die without being a partisan in that sense.'[9] Yet he was the one who had called for Sinn Féin to divide into two separate parties after the Treaty was accepted by the Dáil. During the Treaty negotiations he had insisted that the IRA give unqualified allegiance to the government, but now that he was in opposition, he called for two separate armies. 'I have sufficient faith in the Irish people to believe that they can divide without turning on one another,' he said.[10]

Most of the anti-Treaty animosity at the Ard-Fheis was directed at Collins. At one point de Valera looked straight at him. 'There are people who talk of Ireland being a mother country but who are content to make her the illegitimate daughter of Britain.'[11]

The main issue before the conference was a resolution proposed by de Valera stipulating that 'the Organisation shall put forward and shall support at the coming parliamentary elections only such candidates as publicly subscribe to it, and pledge themselves not to take an oath of fidelity to, or own allegiance to the British King.' This would, of course, have effectively barred any pro-Treaty candidates.[12]

Collins argued repeatedly for the chance to demonstrate the benefits of the Treaty. 'If there is any false dealing with us by England,' he declared, 'they will find I am not a Redmond or a Dillon to deal with.' This was clearly his answer to de Valera's public pronouncement a couple of weeks earlier that Lloyd George's policy was 'to trick the Irish people and deal with President Griffith and Mr Collins as he dealt with Messrs Redmond and Dillon'.[13]

'If we are beaten in the Dáil we cannot go on,' Collins said. He would accept the verdict and resign his office. 'Some people say that England cannot now make war on this country,' he added. 'I know that England can go to war with us, and will go to war, and is at this moment watching for an opportunity to go to war with us.'[14]

'It is for the Irish people to say whether they will have the Treaty or not,' Cathal Brugha, a member of the anti-Treaty committee interjected. 'Put it to the Irish electors and let them decide whether Mr Collins decides to resign office or not. Let the British put someone else in Mr Collins' place.'

There were loud shouts of 'Withdraw!'

'The people of South Cork put me there, not the British,' Collins replied in indignation amid the uproar.

Confusion reigned for some moments before de Valera announced that Brugha would withdraw his statement in substance. 'I had no intention and I have no intention of offending Mr Collins,' Brugha said. 'Mr Collins has been put in that position as a result of the Treaty in London.'

'By whom?' some people shouted.

'By the majority of Dáil Éireann,' Brugha conceded and the gathering applauded. 'Is that sufficient now?'

This was greeted with cries of approval from around the hall.[15]

'Do you know, in spite of it all,' Collins told Piaras Béaslaí, 'I can't help feeling a regard for Cathal.'[16]

The day's proceedings dragged on for some nine hours. Historian Michael Hopkinson contends in his book, *Green Against Green*, that there was 'very probably a pro-Treaty majority at the Ard-Fheis'.[17] He based this assessment on the fact that eleven of the fifteen members of the standing committee of Sinn Féin elected in January were strongly pro-Treaty. But there was a test of strength on a procedural matter about whether there should be an open vote or a secret ballot in relation to de Valera's proposal on election candidates, which showed that de Valera probably enjoyed a majority. The standing committee had recommended a secret ballot, but an amendment was submitted on behalf of de Valera's supporters calling on delegates who were representing their respective clubs to vote openly.

A vote was taken on a show of hands as to whether the voting should be open or secret. De Valera ruled that the majority favoured an open vote. If anyone wished to challenge his decision, he was prepared to agree to a formal vote. Collins admitted there was no doubt whatever about the decision, and de Valera then declared the amendment to have been carried.

Collins realised that his supporters were probably facing defeat at the Ard-Fheis. After a protracted discussion, he suggested that they should adjourn the Ard-Fheis for three months to allow passions to cool and give people a chance to see how things were developing. They would then be in a better position to judge whether the English were breaking faith with them. Even Brugha appeared to agree with the call for a three-month delay. He was prepared to let 'the Provisional Government function in its own way', and also let Sinn Féin function, though he called for equal representation between the two sides on the party's standing committee. 'With these things,' Brugha said, 'unity would be preserved at any rate for three months.'[18]

Minister for Defence Richard Mulcahy proposed the Ard-Fheis adjourn until the following morning to give the leaders a chance to confer privately in the hope of bringing forward proposals that would avoid 'a general election until such time as the constitution was put before them'.

Griffith, Collins, de Valera and anti-Treaty committee member Austin Stack hammered out a formal agreement before the Ard-Fheis resumed the following morning. It was due to begin at 11 a.m., but the proceedings were delayed as they put the finishing touches to their agreement. They agreed to postpone the Ard-Fheis for three months to allow for the drafting of a constitution that would be published before the election. The electorate would then be able to decide between the Republic and the Free State before voting. During the three-month delay all departments were to be allowed to function as before the signing of the Treaty.

'These articles have been signed by President Griffith and myself, Michael Collins and Austin Stack,' de Valera explained. 'Four of us have signed these articles of agreement, and we have agreed that we present them to you without speeches.' They received the overwhelming approval of the conference.[19]

At the Ard-Fheis the delegates from the six counties decided to establish the north-east advisory committee – with two representatives from each council district in Northern Ireland – to brief the Dublin government on northern affairs. The new committee was established to provide a broad consultative role and to attract maximum northern nationalist support, especially the support that Joe Devlin of the old Irish Parliamentary Party might otherwise garner. The new committee afforded the northern nationalists a forum for letting off steam and helped to keep the issue of Northern Ireland very much to the fore within both the Dáil and the Provisional Government. The need to protect northern nationalists also united southern opinion in a common cause. There is little doubt that Collins shared the frustration of Ulster nationalists in relation to what was happening in Northern Ireland.

During the first weekend following the Ard-Fheis, de Valera was again campaigning against the Treaty, this time in Limerick and Ennis. In the circumstances, the pro-Treaty side could not afford to allow him to have all of the running. They felt compelled to respond on behalf of the Treaty. Collins and Griffith therefore addressed a massive rally near Trinity College, Dublin, on Sunday 5 March. Although it was a blustery day with showers, a huge crowd gathered between the college and the old House of Lords building, which later housed the Bank of Ireland. Students gathered on the roof of the college and there was hardly room for people to move by 3 p.m., when the proceedings were to begin.

There were several minutes of cheering when Collins mounted the platform under the portico of the bank opposite Thomas Moore's statue. He took off his hat and coat, walked to the front of the platform and stood there with his hands on the wooden rail until the cheering died down. He then began in a deep, clear voice and his words were broken only by applause, except for a group of women hecklers. The speech was a fine blend of emotional appeal and logical argument. Collins accused de Valera of surrendering the republican ideal when he realised it was 'physically impossible' after meeting with Lloyd George the previous July. 'We could not beat the British out by force,' Collins said, 'but when we have beaten them out by the Treaty, the republican ideal, which was surrendered in July is restored.'

The Long Fellow, who often used figurative speech as an effective oratorical device, had said in Limerick the previous week that the Irish people were like a party that had set out to cross a desert, but on coming to an oasis, some of them argued that they should lay down and stay there, and be satisfied and not go on. 'Yes,' Collins countered, 'we had come by means of the Treaty to a green oasis, the last in the long weary desert over which the Irish nation has been travelling. Oases are the resting places of the desert, and unless the traveller finds them and replenishes himself he never reaches his destination.' Having figuratively reached such an oasis, they had earned a rest, but some in their midst were finding fault with the oasis. 'They are poisoning the wells, wanting now to hurry on, seeing the road ahead short and straight, wanting the glory for themselves of leading the Irish nation over it, while unwilling to fill and shoulder the pack.'[20]

The Treaty provided the opportunity to achieve freedom and the means to end partition, Collins contended. 'We must remember,' he said, 'that there is a strong minority in our country up in the north-east that does not yet share our national views, but has to be reckoned with.' He admitted that arrangements in relation to partition were not ideal, 'but then the position in North East Ulster is not ideal,' he said. If the Free State were established, however, Irish unity would be a certainty, he said. 'Destroy the Free

State now and you destroy more even than the hope, the certainty of union,' he continued. 'You destroy our hopes of national freedom, all realisation in our generation of the democratic right of the people of Ireland to rule themselves without interference from any outside power.'[21]

Freedom was assured because the Treaty guaranteed the Irish Free State the *de facto* status of the dominions. Henceforth, if Britain challenged the country's status, 'she would be challenging the status of Canada, South Africa, and the other dominions'. Those dominions would therefore have a vested interest in defending the Free State's status. 'Any attempt to interfere with us would be even more difficult in consequence in reference to the constitutional status of Canada and South Africa.'[22]

As the deliberations at the party Ard-Fheis were winding up, a crisis began to develop in Limerick, where the local IRA took umbrage at pro-Treaty forces from outside taking over local barracks in breach of an earlier agreement where it was decided that local IRA forces, whether pro- or anti-Treaty, would take over barracks evacuated in their areas. Minister for Defence Richard Mulcahy had ordered Commandant General Michael Brennan from the 1st Western Division of the IRA in east Clare to take over five police barracks being vacated by the RIC on 23 February, along with St John's Castle, from which the British army were departing. Brennan arrived with a force of over a hundred men to take control of the facilities.

Tension increased when the British army evacuated the Strand Barracks and handed the place over to pro-Treaty troops on 1 March, and Brennan and Ernie O'Malley of the 2nd Southern Division began vying for control of the city of Limerick.

O'Malley was already incensed at what he considered an invasion by outsiders. He introduced reinforcements from Tipperary and tried to get personnel from Rory O'Connor to attack the Free State troops. But O'Connor, Liam Lynch and Liam Deasy were all reluctant to co-operate with O'Malley for fear of provoking civil war. However, O'Malley did get support from Cork, from Tom Barry, Seán Hales and Seán Moylan.

President Griffith appeared anxious for the Free State troops to fight. 'The situation is largely the outcome of incitement to indiscipline engaged in, or connived at, by some of Mr de Valera's supporters,' Griffith declared in a public statement. 'The negation of national authority can under no circumstances be acquiesced to.'[23] Initially Collins agreed with him, but Mulcahy thought the Free State soldiers were not properly equipped for war. If they did not stand up, Griffith warned, 'they would go down as the greatest poltroons in Irish history'.[24]

There were 800 armed anti-Treaty IRA in Limerick ready to fight. 'As it is a foregone conclusion that the mutineers will be able to lock us in, I propose cutting down the Limerick garrison to 500 reliable men,' Brennan wrote. 'Some of my men have too many associations with the mutineers to be properly reliable.' Hence he was anxious to get an extra hundred good men from Commandant Seán MacEoin.[25]

Realising that his plan to take control of Limerick city had gone dangerously wrong, Mulcahy jumped at the chance to extricate his forces when Mayor of Limerick Stephen O'Mara intervened to prevent a battle. Liam Lynch, the commander of the 1st Southern Division IRA, and Oscar Traynor, the commander of the Dublin Brigade IRA, met O'Mara, along with Collins, Mulcahy and

Eoin O'Duffy at Beggars Bush on 10 March. They agreed that the police barracks would be handed over to Limerick Corporation and would then be occupied by a small civilian maintenance crew, which would report to Liam Lynch, while the William Street Barracks would be occupied by a token force of Free State soldiers.

Brennan was enraged as, having been ordered to march his troops into Limerick and risk fighting a much larger force of IRA, he was now being told to march out again. He demanded to see Collins and presented him with a letter of resignation. 'So you're going, too!' Collins snapped. 'The rats leaving the ship. Well, go on. Clear out! Leave it all to me. You're all the same, you fellows, putting your bloody vanity ahead of the good of the country.'[26]

Like Arthur Griffith, Winston Churchill thought that the Free State should have taken a firm stand in Limerick. Although disillusioned, he went along with the decision. 'You seem to have liquidated the Limerick situation in one way or another,' Churchill wrote to Collins. 'No doubt you know your own situation best, and thank God you have got to manage it and not we.'[27]

10

'LET THE BASTARD GO'

The first political rally that Collins attended outside Dublin was fittingly in Cork city, the second weekend in March 1922. The crowd 'exceeded in dimensions any similar demonstration held in the south of Ireland in recent years,' Hamar Greenwood reported.[1] Collins travelled to Cork by train, along with Fionán Lynch, Seán MacEoin, Seán Milroy and J. J. Walsh, on the eve of the planned address. A large enthusiastic crowd greeted them at Glanmire railroad station on that Saturday afternoon, and they were taken through the city in triumph, behind a number of bands.

Not everyone was so happy to see them. Some armed republicans had stopped one band on the way to meet Collins, seized their instruments at gunpoint and threw them into the River Lee. One enraged band member jumped into the cold water to recover a drum as it floated down river. Republican protesters later tried to disrupt proceedings by firing shots in the air as Collins was being driven through Patrick's Street.[2]

'The people came out of their own free will to express their feelings, and they came without canvassing and without organisation,' Collins said afterwards. 'Of course, I knew that Cork was for us. I knew that I was as good an interpreter of the desires of the people of Cork as anyone, and I am glad my interpretation was confirmed.'[3]

During the night the republicans dismantled the two platforms which had been prepared for the speeches due to be made on Sunday and threw the wooden planks into the river. The place around Turner's Hotel, where Collins was staying, was littered next morning with republican slogans, along with a number of white flags, strategically placed in prominent positions to intimate that the Treaty supporters were essentially surrendering. Some of the planks from the platforms could also be seen floating in the river.

After Sunday Mass, Collins and his colleagues tried to visit the graves of Tomás MacCurtain, who had been murdered by crown forces in March 1920, and his successor as lord mayor of Cork, Terence MacSwiney, who died on hunger strike the following October. A group of about twenty armed men blocked Collins and colleagues and threatened to shoot any of them who entered the republican plot. Outside Cork, special excursion trains from Fermoy, Newmarket and Youghal were held up by armed republicans, who kidnapped the engine drivers and firemen, leaving the passengers stranded. Had those trains made it to Cork, however, there would hardly have been room for the extra people because, as it was, a crowd of about 50,000 people turned up that afternoon for the rally on Grand Parade. Every vantage point was taken.

As the crowd waited for the rally to begin, one young man began climbing the fountain to take down a white flag from its pinnacle. As he was about to remove the flag a shot rang out and, to the horror of spectators, the young man fell into the empty basin, but he was not injured. Shortly afterwards another young man shinned up a tram pole, topped by another flag. As he neared the top another shot was fired but, much to the amusement of the crowd, he ignored the flag, continued to the top and sat on the cross bar. The laughter of the crowd promptly turned to cheering as Collins and his colleagues made their way to the main platform. It was an impressive sight. 'Old people who have seen Parnell, O'Brien and Redmond meetings all say that they never saw anything like yesterday's display,' Collins gloated the next day.[4]

He delivered a rousing speech, sprinkled with bravado and with indignant swipes at de Valera, who had had the effrontery to suggest in Cork, three weeks earlier, that Collins was either a coward or a traitor. That was some charge from the man who had not only spent most of the terror in the United States, but had also refused to go to London to negotiate the Treaty. 'While the captain was away from the ship – that time in America – there was a hurricane blowing,' Collins said. 'The helm had been left by the captain in the hands of those very same incompetent amateurs who afterwards, in the calm water, had the ship on the rocks, and while he was away, somehow or other, we steered safely through those troubled waters, the roughest through which the ship of the Irish nation had to be navigated in all her troubled history.' *Poblacht na h-Éireann*, the anti-Treaty journal edited by Erskine Childers, contended that Collins was accusing de Valera of cowardice.[5]

Collins explained in his speech that the IRA had not defeated the British militarily. Hence the Irish side was not able to dictate terms in negotiating the Treaty. He left no doubt, however, that they would have stood out for better terms if they had been strong enough to secure them. What they got was the freedom to develop.

'The only policy of our opponents has become, it seems, by hidden manoeuvre, to stir up trouble,' he told the gathering. They were fomenting strife and delaying the withdrawal of the British. In the process they were damaging the chances of unity and causing disunion. 'That disunion in itself encourages the cowardly element in Belfast to an orgy of bloodshed and ruffianism,' Collins said. 'For factionalist ends they are jeopardising the unity of Ireland.'[6]

The meeting was best remembered for the irresponsibility of republican agitators who skirted the periphery of the gathering, firing shots into the air and shouting, 'Up the Republic'. 'There were probably not more than a dozen men doing the shooting,' Collins noted.[7] He commented on the wonderful composure of the crowd. 'If there had been a stampede,' he said, 'women and little children would have been trampled under foot.'[8] Remarkably, the only incident reported requiring hospitalisation was a youth who was shot in the wrist.[9]

'Before Collins' visit, Cork republicans had had the luxury of blaming the passage of the Treaty on political enemies who had not supported them during the War of Independence: the commercial elite, the newspapers, Redmondites, ex-soldiers and the Catholic church,' John Borgonovo concludes in his book, *The Battle for Cork*. 'Yet the city's rapturous reception for Michael Collins clearly demonstrated the mass of public opinion was opposed to renewed hostilities with Britain.'[10]

That evening Collins went to the home of his sister, Mary Collins Powell. On the way a gunman accosted him. 'I have you now,' the gunman said, but MacEoin disarmed the man.

'Will I shoot him?' MacEoin asked.

'No,' the Big Fellow replied. 'Let the bastard go.'[11]

Over the next six weekends Collins held political rallies in Skibbereen, Waterford, Castlebar, Wexford, Naas and Tralee.

Although de Valera professed to be happy with the Ard-Fheis agreement postponing the election until after the publication of the constitution, he soon changed his mind and began adopting further delaying tactics. He demanded that the electoral register be updated, but Griffith contended that this would take over five months, which would necessitate an even longer delay than the three months agreed at the Ard-Fheis. In reply, de Valera argued that the existing register excluded tens of thousands 'of young men who have just attained their majority, who were the nation's most active defenders in the recent fight, and whose voice should certainly not be silenced in an election like the pending one, in which the fate of their country and the ideals for which they fought are to be determined'.[12]

Showing signs of exasperation, Griffith refused a further delay. He was convinced the request had nothing to do with the democratic rights of the unfranchised, but was merely a ploy to stall the elections to avoid certain defeat. As recently as November, de Valera had been instrumental in having the register updated, but now he was asserting that 'the register is invalid', Griffith wrote in an open letter. 'The public can draw its own conclusion.' If they waited for a new register 'an election would be impossible for the next six months,' Griffith argued. 'This would suit the game of those who desire to muzzle the Irish electorate, but I cannot be a party to any muzzling order.'

'You propose muzzling them,' de Valera replied. 'I simply demand a proper register on the existing franchise, so that all who are entitled to vote may be permitted to vote. You would deprive the young men of their right because you believe that their votes would be cast against the London Agreement.'[13]

De Valera's own conduct in recent months and especially in the following days and weeks certainly raised serious questions about his commitment to democracy. On 15 March 1922, for instance, he issued a manifesto announcing the formation of a new organisation, Cumann na Poblachta, which he had initially announced at the Mansion House meeting the day after the Dáil accepted the Treaty. He said the name should be translated as 'the Republican Party Organisation'. Composed of anti-Treaty deputies, it was not supposed to supersede Sinn Féin, but there was no doubt that this party within the party added to the growing split within the movement as he set out on what would be the most controversial tour of his whole career.

'They tell you, you will be prosperous,' he told a gathering in Dungarvan next day. 'Wait till you see the burden they will try to place upon you. You will want to fight for your rights whether you like it or not, if you don't fight today you will have to fight tomorrow, and I say when you are in a good fighting position, then fight on.'[14]

While de Valera was calling on people to fight on, Collins was in his native west Cork proclaiming that 'Dublin Castle has been surrendered into my hands for the Irish nation'. He told the cheering crowd in Skibbereen that 'the British game is up. Dublin Castle has fallen, and with it will have gone all bureaucratic regulations and tyrannies that the people of Ireland suffered from'.[15] With the British departing, Collins asked, who was de Valera proposing to fight against?

De Valera answered that question in both Carrick-on-Suir and

Thurles on St Patrick's Day. Speaking in Thurles he told a crowd which included many armed IRA volunteers that if the Treaty was ratified, they would have 'to wade through Irish blood, through the blood of the soldiers of the Irish government, and through, perhaps, the blood of some members of the government in order to get Irish freedom'.[16]

Next day in Killarney he suggested that he was not just talking about the current generation of volunteers but also future generations. 'These men, in order to achieve freedom, will have, I said yesterday, to march over the dead bodies of their own brothers. They will have to wade through Irish blood.'[17]

'It is not peculiar in our time to have Volunteers and men who are willing to give up their lives for the freedom of their country,' he explained. 'These aspirations will continue, and the next generation will strive to do it, and the road will be barred by their own fellow-countrymen, and feeling that they have a right to complete freedom, they will not allow that to stand in the way. Therefore, they will oppose even the troops of an Irish government set up in accordance with that, because it will be felt that, even if that Treaty were ratified, it would not be ratified with your free will, but under the threat of war.'[18]

Yet in January of that year he had denounced the idea of civil strife. 'I hope that nobody will talk of fratricidal strife,' he had told the Dáil. 'This is all nonsense. We have got a nation that knows how to conduct itself. As far as I can on this side it will be our policy always.'[19] Now in March he was clearly abandoning that policy and talking openly of civil war. It was grossly irresponsible, as his words were widely interpreted as threatening civil war, or even attempting to incite one, and he set off a firestorm of criticism both in the Irish and international press. 'Mr de Valera has shocked the whole country,' *The Times* of London reported.[20]

De Valera contended that he was merely assessing the situation realistically and rebutting the argument that the Treaty contained the freedom to achieve freedom. He accused the press of using his words to do the very thing of which they were accusing him. 'You cannot be unaware,' he wrote to the editor of the *Irish Independent*, 'that your representing me as inciting the civil war has on your readers precisely the same effects as if the inciting words were really mine.'[21] He blamed the press. There were around 7,000 people in Tralee on Sunday 19 March, when de Valera complained that newspaper owners had 'an influence altogether disproportionate to their personal worth'.[22] He warned the people not to allow themselves to be hypnotised by newspapers when making up their minds. Instead, he said, they should realise that anything they read in a newspaper was likely to be false.

Although de Valera was widely blamed for inciting the IRA, he was rapidly losing his influence over the organisation. Collins and the Irish Republican Brotherhood were in control of most of the headquarters staff, which was largely pro-Treaty. Even among the anti-Treaty members of the headquarters staff, de Valera had little influence. Rory O'Connor, the director of engineering, declared that he was 'no more prepared to stand for de Valera than for the Treaty'.[23] The divisional commanders and the rank and file were strongly anti-Treaty, especially in those areas that had been most active in the struggle against the British. O'Connor therefore wanted an IRA convention called to elect a new leadership, but the headquarters staff – realising that their control was tenuous at best – procrastinated. De Valera tried to make the best of his own weak position by siding with those asking for a convention. He suggested that the IRA should split on Treaty lines. Some mistakenly thought de Valera was therefore the instigator when O'Connor announced at a press conference on 22 March that an army convention would be held on 26 March, in defiance of the Dáil cabinet and headquarters staff.

O'Connor openly distanced himself from de Valera at the press conference announcing his plans. 'President de Valera asked that the army should obey the GHQ, but the army for which I speak cannot,' O'Connor said, 'because the minister for defence has broken his agreement.'[24] The IRA had voluntarily submitted to the authority of the Dáil, but O'Connor – who claimed to represent eighty per cent of the organisation – announced that it would be withdrawing this allegiance, because the Dáil had exceeded its authority in approving the Treaty. 'There are times when revolution is justified,' he said. 'The armies in many countries have overturned governments from time to time. There is no government in Ireland now to give the IRA a lead, hence we want to straighten out the impossible position which exists.'[25]

The convention was called to set up a new executive to issue orders to the IRA throughout the country, despite the decision by the Dáil cabinet that the convention should not be held. 'In effect,' O'Connor said, 'the holding of the convention means that we repudiate the Dáil.'

'Do we take it that we are going to have a military dictatorship then?' a reporter asked.

'You can take it that way, if you like,' O'Connor replied.[26]

On the eve of the convention some eighty volunteers associated with the Four Courts garrison seized the Wholesale Fish Market in Halston Street. They held it overnight and then withdrew the following day. The same night some forty or fifty of O'Connor's followers seized the Orange Hall and Fowler Memorial Hall at 10 Parnell Square. There was a social function going on in the Orange Hall at the time when men in civilian clothes and carrying pistols ordered everybody out. The raiders announced they were seizing the building in the name of Catholic workers expelled from the Belfast shipyards. All apparently had southern accents, but they indicated that they expected some of the expelled workers to arrive that night. In the following days fifteen families, totalling eighty-three individuals, from Belfast were put up in the building, and seventy single men from Belfast were provided with three meals a day there.

The convention called by O'Connor was convened in the Oak Room of the Mansion House, with some 233 delegates representing forty-nine brigades. The meeting, which began at 10 a.m., lasted throughout the day and did not break up until after 10 p.m. Only a small group gathered outside, which was a reflection of the meagre public support. Liam Lynch was elected chief of staff of the faction of the army that had broken away from the authority of Mulcahy and O'Duffy. Henceforth there were two armies, both claiming to be the IRA, at least for the time being.

Pro-Treaty elements retained their headquarters at Beggars Bush Barracks, while the others – the self-styled Executive Forces – set up their headquarters in the building seized from the Orange Order in Parnell Square the previous night. Each claimed to be the official or regular IRA, but the pro-Treaty element was frequently referred to as the Free State army or Free Staters, and the anti-Treaty faction, as the Executive IRA or Republicans.

11

'Some of you know nothing about freedom'

As the IRA convention was being held at the Mansion House, Collins went to Waterford for a political rally. Trenched roads, cut power and communication lines, a burned platform and, as in Cork, the stealing of band instruments were features surrounding his visit. The first sign of trouble was when the train carrying Collins, Ernest Blythe, Joe McGrath and Seán Milroy was delayed for over an hour at Ballyhain station because the communication wires with Mullinavat had been cut. This necessitated a porter walking eight miles to ensure the track was safe. When the party finally got to Waterford, the band to welcome them was unable to play because armed men had commandeered their instruments. Several tar barrels that were burning as a welcome were thrown in the river, and the platform that had been erected for them was sprinkled with petrol and set on fire.

Collins spoke, instead, from an upstairs window of the Town Hall. There were frequent interruptions from hecklers, but he parried those effectively, much to the delight of the crowd. 'I have had occasion to give plain talk to some of those slackers during the past few years; to those who were civilians in war, and who are warriors in peace and I perceive that some of you know nothing about freedom,' he said.[1]

From a house on the other side of the Mall, a banner with 'Long Live the Republic' was unfurled.

'I am not ashamed to see that flag flying,' Collins said. 'I can afford to look at it, and that is more than some of you can do.'

The crowd loved it. He was responding to good effect, but the interruptions continued. 'If you with the black hat down there were as brave this time twelve months ago as you are now, perhaps we need not be here today,' he snapped.

Collins went on to berate de Valera over his recent speeches. 'While it was perfectly justifiable for any body of Irish men, no matter how small, to rise up and make a stand against their country's enemy,' the Big Fellow insisted, 'it is not justifiable for a minority to oppose the wishes of the majority of their own countrymen, except by constitutional means.

'Whatever Mr de Valera's meaning, the effect of his language is mischievous,' Collins continued, 'a leader must not be unmindful of the implications of his words. If Mr de Valera really wishes to convince the public that he did not mean to indulge in violent threats and in the language of incitement, and wants to wipe out the impression caused by his speeches, he must take instant action ... His explanation, as published, will not do. He must press home the foregoing truths to all his supporters, and he must publicly disassociate himself from the utterances of the former ministers of defence and home affairs [Brugha and Stack], and from such mutinous views as those expressed by Commandant Roderick O'Connor.'[2]

On the night of 29 March 1922, Rory O'Connor and his men raided the offices of *The Freeman's Journal* and wrecked the equipment, before boldly issuing a statement justifying their actions. 'I was, with my associates, responsible for the suppression of the *Freeman*,' O'Connor announced. 'A free press is admirable, but "freedom of the press", according to the view of the *Freeman*, is the right to refuse publication of articles with which its proprietors do not agree, and the right to undermine the army and seduce it from its allegiance to the Republic.'

De Valera later said that he 'heartily disagreed' with what amounted to O'Connor's repudiation of the Dáil, but he nevertheless publicly defended O'Connor's patently undemocratic behaviour in a series of press interviews in the coming weeks.[3]

***

While de Valera and Collins were talking about the danger of civil war in the twenty-six counties, the situation seemed to be deteriorating even more rapidly in Northern Ireland. Collins was anxious to turn the spotlight on the north. The Provisional Government was eager to re-open talks with the northern government, but Northern Ireland Prime Minister Craig was unwilling to meet the southern representatives while the Ulster Special Constabulary men arrested in Clones were still being held.

Churchill was showing signs of disillusionment with the unionists. If Craig and company refused to talk after those Specials were released, the colonial secretary told the British cabinet that he would not accept this because 'of the heavy obligations in regard to troops and Special Constabulary which we were incurring on their behalf'.[4] The British were not only maintaining troops in Northern Ireland to protect the loyalist community but also funding the operations of the police and the Special Constabulary.

'The state of affairs in Belfast is lamentable,' he wrote to Collins on 14 March. 'There is an underworld there with deadly feuds of its own, and only the sternest and strictest effort by leading men on both sides, coupled with ample military and police will produce the tranquillity which is demanded by the interests of Ireland as a whole.

'Sir James Craig left me with the impression that he would be glad to see the obstacles removed and to have a further parley,' Churchill continued in his letter to Collins. 'You ought to put yourself in the right by either effecting the release of these men or bringing them to trial in a regular way on a definite charge before lawfully constituted tribunals. Sir James Craig would be quite satisfied if they have a fair trial and are dealt with according to law ... This hostage business is more suited to the Balkans than to Ireland, and the sooner we get on to a normal footing the better.'[5]

The same day in Belfast, however, Craig blamed the British for many of his government's problems. He said he would have resigned when the British commuted the death sentences of the three prisoners in Derry, only that he thought it would have suited the British government to have chaos in Northern Ireland. 'If anything of the kind occurs again,' he said, 'I will resign, unless we have full power here to say what is best in the interests of the community.'[6]

Craig announced the introduction of the Civil Authorities (Special Powers) Bill to tackle the existing unrest. It was the first of what would become the infamous Special Powers Acts. Ordinary courts were to be authorised to impose special punishment for 'breaches of ordinary law and offences against the Regulations connected with illegal possession of arms and ammunition,' he explained. 'The courts may order the convicted person, if a male, to be flogged.'[7] The RIC, which was shortly to become the Royal Ulster Constabulary (RUC), was to be backed up by A, B and C Special Constables. There were 6,000 A Specials, who were a full-time force. The 21,000 B Specials were part-time members, while the much more numerous C Specials were only to be called upon as a last resort, but once they enrolled they were entitled to carry arms. As unionists could easily get permits to have arms, the implications of the bill were that nationalists could not get a gun permit and could be flogged for having a gun. The Special Constabulary, which was largely sectarian, was now seen as the Orange counterpart of the IRA, because its members were drawn mainly from the Ulster Volunteer Force which had been set up in 1912 to resist Home Rule and thus fight not only Irish nationalists but the British as well. There were calls for the British to take charge of law and order in Northern Ireland by introducing martial law throughout the area.

'I myself am dead against any suggestion of martial law,' Craig said. 'I feel instinctively that if we hand over the conduct of the affairs of this city to the military, who would be controlled through Dublin from Westminster, we would get back to the same old chaos and confusion as we were in before. If we have martial law our cause in England will suffer immediately and intensely. They will say, "One side is as bad as the other".'[8]

On 14 March Craig announced that Field Marshal Sir Henry Wilson, the former chief of imperial general staff, had agreed to advise the Stormont government on 'the best method of safe-guarding the borders and restoring order within the boundaries'. Wilson was widely credited with leading the British army to victory in the First World War. Like the Duke of Wellington – the hero of the Battle of Waterloo – who was raised in County Meath, Wilson was born and raised nearby in Currygrane, near Edgeworthstown, County Longford. He only retired from the army following his election to parliament in a Down by-election in February 1922. Craig announced that he had pledged that 'whatever scheme Wilson recommended would be carried out in full, regardless of cost and consequence'.[9] The Stormont cabinet approved of the arrangement, but members of the British cabinet clearly had reservations about the northern attitude, especially Craig's naked insistence that any unfavourable decision by the boundary commission would be resisted. This seemed like a re-run of the Home Rule crisis of 1914. Just as the so-called loyalists had threatened to use the UVF to wage a civil war with Britain to stay within the United Kingdom in the 1912–1914 period, Stormont was developing a relatively enormous security force to resist the imposition of an unfavourable finding by the boundary commission. Craig actually warned that 'the loyalists may declare independence on their own behalf, seize the customs and other government departments and set up an authority of their own. Many already believed that violence is the only language understood by Mr Lloyd George and his Ministers.'[10]

'It is difficult to avoid the conclusion that the government of Northern Ireland has succeeded in assuming the military functions specifically reserved to the British government simply by calling their forces "police",' a parliamentary committee noted at Westminster. 'An equivalent force of police in Great Britain would amount to at least 800,000 or in Germany 1,300,000 men. What would France say if Great Britain allowed Germany to maintain well over a million "police" armed with rifles?'[11] The dangers were obvious.

General Macready reported from Dublin that the Provisional Government was building a regular standing army of about 25,000 from units of the IRA that could be relied on. On top of this, however, he added 'that the representatives of the Provisional Government not only maintain their right to raid into Northern Ireland territory in the event of their demands not being acceded to, but that they claim immunity for their formations and units located within the six counties'.[12]

Field Marshal Wilson blamed the British prime minister. 'Owing to the actions of Mr Lloyd George, the 26 counties of the south and west of Ireland are reduced to a welter of chaos and murder difficult to believe, impossible to describe,' Wilson wrote to Craig on 17 March 1922. Britain would lose the empire unless law and order were re-established in Ireland. 'Under Mr Lloyd George and his government this is frankly and laughably impossible, because men who are only capable of losing an Empire are obviously incapable of holding an Empire, and still more incapable of regaining it,' Wilson contended.[13]

Collins complained to Churchill that Craig delivered 'a most reprehensible speech in the Belfast parliament which has created feelings of the gravest alarm and uneasiness not only amongst Catholics of the six counties, but generally among the people of all Ireland'. Collins was particularly critical of plans to introduce flogging. 'I am informed that this degrading work is to be done by "Specials" who will be paid at a rate of 2s 6d per flogging,' he continued. 'The police who are to carry out these plans are all "Specials" who are, as you know, all violent Orangemen and responsible individually for many crimes. To ensure further the purely sectarian working of the Bill, those "Specials" are to be directed by Sir Henry Wilson, an avowed Orange partisan.'[14]

'Southern Ireland desires to coerce Ulster citizens and stir up strife here by bombing our citizens and sniping at them,' Craig had declared in his Stormont speech on 14 March.[15] Collins noted that this was followed by a series of outrages against Catholics in Belfast:

> On the 16th instant, there was much shooting and bombing. A bomb was thrown into Seaforde Street, a Catholic area, from Newtownards Road, a Protestant area, wounding badly seven Catholic young men, one of whom was taken to hospital in a dying state. On this day also Patrick Rooney, barber, was murdered in Ship Street, and a little girl of five years, Mary Wilson, of Norfolk Street, was murdered on her father's doorstep whilst nursing her doll. A villainous attempt was made to massacre little Catholic children by throwing a bomb into the playground of St Matthew's Catholic School, Ballymagarret, which was only frustrated by the timely changing of the play-hour.
>
> Bombing and shooting and general turmoil continued on the 18th instant. Augustine Orange, a member of a well-known Catholic family, was murdered on his way home from a Catholic dance in St Mary's Hall, because he refused to curse the Pope. The same day a hideous atrocity was perpetrated. A bomb was flung into the bedroom of two elderly Catholic women, Rose McGreevy and Mary Mullen, 32, Thompson Street, resulting in the frightful mutilation of both. I am informed that 'Specials' refused to allow an ambulance to be called to bring these ladies to hospital.

> Orange gang attacked 3, 5, and 7, Empress Street, all houses
> owned by Catholics. In No. 5 they deliberately murdered a woman
> named Canon, aged 75 years, and wounded a youngster named
> [Robert] Togue, aged 10.
>
> There seems to be no end to this pogrom on our people, and
> the recent war preparations of the Belfast authorities such as
> the blowing up of bridges and the trenching of roads must only
> intensify the feeling and make matters a thousand times worse.[16]

Collins felt the northern loyalists were getting the better newspaper coverage and he was anxious to exploit the situation for
propaganda purposes. 'I wonder if anything could be done to get
wider publicity for the situation in Belfast,' he wrote to propaganda minister, Desmond Fitzgerald, on 20 March. 'Would it be
possible to arrange a telegraphic news service under competent
management to deal with the English and American press? I feel
they were doing better in publicity than we are.' He wished to interest newspapers like the *Daily Mail* and *Daily Express*. 'Publicity
in these papers would undoubtedly win support from pogrom-
ists,' he added. 'Similar action should be taken in America. What
we want is a decent workable scheme operated by very energetic
people.'[17]

He was already thinking like a propagandist in that he was
particularly selective in referring to events. He was, for instance,
conveniently overlooking the IRA campaign being waged along
the border, such as the attacks on the Ulster Special Constabulary
barracks at Pomeroy in the early hours of 20 March and another
attack on the Special Constabulary barracks at Maghera that night.
Special Constabulary Constable Joseph Stinson was dragged off

his bicycle near Grangemore and shot seven times by the IRA. He managed to survive, but Robert Milligan, 'an Orange farmer', was shot dead on his land near the border. This campaign had direct southern involvement. IRA volunteers from the 4th Northern Division in Armagh and west Down under Frank Aiken, moved over the border into camps at Ravensdale in County Louth and Castleshane in Monaghan, from where they waged their border campaign.

When St Mary's Hall in Belfast was raided on 18 March, the Special Constabulary found a quantity of arms and bombs, along with a cache of IRA documents, which included lists of local members of the IRA. The hall had been the headquarters of Eoin O'Duffy as liaison officer in Belfast during the early weeks of the Truce, and one of the documents found was a message from him directing the officer commanding the Antrim Brigade of the IRA 'to regard the Truce as non-existent', seeing that 'a state of war existed'.[18]

The northern regime suspected the Provisional Government was involved in the attacks on the border, just as it had astutely suspected its involvement in the February kidnappings. Craig was understandably suspicious of Seán MacEoin, the deputy leader of the Northern Command. 'You will recollect that Commandant MacEoin in his speech in Cork quite recently, acknowledged that a flying column of IRA was organised for duty in Ulster and offered to lead it himself,' Craig wrote to Churchill on 21 March. 'It is certain the whole matter has been organised and men imported from the Irish Free State to take part in these raids.'[19]

When *The Times* of London reported the suspected involvement of the Provisional Government in the border raids, Collins wrote a letter to the editor refuting the allegation. 'This is a most sinister statement in more ways than one … To begin with it is utterly false. No members of the IRA stationed in any part of Ireland outside the six counties have crossed into that area and performed any of the hostile acts alleged in the article.'[20]

12

'THREE OF THE MOST DELIGHTFUL HOURS'

On 23 March 1922, two Special Constables – William Cairnside and P. Cunningham – were killed in broad daylight in May Street, Belfast. In the early hours of the following morning five men in police uniforms raided the home of a Catholic publican, Owen McMahon, fifty, who was lined up with five sons – John, Bernard, Patrick, Frank and Thomas. All were shot, along with Edward McKinney, a barman who was lodging with the family. John survived by feigning death and his youngest brother, Michael, who was twelve, survived by hiding under some furniture. It was believed that the killings were a reprisal for the shooting of two Special Constabulary constables the previous day, but Owen McMahon had no involvement with the IRA or Sinn Féin, as he was a close friend and supporter of Joe Devlin of the Irish Parliamentary Party.

Even Churchill believed that Britain had to accept some responsibility for the McMahon slayings because she was paying large sums of money to support the Specials, 'some of whom had possibly been guilty of these murders,' he explained.[1] The notorious District Inspector John W. Nixon was reputed to have been involved. He was as unfit for service as the worst elements of the Black and Tans had been elsewhere on the island before the

Truce. The outrages in Belfast 'were worse than anything which has occurred in the south,' Churchill chided Craig.[2]

Publicly he blamed the Irish as a whole. 'I think one would have to search all over Europe to find instances of equal atrocity, barbarity, cold-blooded and inhuman, cannibal vengeance – cannibal in all except the act of devouring the flesh of the victims – which will equal this particular event. But I can find other instances in other places in Ireland.'[3] The outrages were not confined to any one side. An order to brigade commanders from the headquarters of the 2nd Northern Division of the IRA, which covered Counties Derry and Tyrone, called for all property owned by 'prominent Orangemen' to be destroyed and 'all reprisals must be taken at once. Reprisals must be six to one so as to prevent the enemy from continuing same.' The brigade commanders were told to shoot spies and informers on sight and with 'no mercy'.[4]

Nor were the horrors confined to Northern Ireland. Churchill denounced the killing in Galway of three men in hospital. 'If we are to paint these horrors in lurid terms, with all the resources of powerful descriptive rhetoric, they will have to be painted on both sides,' he said.[5] The Galway killings had happened a week earlier. Two of those slain were members of the RIC, which had recently been withdrawn from the Galway area. Sergeant John Gilmartin – a married man with two children from Leitrim – was in St Bride's Nursing Home suffering from pleurisy and was advised by his doctor to remain behind on medical grounds. Sergeant Tobias Gibbons, forty-three, from Westport, had been in the nursing home for almost three weeks, suffering from chronic nephritis, which was expected to kill him within a couple of months. Four men entered St Bride's and shot Gilmartin and Gibbons dead in their beds. They also shot and seriously wounded a sick constable in the same room as Gibbons. About half an hour later the men went to the Workhouse Hospital, where they shot dead Patrick Cassidy, fifty-five. He was recovering from gunshot wounds received at his home.

'Why is it that Irishmen will go on doing these things to one another?' Churchill asked. 'We seek only the repression and termination of these horrors.'[6]

Neither Craig nor Collins was able to implement their initial pact of January 1922, but neither did they make much effort to do so. Collins was unable to end the economic boycott, but then he went to extremes to encourage a political boycott by encouraging local councils in the six counties that were controlled by nationalists to refuse to recognise the authority of the Stormont government. In the nine weeks after the pact was signed Craig could not, or did not, try to ensure re-employment of any Catholics expelled from the Belfast docks. 'In all that time not one single expelled nationalist or Catholic worker has been reinstated in his employment, nor has Sir James Craig, to my knowledge taken any action whatever or even publicly expressed a wish that his part of the agreement should be honoured,' Collins complained publicly on 27 March. 'There are at present 9,000 workers, all citizens of Belfast, who have been driven out of their employment solely because they happened to hold different political and religious views.'[7]

Craig did not deny this. He just pleaded an inability to keep his side of the agreement. 'There is no law, as far as I know, whereby a workman can be compelled to work alongside someone else whom he does not desire to work with,' he explained next day in an address at Stormont parliament. He said that the 66,926 unemployed in the six counties included 8,000 ex-servicemen and he had made it clear to Collins that these former servicemen would get preference over everyone else.[8] If employment reached its old level, Craig said that he had persuaded the workers to agree to 'allow Catholics back to the yards'. He also indicated that he had no problems with Catholics in the police force and would welcome more and allow them to take charge of their own district 'to see that all the hooligans, the Bolshevists, the bomb-throwers, and the republicans and other classes were kept in their proper place'.[9]

The first pact was undermined by the Big Fellow's attitude to the boundary commission, according to Craig. Collins had kept him 'entirely in the dark' about believing 'that large territories were involved in the commission and not merely boundary lines', Craig explained in a statement on 28 March 1922.[10] Collins had never made any secret of his belief that the boundary commission would transfer large areas, but it was a measure of how little the partition issue had actually figured in the Treaty dispute in the twenty-six counties that Craig could claim to have been unaware of the fact.

With the situation in Belfast becoming steadily more dangerous, Churchill brought representatives from the three governments together in London on 29 March 1922. By the following day the three sides concluded another agreement, signed this time by Collins, Duggan, O'Higgins and Griffith on behalf of the Dublin government; by Craig, Lord Londonderry and E. M. Archdale for Northern Ireland; and by Churchill, Sir Laming Worthington-Evans and Hamar Greenwood for the British.

Collins got on particularly well with the northern delegation, especially the education minister, Lord (Charley) Londonderry. 'I spent three of the most delightful hours that I ever spent in my life,' Londonderry wrote. 'I formed a conclusion of the character of Michael Collins which was quite different from the one which I would have formed if I had only known him as I had read of him before this particular interview.'[11]

The three delegations concluded and signed an agreement which became known as the second Collins–Craig Pact. 'Peace is today declared,' the agreement began. It outlined a reorganisation of the police in Northern Ireland. In mixed areas the police were to be made up of an equal number of Catholics and Protestants, and members of the Special Constabulary not required were to be withdrawn to their homes and their weapons were to be handed in. The uniformed police were also to be disarmed, and all searches were to be conducted 'by police forces composed half of Catholics and half of Protestants', with the military being used as an armed back-up. A joint committee, comprising an equal number of Catholics and Protestants, was to be set up 'to hear and investigate complaints as to intimidation, outrages, etc.' All IRA activity was 'to cease in the six counties', and it was agreed that political prisoners would be released.[12]

Although the agreement had been concluded with Craig and his colleagues, Collins was clearly uneasy. 'I am not very sanguine from any point of view,' he wrote to Kitty Kiernan from London that night. 'The news from Ireland is very bad and "the powers that be" here are getting very alarmed and there may be a burst up at any moment. Were it not for the awful consequences I'd almost welcome it.'

From 18 to 26 March thirty people had been killed and thirty-seven others wounded in the north. People in Britain were incensed. Even Churchill denounced the outrages in the most trenchant terms, which gave Collins hope. 'Last week Belfast and the N.E. was dreadful to everyone here,' he explained. 'A few things are done by our political opponents and all is changed; they stand with Craig again immediately.'[13]

After the McMahon killings there had been comparative quiet in Belfast, with only one person being killed in the following days leading up to the latest agreement in London. The big news was the kidnapping of sixteen constables in Belcoo, County Fermanagh.

'The whole business is casting a gloom,' Collins wrote. 'I cannot help feeling that as a people we are destined to go on dreaming, vainly hoping, striving to no purpose until we are all gone. When I think of how the position is given away behind our backs.'[14] In this case, however, it was not his opponents but Seán MacEoin who was behind the kidnappings. Some fifty men under his command had raided a police barracks at Belcoo on the night of 28 March. They seized a quantity of arms and took five members of the RIC and eleven Special Constabulary as their prisoners.

Back in Ireland, on the evening of 1 April, Collins stopped in Athlone en route to Castlebar for a political rally the following afternoon. The local weekly *Westmeath Examiner* was highly exercised over recent events in Northern Ireland. 'The Belfast scandal reached its climax by the savage massacre of a whole family whose sole offence appears to have been that they were Catholics,' the newspaper complained in an editorial. 'Sectarian trouble and outrage abound through the Craig confines. The intensity at the border is such that any day it may precipitate a disaster.' With Craig assuring support to Field Marshal Wilson 'regardless of cost and consequence', the danger to northern nationalists and Catholics was obvious, but the remainder of the island seemed preoccupied with its own difficulties. 'Preparations are in progress in the rest of Ireland for a struggle that may well plunge Ireland into chaos and ruin,' the editorial continued. 'Most, if not all, the Sinn Féin organisations, male and female, have met only to emphasise the division in the ranks as well as amongst the leaders.'[15]

While in Athlone that evening Collins pointedly emphasised the northern problem in a brief address. It was obvious that he was trying to use it as a rallying cry. 'If we all join together and present a solid front to the north-east, I can guarantee everyone in Ireland will be united,' he said.[16]

The police taken at Belcoo a couple of days earlier were secretly being held at Athlone military barracks as hostages for the return of members of the IRA arrested in other raids across the border. Collins inspected the barracks and MacEoin escorted him 'around the area and attempted to hustle him past a tool-shed into which the hostages had been pressed', Padraig O'Farrell wrote in his biography of MacEoin. 'Here at least he belied the claim of being a "blind follower" of Collins. He was intent on protecting his own officers who had made the capture.'[17] If MacEoin was hiding the hostages from Collins it was probably because he suspected that the Big Fellow would officially wish to be able to deny any involvement. Some of the hostages called for help and Collins demanded to know who they were. MacEoin told him, but they were not released for over three months.

Unlike the cross-community acceptance that initially welcomed the first Collins–Craig Pact, the second agreement never really got off the ground after it was published on 31 March.

Next day RIC Constable George Turner, a native of Donegal, was shot dead in Belfast. That night a group of men arrived in lorries and went on a violent rampage in Arnon Street. In the first house they broke into they shot dead Joseph Walsh, twenty-nine, a former soldier. He was killed in his bed where he had been sleeping with his seven-year-old son. Walsh tried to shield the child, but three of the bullets passed through his body, seriously wounding the boy. Locals believed a Special Constabulary murder gang was responsible. Shortly afterwards, when a woman was crossing the street with Walsh's infant son in her arms, the baby was shot dead. The death toll that night in Belfast was seven dead and forty-three wounded. Those Belfast killings rendered the latest agreement with Craig a mere 'scrap of paper', de Valera told a public meeting in Dundalk next day.[18]

Craig ignored repeated requests from Collins for the proposed bipartisan committee to investigate the killings, along with the killing of Constable Turner. It would be 'injudicious' to go back over any of the Arnon Street killings, or that of the policemen, Craig wrote on 4 April, 'in view of the pleasing fact that peace has reigned for over twenty-four hours'.[19]

'It is imperatively necessary to have inquiry into all cases,' Collins insisted. 'We believe continuation of peace and restoration of confidence depend on the inquiry. The conditions of the Agreement must apply rigidly from date of signing; otherwise they are valueless.'[20]

'I differ profoundly,' Craig replied. 'A few days were required to establish the peaceful conditions now prevailing. I cannot consent to rake up past cases. Such action might cause fresh outburst of bitterness which we are so anxious to avoid.'[21]

Collins was not even demanding an inquiry into the McMahon case; he was just insisting that the outrages that had occurred since the signing of the latest agreement be investigated. Those had occurred only a couple of days earlier, yet Craig was already referring to them as 'past cases'.

'Have seen Bishop MacRory and several prominent Belfast Catholics,' Collins telegraphed back. 'They are all at one in stressing the necessity for an inquiry. They are emphatic that it is necessary both for the purpose of carrying out the agreement and for showing that both sides are determined to do all that is required for peace. I therefore urge you to make necessary announcement without delay otherwise situation may become critical.'[22]

'Can't submit issue to either the police committee or to an enquiry,' Craig replied the following day.[23]

'I waited to consult colleagues and advisers,' Collins telegraphed on 8 April. 'All of opinion that if inquiry not held into all cases which have occurred since the agreement, the hopes of peace will be greatly diminished and the situation will again revert to the pre-agreement conditions.'[24]

Collins had a particularly stormy meeting in Castlebar on Sunday 2 April 1922. Initially motorcars and trains were held up to prevent Treaty supporters from getting to the meeting. A train from Ballina had to be cancelled, but its prospective passengers were luckier than the 300 people who set out from Sligo at about 11.30 a.m. In Swinford they were informed the rails had been lifted down the line, about two miles from Kiltimagh. It was 3 p.m. before they were able to continue their journey. Then fourteen armed republicans held them up and forced them to lift the rails again at the spot where they had just been replaced. The train had to reverse to Swinford before returning to Sligo, which they reached about 9 p.m.

Meanwhile the Castlebar meeting had to contend with persistent interruptions, some of which were particularly dramatic. As Collins was speaking from a makeshift platform on the back of a lorry, a motorcar drew up beside him and Thomas Campbell, a solicitor from Swinford, produced a list of typewritten questions to which he demanded answers. Collins invited him to hand over the questions and there was a brief private exchange between the two of them. 'He won't give them to me,' Collins shouted to the crowd and then stressed that the national struggle was for freedom, no matter what they called it. 'We struggle for it under many different titles throughout our history, and we struggle no less against the republican Cromwell than against the monarchical Elizabeth,' he said. 'We wanted the fullest amount of freedom that could be won at any time.'[25]

As Campbell continued to interrupt, some men had to be restrained from rushing him. He pointed at Collins and shouted: 'The faithful subject of King George!'

'Your conduct is worthy of your record,' Collins replied as he swung around angrily. 'You took good care to be in jail when there was danger.'[26]

Suddenly there was further commotion as some men tried to drive away the lorry that was being used for the platform. Alex McCabe, one of the pro-Treaty deputies on the platform, drew his revolver and threatened the would-be hijackers, generating moments of electrifying tension. Numerous revolvers were produced. Portions of the crowd took flight and an anti-Treaty officer in uniform announced they were going to arrest McCabe.

An angry scene ensued, as a priest pleaded with the uniformed officer and his men.

Charles Byrne, a tall, young Dubliner, dashed through the highly strung crowd, pursued by officers in uniform. He raced down a side street and several shots were fired. Many women screamed and some even fainted. One woman received a bullet wound, but the crowd around the lorry held their ground. In the brief lull that followed Collins proceeded with his address, only to be interrupted again.

'Aren't you ashamed of the man who shot the woman?' a uniformed anti-Treaty officer shouted.

'Everyone here knows I am not responsible for that,' the Big Fellow replied and the crowd cheered.

Another anti-Treaty officer then announced that the meeting was being terminated 'in the interests of peace'. Somebody started up the lorry and Collins promptly jumped off as the vehicle was driven away, much to the consternation of the platform guests. Thus the meeting ended in disarray.[27]

Collins went to a hotel with some colleagues. An anti-Treaty officer came and announced that nobody would be allowed to leave until they surrendered their arms, but Michael Kilroy, the divisional commandant, was called and he rescinded this order.

13

'Civil war can only be averted by a miracle'

De Valera was widely blamed for the disruptive tactics of the anti-Treaty volunteers, because he had initially stoked radical republican passions and then was not able to control them. He was pretending to lead but his supposed followers were actually dragging him along. He made approving statements to conceal his differences with them, and he soon found himself a prisoner of his own deception. He was like a man floundering in quicksand, sinking deeper every time he tried to move.

'If the Irish people were allowed a free choice,' de Valera told a public gathering in Dun Laoghaire on 6 April 1922, they would choose by an overwhelming majority exactly what the breakaway section of the IRA desired. But he still paid lip service to democracy. 'Everybody regards the will of the Irish people as supreme … This nation, taking away all force, should have the right to do with itself what it wants, but I would say further, that even in the circumstances of the moment – even with the threat of war – the Irish people would have the right, if they wanted to, to avoid war by taking another course.'[1]

'The threat of war from this government is intimidation operating on the side of Mr Griffith and Mr Collins as sure and as definite as if these gentlemen were using it themselves, and far more effective, because indirect and well kept in the background,' he argued. 'Is our army to be blamed if it strives to save the people from being influenced by, and from the consequences of, giving way to this intimidation?'[2] Yet he was doing the same thing himself and he was talking out of both sides of his mouth, or as some would probably say, out of both ends.

Collins condemned de Valera for using the emotive language of a despot. 'And not the avowed despot,' he told a gathering in Wexford on 9 April, 'but a more dangerous one – of the despot posing as a greater lover of liberty than other men, of a despot who shouted the name of liberty louder while he tramples the forms of liberty underfoot.'[3]

He continued, 'We are told that the Treaty will not bring us peace. The Treaty has already brought us peace with our British enemy. If it will not bring us peace now, it will be because there are those who do not wish it to bring us peace. Was it by civil war, by shedding the blood of our brothers, that we could win peace and freedom? This is the language of treason, not of patriotism.

'If civil war breaks out – and unless there is an immediate change of tone and tactics it looks as if civil war can only be averted by a miracle – there is little doubt that the British will return,' Collins warned.

'If we proceed to fly at each other's throats, the British will come back again to restore their government, and they will have justified themselves in the eyes of the world. They will have made good their claim that we were unable and unfit to govern ourselves. Would not Mr de Valera, then, pause and consider where his language, if translated into action, was hurrying the nation? He had much power for good or evil. Could he not cease his incitements – for incitement they were, whatever his personal intentions. Could he not strive to create a good atmosphere, instead of a bad one?'[4]

He also warned about the consequences of violence in the six counties. 'If the so-called government in Belfast has not the power nor the will to protect its citizens then the Irish government must find means to protect them … We all know only too well the hopes and aims of Orange north-east Ulster. They are well expressed in the world with the lightly veiled brutality in the language of Sir Henry Wilson. They want their ascendancy restored.' He added that 'mischief makers of the Sir Henry Wilson breed are leaving no stone unturned to restore British domination in Ireland.'[5]

Edward J. Byrne, the Roman Catholic archbishop of Dublin, took the initiative in helping to organise a peace conference between the two factions of Sinn Féin. Byrne, who had taken over as archbishop the previous November, had always kept a low political profile. 'Nobody had ever known him either to make a political speech or to write a political letter,' Robert Smyllie of *The Irish Times* noted.[6] The archbishop joined with the lord mayor of Dublin, Laurence O'Neill, in arranging a peace conference by inviting the leaders of both sides to meet on Thursday 13 April at the Mansion House. Griffith and Collins were on one side and de Valera and Brugha on the other. In addition to the archbishop, the attendees also included the lord mayors of Dublin and Limerick.

'We did nothing at the conference yesterday except talk,' Collins wrote to Kitty Kiernan, 'talk all the time – it's simply awful. And the country! But they never think of the country at all – they only think of finding favour for their own theories, they only think of getting their own particular little scheme accepted.'[7]

As it was Holy Week, one of the busiest times of the year for the archbishop, the only agreement that the two sides could reach was to postpone the discussions until the following week. But at least the two sides were talking to one another around a table.

In the early hours of Good Friday, 14 April, the anti-Treaty IRA, under Rory O'Connor, occupied the Four Courts and a number of other buildings in Dublin. It was estimated that over 300 men were involved in the seizures. Next day they seized Kilmainham Gaol, which had been closed for some time and had been under the control of a caretaker. There were all kinds of rumours of an impending *coup d'état*, but O'Connor said that they only occupied the buildings because they did not have enough room elsewhere. He added, however, that scrapping the Treaty was the only way of avoiding civil war.

The similarity with the start of the Easter Rebellion, six years earlier, was unmistakable. The Irish Volunteers had merely seized prominent buildings in 1916. The fighting began when the government forces tried to regain the buildings. O'Connor and company were now throwing down the gauntlet to the Provisional Government, but, much to Churchill's initial frustration, Collins was not about to behave the same way as the British had done.

Although many again assumed that de Valera was behind the takeover, he had nothing to do with it. 'I remember the day shortly after occupying the Four Courts when Rory O'Connor told Erskine and me that he had acted without consulting or even informing you of what was planned,' Erskine Childers' wife, Molly, later wrote to de Valera. 'He made his reasons clear. He and his staff had decided to act independent of political leaders.'[8] In fact, de Valera was not even informed, much less consulted, in advance. Nevertheless he did nothing to disabuse the public misconception. A Labour Party deputation that called on him later the same day found him particularly unreceptive to their pleas for peace. 'We spent two hours pleading with him, with a view to averting the impending calamity of civil war,' J. T. O'Farrell, a member of the deputation, later recalled.[9] 'The majority have no right to do wrong,' de Valera told them. 'He repeated that at least a dozen times in the course of the interview.' The Long Fellow refused to accept he had a 'duty to observe the decision of the majority until it was reversed', according to O'Farrell.[10]

De Valera indignantly refuted the idea that he was trying to incite civil war. 'If you got a unanimous vote of the people telling you to go and shoot your neighbour, you would be quite in the wrong in carrying out that majority will,' de Valera explained years later. 'You would not be right. Therefore, the majority rule does not give to anybody the right to do anything wrong, and I stand by the statement that a majority does not give a right to do wrong. What was wrong in that statement?' he asked. 'It was simply the truth. To quote Kipling, the truth I had spoken was "twisted by knaves to make a trap for fools".'[11]

In a purely abstract sense he was undoubtedly correct, but he was not talking in the abstract on that Good Friday. Taking his remarks in their proper context, he was contending that the anti-Treaty IRA had a right to ignore the wishes of the majority of the Irish people. He actually issued an inflammatory proclamation that weekend which ended with an emotional appeal to the youth of the country: 'Young men and young women of Ireland the goal is at last in sight. Steady; all together; forward. Ireland is yours for the taking. Take it.'[12] It is hard to understand how such a statement could have been interpreted as other than an appeal for young people to support the anti-Treaty IRA which had just seized the Dublin buildings. John Devoy – the Clan na Gael leader in the United States and editor of the *Gaelic-American* – was blisteringly critical: 'It might have been issued from a lunatic asylum, for all the sense there is in it,' the *Gaelic-American* noted.[13]

At a rally in the Theatre Royal, Dublin, on Easter Sunday, de Valera said that they had been hearing wails about disunion. Although none of them wanted disunion, he warned that a certain section of the Irish people, followers of those who had died for Ireland – would go marching on. It did not matter whether they would be few or many, they were that section of the Irish nation which had been the point of Ireland's spear in the past. If people wanted to unify the nation they only could do so by uniting behind that section.

Collins spoke in Naas that day. It was very different from his recent rallies. 'Large numbers of troops loyal to GHQ were assembled in the vicinity of the meeting under their officers,' the *Kildare Observer* reported. 'Fortunately there was not the slightest need for their interference, the only "counter demonstration" being a youthful voice at the back of the platform and well away from the crowd which once uttered the cry of "Up de Valera" and was heard no more.'[14]

Some of those who preceded Collins on the platform had raised questions about de Valera's decision not to go to London for the Treaty negotiations. 'I am not going to argue as to why de Valera stayed behind,' he told the crowd, 'but I know the reason, because I spent five hours with him. I can say if he had gone over you would not have got what we got in the Treaty.' The crowd cheered loudly.

'We might as well tear off the veil of sanctity surrounding Mr de Valera,' Collins added.

'It is time,' someone in the crowd shouted.

'I am going to do it from this time forward, and I am going to tell the people where we all stand,' Collins said. 'The position is rapidly developing into a state of civil war.' Eight men had been killed and forty-nine wounded in clashes between IRA factions in recent weeks. 'The condition of the country is unstable,' he added. 'Life is insecure. Liberty is imperilled. This state of things must be brought to an end. It is a question now between ordered government and anarchy. The people want ordered government. They must, and will, have it.'[15]

When Collins talked about life being insecure, he could hardly have envisioned what would happen on his return to Dublin that night. He was dropped off outside Vaughan's Hotel. As he got out of his taxi, he paused to talk with Seán Ó Muirthile and Gearóid O'Sullivan on the footpath outside the hotel. A group of republicans suddenly rushed out of No. 44 and began shooting. It was initially reported that they had tried to kill Collins, but this was not the case. The garrison in the Four Courts later issued a formal statement emphasising 'definitely and emphatically that an attack on Mr Michael Collins was not in any way intended or contemplated. He happened to be in the vicinity during the incidents at Parnell Square, and thus got implicated in the matter.'[16] A number of incidents had occurred in the area earlier in the evening, when some pro-Treaty soldiers cruising around in a car had exchanged shots with those in No. 44. During the later incident Collins never thought they were firing at him, but he still chased one of the men into a doorway and took a pistol from him. The young man was promptly seized. Some time afterwards Fr P. J. Doyle, a staunch Collins supporter who had presided at the dinner in Naas, asked the Big Fellow what had happened to the young man who had attacked him in Parnell Square. 'He had a good face,' Collins replied, 'so I sent him home to his mother.'[17]

Next day there was a national strike called by the Labour Party to protest against militarism in the country. The strike received overwhelming support from workers, the public and the media. In Dublin between 6 a.m. and 9 p.m., there were no trains, trams, taxis, hackney cars or transport vehicles. Pubs, banks, theatres, law courts, restaurants and the Stock Exchange were all closed, and there were no public services, hotel or club services available. No newspapers were published in Dublin that day, the Punchestown race meeting was postponed until later in the week and even the Kildare Street Club was closed for the first time in its existence. 'This may be taken as an indication of the success of the stoppage of the work,' the *Irish Independent* noted.[18]

As a result of the success of the national strike, Labour leaders were invited to take part in the Mansion House peace conference when it reconvened on 20 April. William O'Brien and Cathal O'Shannon accompanied Thomas Johnson, the English-born leader of the Labour Party. The conference lasted little over an hour before it was adjourned for another six days. The atmosphere was poisoned by the intense personality differences. Brugha accused Griffith and Collins of being British agents. Both protested. They were standing in indignation. De Valera was standing, too, but

Brugha remained quite composed. Archbishop Byrne demanded that the accusation be withdrawn. Brugha agreed, explaining that he considered those who did the work of the British government to be British agents. Standing with his hand on the table, Collins leaned towards Brugha. 'I suppose,' he said, 'we are two of the ministers whose blood is to be waded through?'

'Yes,' Brugha replied quite calmly. 'You are two.'

For months vile accusations had been hurled at Griffith and Collins, while de Valera stood by indifferently, depicting himself as having consistently tried to maintain the republican position. He never denied his willingness to compromise with the British, but he now contended that there was never any possibility that this compromise would have been inconsistent with the republican ideal.

'Was that your attitude?' Griffith asked. 'If so a penny postcard would have been sufficient to inform the British government without going to the trouble of sending us over.'

De Valera tried to explain himself, but Griffith interrupted. 'Did you not ask me to get you out of the straight-jacket of the republic?'

'Oh, now gentlemen, this won't do any good,' the archbishop interjected.

'I would like to explain,' de Valera said, 'because there is a background of truth to the statement.' He said he was thinking of the straitjacket of the isolated republic when he asked Griffith to head the delegation to London.[19]

There was so much bitterness now between Griffith and Collins on one side and de Valera and Brugha on the other that the two sides had to withdraw to separate rooms while others vainly tried to mediate. The discussions were then suspended until the following week and the various leaders headed off for rallies around the country that weekend.

14

'WE WILL CO-OPERATE IN NOTHING'

Collins headed for Kerry, where the IRA had gone strongly anti-Treaty. There was a split in north Kerry within the No. 1 Brigade going back to before the Truce, as a result of problems after Brigadier Paddy J. Cahill was replaced by IRA headquarters. The Kerry No. 1 and No. 2 Brigades both went anti-Treaty. The two brigadiers, Humphrey Murphy and John Joe Rice, proscribed the pro-Treaty rallies planned for Collins in Killarney on Saturday 24 March 1922 and in Tralee the following day.

Accompanied by Seán MacEoin, Kevin O'Higgins and Fionán Lynch, Collins arrived in Killarney by train, along with a twelve-man army guard under Joe Dolan. An anti-Treaty officer met them at the railway station and told them that their meeting would not be allowed. Posters had already been put up around the town banning the gathering and the platform built for the occasion had been burned down. The heavily armed contingent of anti-Treaty men had a Thompson sub-machine gun, but their threats were withdrawn following the intervention of a Franciscan priest and the meeting was then held in front of the Franciscan church, where the sloping ground formed a natural platform. '"Maintain the Republic", Mr de Valera and his followers exhort us,' Collins exclaimed. 'What republic? Do they mean the republic we have had during the last few years with the British here – a republic functioning incompletely, with British laws, British taxation, British stamps affixed to our cheques and agreements, paying our revenue to the British? Is that the republic we are to maintain? A republic during which the enemy was here hunting, imprisoning, torturing, shooting and hanging our people.'[1]

Next day Collins and company went on to Tralee, where they met more opposition. Special trains had been put on for the Sunday meeting, but only the Dingle train reached Tralee. Others from Killarney, Kenmare and Newcastle West were stopped because rail lines had been taken up. Virtually every road leading to the town was also heavily obstructed. Collins and his colleagues were at morning Mass when the dean of Kerry denounced the efforts to prevent the meeting.

The military escort under Joe Dolan had been strengthened with the addition of twenty-four extra men under Commandant Dinny Galvin of Knocknagoshel. Galvin arrested a number of the Tralee republicans and seized their weapons. Humphrey Murphy, the new brigadier of the Kerry No. 1 Brigade and one of the more active members of the IRB to go anti-Treaty, protested to MacEoin about Galvin's actions. MacEoin, who was clearly unwilling to allow old IRB ties to influence his attitude, attacked Murphy, knocking him down some stairs. 'I jumped on him at the bottom of the stairs and I was giving him a few pucks when Collins caught me by the collar, hauled me up, slammed me into a little room near the front of the stairs and locked the door,' MacEoin recalled.[2]

When MacEoin cooled down, Collins ordered him to shake hands with Murphy, which he did grudgingly, and a kind of truce was arranged. The men arrested by Galvin were released and the gunmen from each side withdrew to different sides of the town and agreed not to disrupt the meeting.

One of the early speakers was local curate Fr J. J. Brennan, who recalled the Holy Saturday morning six years earlier when Roger Casement was walked through the streets of Tralee, escorted by only three or four RIC men, on the start of his journey to London, where he was tried and executed. 'If Michael Collins, who was so much blackguarded, was in charge of the Volunteers of Kerry on that day, [Fr Brennan] doubted very much if Sir Roger Casement could be brought away as he was.'[3]

The *Kerry Leader* newspaper had come out that Friday with a series of questions that the Treaty signatory Robert Barton had posed for Collins to answer in Tralee. They were the kind of questions that would be asked again and again over the next fifty years.[4] 'Did the Irish plenipotentiaries sign the Treaty without fulfilling their commitment to the cabinet?' Barton asked. It was ironic that he asked that question because he was one of those who signed the Treaty in the belief that they had fulfilled all their obligations to the cabinet before signing. It was only later that Barton came to the conclusion that Griffith's promise not to sign the draft treaty presented to the cabinet on 3 December 1921 had put the delegation under a further obligation. Collins ducked the question about Griffith's promise in his reply. 'Not one of the plenipotentiaries when they gathered together in their own house in London that night ever raised this question whatsoever,' he replied quite truthfully.[5] Barton, Childers or Duffy had not remembered the promise on the crucial night.

Barton's second question was whether Collins and Éamonn

Duggan had refused to present counter-proposals following their return to London on the Sunday before the Treaty was signed. They certainly had, but Collins brushed aside the question by appealing to the emotions of the crowd.

'No,' Collins lied. 'We did not definitely refuse. There are members of the Dáil cabinet who will bear me out on this.' Brugha had complained at the cabinet meeting about the exclusion of Barton from the talks, and now Collins said that when they got back to London he adopted the attitude that Barton could try for himself.[6] 'Go on now, Bob, go ahead and see what you can do,' the Big Fellow told him at the time, according to himself. 'That is the reason that I did not go, and my staying away got better proposals than we would get otherwise, because they thought that I was going to take the field against them again.' The crowd cheered loudly.[7] This was a time when emotion had more influence than reason.

The whole thing passed off so peacefully that at least one leading journalist saw the meeting as a really encouraging sign. Hugh Martin of the *Daily Mail* was making his first visit to Tralee since the height of the terror on 1 November 1920 when the Black and Tans told a group of reporters that they were looking for Martin, not realising that he was present. Their threats at the time made international news.[8] 'Personal memories of Tralee 18 months ago,' he wrote 'perhaps not unnaturally made today's evidence of approaching peace with honour seem particularly cheering.'[9]

***

Although President Griffith was now nominally in charge, Collins was recognised as the real power on the Treaty side. 'I deal with

Collins only because he is alone responsible for the split,' Mary MacSwiney wrote. 'All the young men who follow him – the young soldiers of the IRB – would not have followed Griffith two steps. But they believed and still believe in Mick.'[10]

Both Griffith and de Valera were effectively being sidelined, but few realised at the time that the Long Fellow had lost most of his influence over hardline republicans. 'If de Valera were on your side,' Mary MacSwiney wrote to Richard Mulcahy, 'we should still fight on. We do not stand for men but for principles, and we could no more accept your Treaty than we could turn our backs on the Catholic Faith.'[11] She was in for a rude awakening a couple of days later when the Catholic hierarchy issued a statement to be read out at all Masses around the country the following Sunday. It was a blistering condemnation of the 'immoral usurpation and confiscation of the people's rights' by those in the Four Courts 'who think themselves entitled to force their views upon the nation'. According to the bishops, 'the one road to peace and ultimately to a united Ireland, is to leave it to the decision of the nation in a general election, as ordered by the existing government, and the sooner the election is held the better for Ireland'.[12]

The Executive faction was determined to prevent elections, but de Valera adopted a somewhat contradictory approach. He declared that the people had a right to accept the Treaty, even when faced with the British threat of war. Yet, he publicly supported their opposition to the elections by contending not only that the electoral register was out of date, but also that the British were really making a mockery of the democratic process by using their threat of war to bolster support for the Treaty.[13] Indeed, Winston Churchill was deliberately exploiting 'the fear of renewed warfare' as a means of getting the Irish electorate to 'go to the polls and support the Treaty'.[14]

***

It had been decided at the Sinn Féin Ard-Fheis in February to establish a committee of northerners to advise Dublin in relation to the six counties. The inaugural meeting of the committee took place at the offices of the Provisional Government on 11 April 1922. In seeking to select members of the northern committee to advise the Provisional Government in relation to Northern Ireland, Collins explained that the intention of his government 'is to get the best possible advice from representatives of people in the north-east, in order to help and direct its general policy in regard to the whole question'. In particular his government was looking for advice in relation to the boundary issue, the Belfast pogrom, the 'possible re-institution of the boycott', as well as 'all governmental functions as affected by or as affecting the Belfast parliament'.[15]

The gathering consisted of fifty-one people. Thirteen of those were Dáil deputies who were essentially only observers, while the other thirty-eight were northerners from different walks of life, with thirteen of them being clergymen. Collins quickly indicated that he was only ready to implement the latest agreement with Craig if he could get anything out of it. He wished to use it to get an inquiry into the outrages in Belfast, to secure the release of IRA prisoners and to stop the raids of the Special Constabulary. 'The attitude we take is that we will co-operate in nothing, that we will just make time until we get these things,' he explained. 'If we can get this inquiry, the prisoners released, and raiding stopped by the "Specials", we are in a much better position from our point of view in any co-operation we undertake. On the other hand, if we don't get these things done we are in a much better position by breaking off.'[16]

The Big Fellow seemed to be using the second agreement with Craig merely for his own ends. He made no effort to rectify the situation in which Catholic schools in the north were refusing to recognise or co-operate with the Northern Department of Education. Northern Minister for Education Lord Londonderry, who had been positively effusive about his meeting with Collins in London in the lead-up to the second agreement with Craig, found that the Big Fellow was either misinformed or had misled him about the payment of teachers in Catholic schools in the north. 'You told that, as far as you were aware the Provisional Government was not responsible for these payments,' he wrote to Collins the following week. 'I find that we have definite evidence in the Ministry here that the salaries of certain teachers in National Schools under R.C. management in Northern Ireland are being paid from Dublin.' What was more, 'the extent to which the practice exists is very considerable,' he noted. 'Under whose authority this is being done I am unable, at the moment to say,' Londonderry added.[17]

Two days later he wrote again. 'I find that we have conclusive evidence in this Ministry that the education authority of the Provisional Government is proposing to conduct the Easter Examination of Monitors, Pupil Teachers, candidates for training etc. at centres inside the Northern area — vis: Armagh, Belfast and Londonderry.'[18] There was no escaping the conclusion that Collins was either double-dealing or out of touch with what the Provisional Government was doing.

Although critical of Craig's failure to ensure that ejected Catholics were returned to their homes in Belfast, Collins made no effort to get the republicans to evacuate the Orange Lodge in Parnell Square, Dublin. But then there was probably little that he could do about it or about the Belfast boycott, because the Executive IRA and its supporters were intensifying the boycott as a way of demonstrating their opposition to the Provisional Government. 'A certain lawless section in the country has illegally re-imposed the Belfast boycott and undertaken the destruction of goods consigned from Belfast,' Collins wrote to Craig. He added that many of those culprits had been actually driven out of Belfast themselves.[19]

'Although I fully appreciate the difficulties with which your government is confronted,' Craig wrote to Collins on 15 April, 'I feel sure that your government would strengthen its position if it took prompt action in dealing with every case of illegality that may arise.'[20] Craig was under pressure from Field Marshal Wilson, who was particularly critical in his diary that same day. 'A man caught eight days ago with bombs on his person had not yet been flogged,' Wilson wrote. 'I am determined to wake up this place but the real culprit of course is James Craig away on "several weeks holiday." It is disgraceful.'[21]

Wilson, who spent the week in Northern Ireland, was deliberately outspoken during his meetings with members of the northern government. 'Who is governing Ulster, you or Collins?' he asked them. Stormont could not act on 'my advice and the orders of Collins at the same time,' he said.[22]

In the meantime, Churchill had agreed to use his influence in an attempt to get Craig to inquire into the Belfast outrages that had occurred since the signing of the latest pact in London. 'I will talk with Sir James Craig and let you know the result,' he wrote to Collins. 'They will be greatly helped by the release of the Clones Specials, which I am very glad to see you have achieved.'[23] The Specials had been released on 10 April.

Churchill should have understood better than most the difficulties facing Craig, in view of his own role as secretary for war during the Black and Tan period. The same day that he was writing to Collins about talking to Craig, for instance, Churchill was challenged in the House of Commons about the outrageous behaviour of the Black and Tans at Balbriggan in September 1920. He defended what had happened. 'When officers of the crown, military and police, were ambushed and murdered under circumstances of the grossest treachery, it was quite impossible to prevent the police and military making reprisal on their own account. It would exceed the limits of human nature, however lamentable or however regrettable,' he explained.[24] 'Everyone knows that armed men will not stand by and see one after another of their number shot down by treachery, without to some extent taking the law into their own hands. Although the government did their best to restrain them,' he added, 'it is perfectly true that we did not punish with the full severity persons who had been mixed up in this sort of affair. We have never concealed that. How could we punish them while there was no other redress open to them, while no court would convict, while no criminals were arrested, while there was no means whatever of affording these men the satisfaction of a sense of self-preservation when they saw comrades weltering in blood from a foul blow?'[25] The Black and Tans had hit out blindly at innocent people, even children, and this was what the loyalists were doing in Northern Ireland. They were lashing out at children in an even worse way, such as the throwing of a bomb among children playing in Weaver Street and the murder of the McMahon children. Churchill had privately denounced the Weaver Street outrage, but he still seemed to be trying to defend this indefensible behaviour that was threatening to convulse the whole island.

Churchill had been uneasy about developments in the south for some time. At the end of March he had expressed reservations about arming the Provisional Government in Dublin. 'There can be no question of handing over further arms until we are assured that persons to whom they are entrusted will use them with fidelity to the Irish Provisional Government and will not allow them simply to pass into republican hands.'[26] But he was embarrassed by the news that the *Upnor*, a British naval armament freighter, had been highjacked by republicans off the Cork coast the previous day. They captured its cargo, which included 381 rifles, 727 revolvers, 33 Lewis guns, along with 29,000 rounds of ammunition.[27] To Michael Collins this capture of arms was a godsend, because it allowed him to justify asking the British for extra arms on the grounds that the republicans were better armed as a result of the *Upnor* seizure.[28]

'It is generally believed here that there was collusion between those responsible on your side and the raiders,' Collins complained to Churchill. 'We do not charge collusion from high responsible authorities but we are convinced there has been collusion from subordinates. It is absurd to believe that a vessel containing such quantities of arms and ammunition be left open to seizure in an area where it is notorious our opponents are well armed.'[29]

'I am quite sure there was no collusion between admiralty authorities and raiders of *Upnor* nor has such an idea the slightest foundation,' Churchill replied.[30] But he did agree to supply some of the requested weapons. He authorised Andy Cope, one of the assistant under-secretaries at Dublin Castle, to issue the Provisional Government with up to 6,000 rifles and 4,000 pistols at once, but he drew the line at providing a large assortment of grenades. 'I do not recommend you drawing, as requested by Dalton, 25,000 Mills Bombs, and 5,000 rifles grenades,' Churchill had already written to Collins a week earlier. 'These are the weapons far more of revolution than of government. If they fall into bad hands they could be a most terrible means of aggression on the civil population. I am quite ready to issue a small number for the defence of particular posts. Perhaps you will talk it over with Cope tomorrow. You never know whom a bomb will kill; very likely a woman, probably a widow.'[31]

Never the most patient of politicians, he was becoming uneasy at the way Collins repeatedly backed down rather than confront the republicans. Members of the Provisional Government 'were obviously afraid of a break with their extremists and have not shown themselves on any single important occasion capable of standing up to them,' Churchill complained. 'The Irish have a genius for conspiracy rather than government,' he concluded. 'The government is feeble, apologetic, expostulatory; the conspirators active, audacious and utterly shameless.'[32]

'A point might come when it would be necessary to tell Mr Collins that if he was unable to deal with the situation,' Lloyd George warned Churchill on 5 April, 'the British government would have to do so.' Churchill drew up contingency plans in case the Irish abandoned the Treaty and declared a republic again. Britain would introduce a blockade and exert economic pressure. 'The effect of a blockade would not starve the Irish people, but it would at a stroke ruin their prosperity,' he wrote. In 1921 Irish exports were worth £205 million, and £203 million of those went to Britain. 'This fact alone is decisive,' he wrote. Britain would set up some enclaves with aerodromes in the north and in the neighbourhood of Dublin, from where 'hostile concentrations may be dealt with from the air, or retaliatory measures taken if we are ourselves aggressively attacked,' he added. 'In this posture I think we could sit down for a considerable time until Ireland came to her senses, without any great expense or inconvenience.'[33]

Churchill warned Collins that the London government was about to adopt a stricter approach. He wrote that the 'Cabinet have instructed me to send you a formal communication in course of next few days as to the increasing gravity with which they regard the situations and urgent need that it should be coped with effectively by Prov. Govt. They have instructed me to state explicitly at Dundee on Saturday that they will in no circumstances recognise or negotiate with a republic should it be set up but of course they will stand by the Treaty as representing the full and final offer of Great Britain.' During his speech in Dundee, Churchill stated that Britain would 'in no circumstances recognise or negotiate with a republic if it be set up'.[34]

Collins responded by trying to put him on the defensive. The Provisional Government had been insisting that the people had a democratic right to endorse the Treaty, but in his Dundee speech, Churchill essentially suggested that the Irish had no democratic right to reject the Treaty, or do anything without

Britain's approval. 'The people here are not able to fully grasp the implications of such a statement,' Collins warned.[35]

15

'DRIFT ABOUT IN RECRIMINATORY CORRESPONDENCE'

Collins and Craig were becoming exasperated with one another over the inquiry issue, and they reached an impasse over the release of prisoners. 'Unless immediate actions were taken by Sir James Craig to show his good faith,' the Provisional Government decided on 21 April, Collins should warn Churchill it 'would be obliged to regard the agreement as broken'.[1]

'All here agreed that it is impossible to make further progress until vital clauses of the agreement are fulfilled by you,' Collins telegraphed Craig next day. 'Consider your attitude with regard to prisoners most unsatisfactory and entirely out of accord with letter and spirit of agreement.'[2]

Collins telegraphed Churchill on 25 April: 'General impression amongst our people in Belfast is that the northern government has no intention of abiding by the agreement. You will I am sure agree that unless something is done at once to remove that impression no arrangement that I could make with Sir James Craig would be of any value.'[3]

'I am sure it is much better to talk it over as we did last time rather than to drift about in recriminatory correspondence,' Churchill replied the same day.[4] There had been some positive results from the agreement, so he suggested they should meet again. He invited Craig and Collins to come to London for further talks. But relations between the two deteriorated even further when Craig provided the press with an advance copy of his reply to Collins, who resented 'the great want of courtesy' in releasing the letter to the press before Collins had a chance to receive it. 'In view of this publication,' he wrote to Craig, 'I propose handing all further communication to the press at the time of dispatch.'[5]

'I was obliged in interests of northern government to publish letter in consequence of your statement of Wednesday morning which directly charges us with failure to carry out the agreement,' Craig telegraphed in reply.[6] The letter to which he was referring was a detailed, clause-by-clause rebuttal of the Big Fellow's public allegation that the Stormont regime had violated the pact. A careful consideration of his complaints suggests that Craig did have legitimate grievances. All the wrongs were certainly not on one side. He regretted that the violence had not been quelled in Belfast. 'I had hoped the establishment of a Catholic constabulary force, intended to protect Roman Catholic areas in Belfast, would have been in operation before this date,' Craig wrote. 'We have been waiting for the formation of the Roman Catholic Advisory Police Committee, but I have not yet received the name of your representatives for this committee.'[7]

Craig recognised the 'grave troubles' confronting the Provisional Government and therefore stated that he refrained from making trouble over the Provisional Government's failure to curb outrages along the border. 'Almost a score of persons who were kidnapped from our area are still illegally detained in southern Ireland,' he added. These included the sixteen constables kidnapped at Belcoo who were being held hostage by forces of the Provisional Government. 'Although you have assured me that the boycott of Northern Ireland is absolutely contrary to the wishes of the Provisional Government', Craig pointed out that interference with northern trade had been greater in the past month than at any time since the boycott was introduced. The week after the agreement was signed, some 200 members of the IRA raided the bonded stores of the Dublin Custom House and destroyed 6,000 casks containing 500,000 gallons of whiskey, the property of Dunville of Belfast. Craig was aware of this because he was the chairman of the board of Dunville. 'Damage has been done to Northern Ireland goods aggregating in value many of hundreds of thousands of pounds,' he wrote. 'Our traders have shown great restraint, and our government has urged them to adopt no methods of retaliation, but has advised them to apply in your courts for reparation and compensation for which we understand your government will assume ultimate responsibility.'[8]

With Collins doing little about the Belfast boycott, Craig would only express platitudes about ensuring that expelled Catholics would be able to return to their homes and their jobs. He noted that his difficulties in this regard were 'aggravated by the hostility of certain sections of the people in southern Ireland towards members of the RIC who wish to return home on disbandment'. Former members of the RIC were being murdered regularly in various parts of the twenty-six counties, especially in those areas where the independence struggle had been most intense.

Much to the annoyance of Collins, St Mary's Hall in Belfast had still not been returned to its owners since it was seized in the raid by Special Constabulary officers on 18 March. Craig expressed the hope that it would be handed back to the owners 'as soon as they were in a position to guarantee that it will no longer be used for criminal purposes'. Of course, when it came to holding buildings, he noted that the IRA was still occupying the headquarters of the Orange Order in Parnell Square, Dublin, and in recent days they had also occupied the Freemasons' Hall in Molesworth Street, Dublin.

On the other major issue – the release of prisoners – Craig stressed that he had 'made it quite clear at our conferences in the Colonial office that we could not acquiesce in a general release of all prisoners for offences committed prior to the date of agreement, and that we could not countenance the liberation of those convicted of grave civil offences. In your list of nearly 170 prisoners for whose release you make request, there is a very large proportion of criminals convicted of murder and other serious crimes. The Minister for Home Affairs of Northern Ireland has carefully reviewed all those cases, and is prepared to recommend to our government – in accordance with the terms of our Agreement – the release of a number of persons convicted of technical offences of a so-called political character.'9

***

With opponents in control of the Four Courts, the symbolic seat of the court system, and its nascent police force still only in its training phrase, the Provisional Government was not really governing. Churchill was encouraged by reports that Griffith and Collins were likely to 'put their foot down and assert their authority strongly', according to General Macready. 'I am convinced that they would have the country behind them, except a few hundred, or possibly thousand, extremists like Rory O'Connor & Co., who will resist *any* form of settled government.'[10]

'There is no doubt a great deal to be said for the Provisional Government waiting its moment,' Churchill wrote to Lloyd George. 'Whether the moment will ever come is another question.'[11] He suggested in a further note a couple of days later that 'the personal prestige' of Collins, Griffith and several other Free State leaders had been 'greatly enhanced by recent events'. Churchill was clearly encouraged by developments. 'The Free State troops are now standing firm and firing back when attacked,' he assured the prime minister. 'I think the government is wise to put up with the occupation of the Four Courts until public opinion is exasperated with the raiders. I feel a good deal less anxious than I did a fortnight ago.'[12]

When the Mansion House conference reconvened on 26 April, the holding of an election was the central issue. President Griffith advocated a prompt general election, but de Valera demurred on a number of grounds. He contended that this would amount to a recognition of partition, because the election would only be held in the twenty-six counties, and he repeated his complaint that the electoral register was out of date. He also noted that it would breach the Ard-Fheis agreement, which provided that the election would not only be on the Treaty but also on the new constitution, which was to be published before the voting.

Collins offered to submit the issue to a straight referendum in which all adults could participate – whether their names were on the electoral register or not. The people would meet at the same time in designated localities throughout the country and would vote by passing through barriers where they would be counted, but de Valera refused to consider such 'stone age machinery', which he contended would still only apply in the twenty-six counties anyway.[13]

He was much more interested in proposals put forward by the Labour Party, which advocated that Dáil Éireann be recognised as the supreme authority and that it should invite representatives from all parts of Ireland to act as a constituent assembly to draw up a constitution for submission to the electorate. It should invite members of the Dáil and outsiders to act as a Council of State to delegate administrative authority to the Provisional Government. The Labour Party also proposed that the IRA should be united and confined solely to preparations for national defence. The army would be responsible to the civil authority of the Council of State, which would also take over the organisation and the running of a civil police force.

For a time it seemed as though the Labour proposals might be accepted, but they were contingent on the holding of a general election. Griffith and Collins insisted on holding the election in June, while de Valera wanted the election delayed for at least six months. 'Time would be secured for present passions to subside, and for personalities to disappear, and the fundamental differences between the two sides to be appreciated – time during which Ireland's reputation could be vindicated, the work of national reconstruction begun, and normal conditions restored,' de Valera explained afterwards. 'I promised that if Mr Griffith agreed, that I would use whatever influence I possessed with the Republican Party and with the army to win acceptance for the proposal, not indeed as a principle of right or justice, but as a principle of peace and order.' Mr Griffith refused.[14] The conference therefore collapsed, as 'no basis for agreement was found'.[15]

'We all believe in democracy,' de Valera told John Steele of the *Chicago Tribune*, 'but we do not forget its well-known weaknesses. As a safeguard against their consequences the most democratic countries have devised checks and brakes against sudden changes of opinion and hasty, ill-considered decisions.' In America a treaty needed the approval of a two-thirds majority of the United States Senate for ratification. As the Irish system had 'not yet had an opportunity of devising constitutional checks and brakes', he intimated it was legitimate for the anti-Treaty IRA to do so. 'The army sees in itself the only brake at the present time, and is using its strength as such,' he said.[16] For one who had championed the right to self-determination for years, de Valera had drifted into an untenable position in his efforts to obscure his own differences with republican militants such as O'Connor.

***

'The great swing of Irish opinion is increasingly towards the Free State and the Treaty and those who stand for them,' Churchill wrote to Collins on 29 April. 'From this point of view the delay has not turned out so badly as we in this country feared. You have not lost hold on public opinion; you have indeed strengthened it.'[17] Collins had become so conscious of public opinion that he became involved in a squabble with *The Irish Times* over what he considered its biased reporting. He complained of an inaccurate report in the newspaper about the alleged murder of five former RIC men in Counties Kerry and Clare, and the dangerous wounding of another. 'Three of the men were killed in County

Clare, and the others were shot in Tralee, County Kerry,' *The Irish Times* reported as its lead news story on 7 April. 'An early report stated that three were dead in Kerry, but a subsequent message says that two sergeants were killed there, and that a constable was badly wounded.'[18] The story of these killings in Clare and Kerry was unfounded, but the supposed killings received international coverage due to *The Irish Times*. The London *Times* and *Morning Post* both published similar reports 'in their most prominent columns', according to the Big Fellow. It so happened that John Edward Healy, the editor of *The Irish Times*, was also the Dublin correspondent of the London *Times* and another member of his editorial staff was the Dublin correspondent of the *Morning Post*. As the stories were groundless, Collins accused *The Irish Times* of essentially engaging in a smear campaign.

'It is regrettable,' he said, 'that any reputable journal should go out of its way to lend itself to that sort of campaign, but *The Irish Times* had consistently suppressed reports transmitted to it by the Provisional Government, from the official investigator in Belfast, as to the atrocities and outrages against Catholics in that city.' This, he added, 'was in striking contrast to the prominence *The Irish Times* had invariably given to reports of the atrocities alleged to have been committed by the IRA, and supplied by the Dublin Castle Publicity Department during the war in Ireland.'[19]

Later Collins protested over the coverage in *The Irish Times* of 25 April of what was happening in Belfast. 'In Tuesday's issue of your paper you devote twenty-seven lines to the persecution of Belfast Catholics dealing with the three days period of Saturday, Sunday and Monday,' Collins wrote to the editor. 'In these three days seven people met their deaths as a result of the pogrom, and twelve persons were wounded seriously. The activities of the pogromites went to the extent of bombing the congregation at St Matthew's Catholic church on Sunday evening, and the sniping of those who went to the aid of the dying and wounded. The evil work of the three days included the murder, wounding, looting, burning of houses, wrecking, and eviction of numbers of Catholics. Neither age nor sex was spared, and one of the victims was a baby of 5½ hours old.'[20]

While the Big Fellow accepted that the amount of space devoted to any story was a matter for the editor, he protested that the only victim whose religion was mentioned was the one Protestant fatality. 'You do not tell your readers whether all the others were Turks, Jews, or atheists,' he wrote. 'Could they by any possibility have been Catholics?' In his letter to the editor, which was published on 27 April he asked, 'Do you think this is fair or candid journalism? And do you still think my references to your paper published in your issue of the 11th instant were not fully justified?'

Healy had no answer to the complaint made by Collins on 11 April, because the report of the supposed killings in Clare and Kerry had been unfounded, but the insinuation of biased reporting on 27 April was much easier to answer. 'The report which Mr Collins censures had been followed immediately in the same column, by the full text of the Belfast Catholic Protection Committee's statement,' according to Healy. This statement noted that 'atrocities committed on the Catholic community of Belfast' in the previous three weeks involved the murder of seventeen Catholics, including three women and four children, the attempted murder of thirty-seven, and the wounding of thirty-nine other Catholics. In addition, the report noted that eighty Catholic families, totalling 357 people, were evicted from their homes, and seventy-five houses owned by Catholics were looted and burned. 'Why does Mr Collins fail to notice our publication of the committee's statement?' Healy asked. 'Is this fair or candid criticism?'[21]

Collins responded by providing *The Freeman's Journal* with a somewhat revised version of his letter to the editor of *The Irish Times*. It was altered to respond to Healy's comments. 'I cannot allow to pass unchallenged your throwing of bouquets at yourself for the "accuracy and impartiality" of your reports of the Belfast atrocities,' he wrote in the revised version. 'You plume yourself on publishing the report of the Belfast Catholic Protection Committee on the same day. Do you mean to say that this is an answer to the charge of your suppression, or ignoring, of the tragic happenings of the 3 days to which I drew your attention?'[22]

Sectarian murders were no longer confined to Belfast. While Collins was arguing about *The Irish Times'* biased coverage of the events in Belfast, thirteen Protestants were killed at the other end of the island in the Dunmanway area of west Cork. Their violent deaths were underplayed in Irish nationalist newspapers as hundreds of terrified Cork Protestants packed the trains and sought refuge in England and Northern Ireland. Similar scenes were taking place all over Ireland. Some 40,000 southern Protestants fled.[23]

In the circumstances Churchill wrote that he could not understand why Collins did not adopt a more understanding attitude. 'This makes me wonder all the more why you adopt such a very harsh tone in dealing with Sir James Craig,' Churchill wrote to Collins on 29 April:

I am sure he has made a very great effort to fulfil the agreement in the letter and in the spirit, and that he is continuously and will continue striving in that direction. Of course, no one expected that everything could be made right immediately or that the terrible passions which are loose in Ireland would not continue to produce their crop of outrages dishonouring to the island and its people and naturally you have many grounds of complaint against him. He, too, has furnished me with a long set of counter-complaints, and the Protestants also have suffered heavily in the recent disturbances. Belfast goods of very great value, running into millions, have been destroyed, debts owing to Belfast have been collected illegally and intercepted, and the boycott I am assured is more injurious in fact than ever before.

Perhaps you get some political advantage for the moment by standing up stiffly against the north, when you feel moved to anger by some horrible thing that has happened in Belfast, it may perhaps give you some idea of our feelings in Great Britain when we read of the murder of the helpless, disarmed Royal Irish Constabulary and now, this morning, of what is little less than a massacre of Protestants in and near Cork. Twenty constabulary men have been shot dead and forty wounded, together with six or seven soldiers, and now these eight Protestant civilians within the jurisdiction of your government since the Treaty was signed. All these men were under the safeguard of the Irish nation and were absolutely protected in honour by the Treaty. Their blood calls aloud for justice and will continue to call as the years pass by until some satisfaction is accorded. As far as I know, not a single person has been apprehended, much less punished, for any of these cruel deeds.[24]

Churchill was, of course, justified in suggesting that these killings were outrageous. It was understandable that people should be annoyed that nobody was apprehended for those deaths, but this did not justify in any way what had been happening in Belfast, where innocent children were being targeted, any more than anyone could cite the outrages in Belfast as justification for the killing of Protestants in the Dunmanway area.

President Arthur Griffith promptly denounced 'the terrible murders' in west Cork. 'Dáil Éireann, so far as its powers extend, will uphold, to the fullest extent, the protection of life and property of all classes and sections of the community,' he declared. 'It does not know and cannot know, as a national government, any distinction of class or creed. In its name, I express the horror of the Irish nation at the Dunmanway murders.'[25]

Collins also denounced those murders. 'I hope every friend of Ireland in south Cork will aid in bringing the guilty parties to justice and in protecting their fellow-citizens who may be in danger of a similar fate,' he declared.[26] He, no doubt, would have been mindful that Sam Maguire – his initial mentor in the IRB during his emigrant days in London – was a Protestant from Dunmanway.

16

'WE ARE FAST VERGING
TO ANARCHY'

There were various indications that the civil unrest was descending to anarchical levels, with a whole series of outrages in the twenty-six counties which involved different aspects of life. Any one of the incidents would have been sensational in normal times. Nobody was safe or immune from the dangers, and the challenges for the Provisional Government headed by Collins were as enormous as they were obvious.

On Saturday 22 April 1922, about fifty armed men boarded and set fire to the Ulster Steamship Company's ocean-going vessel, *Rathlin Head*, which had a cargo of phosphate from New Orleans. It was moored at Sir John Rogerson's Quay, Dublin. Ex-Sergeant John Dunne, a native of Glenart, County Wicklow, was killed the next day in Ennis. He had served for over thirty years in the recently disbanded RIC. The day after this Brigadier General George Adamson – a veteran of the First World War who returned home to serve in the IRA in the War of Independence – was killed in Athlone and on Tuesday eighteen-year-old Thomas O'Malley was killed in Garbally, County Galway. He was a passenger in a lorry that was stopped by 'a party of desperadoes', who shot him for no apparent reason.[1] All of these events, along with the killing of thirteen Protestants over the next three days, were generally attributed to republicans, but there may well have been an element of greedy opportunism on the part of some people. Some of the robberies around the country were undoubtedly freelance operations, contributing to a growing sense of lawlessness that seemed to border on chaos.

On 26 April three British army officers – Lieutenants R. A. Hendy, G. R. Dove and K. L. Henderson – were kidnapped in Macroom, held for two days and then taken to an isolated bog, where they were shot and buried. Also on 26 April, republicans in Mullingar took six soldiers attached to the Beggars Bush command hostage. The following day, their colleagues retaliated by killing a lorry driver and seizing the lorry along with twenty-five anti-Treaty soldiers. They were held as hostages and a prisoner exchange was quickly arranged, thereby ending the standoff.

Mayo County Council had an extraordinary meeting in which Thomas Campbell, the Swinford solicitor who confronted Collins at Castlebar, moved that the council strike a rate of six pence in the pound to raise £2,000 to pay the IRA's local debts. The chairman ruled the motion out of order because the minister for local government and the minister for defence had stated that the Provisional Government would pay the IRA's legitimate debts and if the council interfered it would lose other grants, such as £12,000 to provide for unemployment relief in the area. 'The people of west Mayo recognised the authority of Dáil Éireann,' one member said. 'They wanted none of the hooliganism displayed by Mr Campbell' while Collins was in Castlebar. The chairman announced the meeting was concluded and he left the room. As the secretary was gathering his papers another member took the chair. Two men then stopped the secretary as he tried to leave and forced him to return at gunpoint. Even though the chairman and other members had left, the same motion was put to those remaining, and it was 'passed unanimously'.[2]

The anti-Treaty IRA ordered the *Clonmel Nationalist* newspaper to submit its copy for censorship and when the editor refused, the publication of his newspaper was blocked. *The Freeman's Journal* had returned to full publication on 25 April 1922, following the destruction of its machinery by Rory O'Connor's men at the end of March.

Some opponents of the Treaty believed that civil war would be worse than accepting the Treaty, especially when the majority of the Irish people clearly supported it. Seán O'Hegarty – the officer commanding the Cork No. 1 Brigade, who had organised the seizure of the arms ship, *Upnor* – approached Collins on Friday 28 April with a view to trying to prevent civil war. 'We talked over the situation generally,' O'Hegarty noted afterwards. Next day they met again, this time in company with Dick Mulcahy. They decided to get a number of anti-Treaty and pro-Treaty military people together 'to endeavour to come to some agreement'.[3]

The Big Fellow was probably always more interested in talks with army leaders than with politicians. 'What troubled Collins was the split in the army,' Seán Ó Muirthile wrote. 'There were men in the army that he would go almost any distance to satisfy. He would rather, as he said to me more than once, have one of the type of Liam Lynch, Liam Deasy, Tom Hales, Rory O'Connor or Tom Barry on his side than a dozen like de Valera.'[4]

Over the last weekend in April and the start of May there were further indications of growing unrest. Anti-Treaty forces seized control of the jail in Kilkenny and then seized whiskey from bonded stores. They alleged the whiskey was from Northern Ireland, but it was actually from Powers of Dublin. They brought the whiskey to the jail. Next morning, at 6 a.m., Colonel Commandant J. T. Prout's troops, who were loyal to the Beggars Bush command, issued an ultimatum to the forces in the prison to give up the whiskey and vacate the jail within twelve hours. With the help of Mayor Peter DeLoughry, the whiskey was given up and the occupying forces left the jail before the ultimatum expired.

Also over this weekend, trains were held up and raided at Kenmare, Lismore, Nenagh, Bridgetown and Limerick Junction. RIC Constable Benjamin Bentley, a native of London, was ambushed and killed near Drogheda on Sunday morning on his way to collect a preacher for Sunday services at Gormanston Camp, where the remnants of the RIC were encamped.

On Monday afternoon branches of the Bank of Ireland were simultaneously robbed at locations around the country – Waterford, Sligo, Wexford, Tralee, Westport, Clonmel, Ballina, Mallow, Ennis, Claremorris, Mitchelstown, Sharpeville and Limerick. A statement was issued from the Four Courts stating that this was being done because Richard Mulcahy had not fulfilled his obligation to pay all Irish army debts, including those of the Executive IRA. Banks at Boyle, Gorey, Enniscorthy, Tipperary, Castlebar, Roscrea and Ferns were also robbed. The funeral of Constable Bentley was held and afterwards some of his colleagues travelled through Drogheda, shooting indiscriminately through windows, reminiscent of the behaviour of the Black and Tans.

Ten different military leaders got together on that Monday. In addition to Collins, Mulcahy, O'Hegarty and O'Duffy, were Gearóid O'Sullivan (adjutant general, pro-Treaty IRA), Florrie

O'Donoghue (adjutant general, anti-Treaty IRA), Dan Breen, who held no official position at this time, and three other commanding officers – Tom Hales of Cork No. 3 Brigade and Humphrey Murphy, Kerry No. 1, who were both anti-Treaty, and the pro-Treaty Seán Boylan of the 1st Eastern Division. Seán O'Hegarty suggested that the meeting should agree on a public statement to be issued. Two of the anti-Treaty people drafted this statement. 'If the present drift is maintained, a conflict of comrades is inevitable. This would be the greatest calamity in Irish history, and would leave Ireland broken for generations,' they warned.[5]

'To avert this catastrophe we believe that a closing of the ranks all round is necessary … We suggest to all leaders, army and political, and all citizens and soldiers of Ireland, the advisability of a unification of forces on the basis of the acceptance of the utilisation of our present national position in the best interests of Ireland.' They went on to call for 'acceptance of the fact, admitted by all sides, that the majority of the people of Ireland are willing to accept the Treaty'. The draft called for 'an agreed election, leaving undisturbed the present representation'. Holding an election just to return the same people seemed pointless. Collins suggested it was necessary to provide for Labour Party representation, so all agreed to redraft the clause to call 'an agreed election with a view to forming a government which will have the confidence of the whole country'.[6] Liam Mellows of the Four Courts Executive denounced the initiative as 'another political dodge'.[7] But *The Freeman's Journal* described the military initiative as 'the most hopeful event that has occurred in Ireland since the unity of the nation was shattered last December'.[8]

The officers involved in the peace initiative were invited to appear in the Dáil. Seán O'Hegarty became the first non-member to address the Dáil. 'You have two sections of the army in Ireland and you have for many months feverish activity on both sides, recruiting on both sides, and putting arms into the hands of men that never saw a gun,' he told the assembly. 'For the last week little conflicts have occurred here and there, most of them in places where there never was anything done when hostilities were on.'[9]

'The condition of the country at the present moment is one that should give us all concern,' Collins warned. 'The country quite apart from any political differences is drifting into economic chaos.' The way things were going, doing business was going to become impossible. 'The banks are going to close down over large areas of the country,' he said. 'What will be the economic substitute for the banks?'[10]

The press was already becoming disillusioned with the politicians. That day the *Irish Independent* had an editorial that was blisteringly critical of de Valera. 'It is scarcely necessary to treat Mr de Valera's tactics seriously,' the editorial contended. 'He objects to the present register as a basis for the coming election; in the same breath he scoffs at a plebiscite of every person over 21. A minority may, he tells us, uphold certain rights as against a majority by force of arms.' This amounted to championing 'military dictatorship'.[11]

'Is this Mr de Valera's interpretation of democracy?' the newspaper asked. 'If the elections be postponed for six months, Mr de Valera tells us, the work of national reconstruction can meanwhile be begun. Yet his every act is to obstruct the Provisional Government, the only body which has the power and the machinery to undertake this work. A leader who uses such arguments should not be taken seriously.'[12]

The officers involved in the peace talks continued their discussions, and they were joined by Liam Lynch, Rory O'Connor and Liam Mellows on the anti-Treaty side. The Dáil set up a ten-strong committee, with five from each side, to explore every possibility of agreement. Their main aim was to organise an agreed election from which a coalition of the two sides of Sinn Féin would emerge to preserve peace as a united government.

The thought of going to war against those old comrades was abhorrent to Collins. Recently Paddy Daly, one of those who had helped him in Liverpool, had notified him that he felt obliged to oppose the Treaty. Collins wrote back defending his own stance and wishing Daly well. 'Believe me the Treaty gives us the one opportunity we may ever get in our history' to achieve independence, Collins wrote. 'I am perfectly conscious that you are influenced only by what you think right in the matter, and with an expression of my sincere appreciation of your past service, and a hope that we may work in the same company again I leave the matter.'[13]

Collins felt the peace committee set up by the Dáil was a last desperate effort to patch up a peace agreement. 'Every avenue of co-operation has been explored, and we will have to take strong action to restore order in the country,' Collins told John Steele of the *Chicago Tribune*.[14] The interview took place in the Big Fellow's new office in the College of Science in Merrion Street. 'It is probably one of the most handsome and convenient government buildings in the world,' Steele wrote. 'If it had been built specially for the purpose it could not have been better.' He suggested that it would 'probably become the permanent home of the Irish government'.[15] Over sixty years later the state purchased the building and converted it into the taoiseach's office and department. The room that Collins occupied was modest and plainly furnished. He had a table and an American roll-top desk. There were a host of secretaries, typists and other staff in an adjoining room. Collins told Steele that he had just returned from the country where he had spent the weekend reading an account of the American Revolution and the early years of the United States by John Marshall, the first chief justice of the US Supreme Court. He proceed to quote an extract from Marshall's work:

> To be more exposed in the eyes of the world, and more contemptible than we already are, is hardly possible. No morn ever dawned more favourably than ours did, and no day was ever more clouded than the present ... We are fast verging to anarchy. Good God, who beside a Tory could have foreseen, or a Briton predicted, the disorders which have arisen in these states?

It was an apt quotation. 'It might pass for a history of the present days in Ireland,' Collins said. 'There are the same divisions, the same disorder, the same rebellious elements, America won through. So shall we.'

He confidently predicted that the pro-Treaty side would win the upcoming election. If de Valera and his followers continued their campaign of anarchy after losing the election, Collins said that he was prepared to take them on, but he added that there would not be civil war. It would simply be a police measure. His jaw stuck out, as he told Steele that the current peace initiative would be the last. 'If this peace effort fails, then there will be no other,' he emphasised. 'Every avenue of co-operation will have been explored and we shall have to take action to restore order in the country. It is not an easy problem; for a revolutionary government, in the nature of things, must take some account of motives. There is a lot of plain looting, robbery, and violence going on. That is common criminality, and must be punished. Also, there is a certain amount of commandeering from what, after all, is a patriotic, if misguided motive. That, too, must be stopped; but it requires a different method.'[16]

For one thing, gun control was necessary. 'There are too many guns in the country – uncontrolled guns,' he explained. 'A gun is a dangerous thing for a young man to have. Some day he may use it in a quarrel over a girl, or over a shilling, or over a word. That is one of the problems the revolutionary government has got to solve, and is determined to solve; but it cannot be done in a day or two.'[17]

With law and order clearly breaking down, the difficulties facing Collins must have seemed all the greater when the new Civic Guard mutinied. The force had moved its headquarters from the RDS in Dublin to the Curragh on 25 April. Between six and seven per cent of the men were former members of the RIC. About half of those had resigned for patriotic reasons and the other half had secretly been involved in the IRA. With only a few exceptions, the Commissioner Michael Staines, who was the son of an RIC man, appointed former RIC men to the most influential positions in the new force. The IRA men did not object to the presence of the former RIC, but they did object trenchantly to the prominent positions that they were given. Some of the former IRA volunteers formed their own committee and issued an ultimatum to Staines on 15 May. He addressed all the men and called on those who supported him to stand to one side, but, of the hundreds present, only about a dozen complied. He and most of the senior ex-RIC men then withdrew and headed for Dublin, where they set up their headquarters at the Clarence Hotel on Wellington Quay. Staines submitted his resignation as commissioner of the Civic Guard to the Provisional Government, but this was refused.

The following day select members of the committee formed at the Curragh visited Éamonn Duggan, the minister for home affairs, in Dublin. An effort was then made to collect the arms at the Curragh on behalf of the Provisional Government, but the men there refused to admit the superintendent sent from Dublin. The committee took over the running of the Civic Guard at the Curragh. They stressed that they supported the Provisional Government, but they were just protesting against the preference given to the former members of the RIC. About eighty men from the Curragh joined the contingent at the Clarence Hotel, while some 340 others at the Curragh continued their mutiny, which lasted for about six weeks. During that period some of the men at the Curragh defected with their weapons and joined the IRA.[18]

Collins and the Provisional Government had to deal with situations like this, and they were not coping. They were not governing, but then they had little opportunity to do so because so many people were frustrating their every move.

17

THE ELECTION PACT

De Valera seemed to be straying into the mists of metaphysical fantasy and the realms of unreality with his refusal to accept the authority of the Provisional Government. It was one thing to argue in the abstract that the Irish people had no right to do wrong, but he was insisting that they had no right to establish the Provisional Government, even if they wished to do so. He seemed to be suggesting that the people had no right to disagree with him and his supporters, yet he did suggest that the same Provisional Government – which had no right to exist – 'could use any machinery' set up under the Treaty, provided they did not depart from fundamental principles. In short, he was ready to co-operate with the Provisional Government in matters which he thought would advance the cause of Irish freedom.[1]

Collins waded into the same mists to take on the Long Fellow. 'Any people has a right to go wrong if it wishes, and no one has the right to deny it that right, or to deny it the right to exercise it,' Collins insisted. 'No man, and no army, has got the God-given right to say what a people may or may not do. Not even the Kaiser or the Tsar in the days of their greatest glory made such an extravagant claim.' Even where there were checks on the power of government, like the presence of a second chamber, these did not have a right to override the wishes of the people. 'Even the House of Lords never made any claim to deny the right of democracy,' Collins emphasised. No modern state existed on the army alone. The strength of each depended on the extent to which its executive and legislative branches were 'supported by a strong army, thus enabling it to carry out a virile policy'.[2]

Surely some of the conduct of the Black and Tans should have been a salutary reminder of the absurdity of the right to do wrong? What Collins was saying was as absurd in the abstract as de Valera's statement in the Dáil on 17 May. 'We cannot do anything that would give the impression that we did accept the policy of the majority,' he said.[3]

***

The way the country was going something had to be done to stop the descent into anarchy, and the discussions in early May with anti-Treaty military people such as Seán O'Hegarty, Dan Breen and Florrie O'Donoghue seemed to open the prospect of forging unity on the military side of the movement. Tackling the partition issue seemed to offer an avenue towards co-operation and on 17 May, Frank Aiken headed a delegation of northern nationalists that visited Dublin with the aim of putting pressure on military leaders to set aside their differences in view of the deterioration of the situation in Northern Ireland. 'If a Coalition government is formed here on a basis of good-will carrying through, let us say, the advantages of the Treaty position ...' Collins argued, 'we shall be on the road to a united Ireland.'[4]

Collins and O'Duffy had been secretly supplying the IRA in Northern Ireland not only with their old weapons but also with new weapons as the British armed the forces of the Provisional Government. Many people were employed filing off or obliterating the serial numbers so that the weapons could not be identified as having been supplied by the British, though the latter were never likely to be fooled. One of the men who actually delivered the guns in Northern Ireland was Seán Haughey, an officer attached to the Beggars Bush command and a native of Swatragh, County Derry. He was the father of the future taoiseach Charles J. Haughey.

At the Four Courts Rory O'Connor was aware of this secret co-operation. He believed that the occupation of the Four Courts suited Collins. When somebody suggested during the army unity talks that the Four Courts should be evacuated, for instance, 'Mulcahy laughingly said that as long as we held that place, the war against N.E. Ulster would be attributed to us,' O'Connor reported. 'We, of course, had no objection.'[5] In secretly agreeing to support a concerted campaign of action in the north, Collins was essentially playing with the idea of a military campaign to ensure the ending of partition as a means of reuniting the nationalist movement.

Griffith, on the other hand, had been anxious to clear out the Four Courts. When this was mentioned at cabinet meetings, Collins would thump the table and say, 'By God, we will!' But then he would do nothing.[6] He was playing a devious and dangerous game. Who was he misleading – the British, the radical republicans or his own colleagues?

'I suggested to Michael Collins that he and I should retire from public life and go to the north of Ireland on a defence crusade in favour of our people there,' anti-Treaty committee member Cathal Brugha told the Dáil on 17 May. 'If this proposal be not accepted and there are no further efforts at peace it is quite obvious that we will have fighting here in what are called the twenty-six counties.

'I am never going to fire a bullet at any of these men,' he added, 'and I hope that I am not going to die by a bullet from any of them.'[7]

As the talks were going on, Collins noted that some on his own side thought that he 'had gone beyond the limit of concession'. Some of the opposition were looking for a coalition simply to destroy the Treaty. Collins could not agree to this and, hence, he warned, 'from this stage it was quite clear that no agreement could be reached'.[8]

The anti-Treaty proposals called for a declaration 'that no issue is being determined by the election'. This was fundamentally objectionable, because it 'would make anybody subscribing to it a laughing stock and would make the election farcical' as far as Collins was concerned. 'There was no inherent thought or wish to interfere with the free choice of the electorate,' he insisted in his note covering the discussion. 'We would ask the people to regard the recommendations agreed on, if any, as entirely subject to their approval and backed by whatever influence we had in consideration of the national situation.' Throughout the talks he insisted that other parties and independents would be free to contest any election, no matter what the Sinn Féin factions might decide.[9]

Churchill was alarmed by reports of a possible election pact between Collins and de Valera. 'It seems to me absolutely necessary,' he wrote to Austen Chamberlain, 'to tell Griffith on Monday that we will have nothing to do with such a farce.' He suggested that Westminster demonstrate its displeasure by not passing the legislation necessary to create the Irish Free State after such an election. 'The Irish terrorists,' he added, 'are naturally drawn to imitate Lenin & Trotsky; while we should take our stand on the will of the people freely expressed.'[10]

Churchill wrote to Collins on 15 May. 'I think I had better let you know at once that any such arrangement would be received with world-wide ridicule and reprobation. It would not be an election in any sense of the word, but simply a farce, were a handful of men who possess lethal weapons deliberately to dispose of the political rights of the electors by a deal across the table.' He added that, 'It would be an outrage upon democratic principles and would be universally so denounced.'[11]

The ministers of the Provisional Government 'live far too much in the narrow circle of their own associates and late associates, and they think only of placating the obscure terrorists who spring up one after another all over Ireland,' Churchill told the British cabinet on 16 May 1922. The position was lamentable. 'The election should have taken place six months or three months ago.'[12]

'There is no likelihood of agreement between Collins and de Valera,' Tom Jones wrote to Lloyd George on 17 May. 'This is good news as what I most feared is an agreement in which Collins would be still further paralysed and the constitution compromised.'[13]

Collins offered a pre-election pact provided the pro-Treaty side was assured of a six to four majority and the minority gave an assurance that they would not try to wreck the Treaty. 'He was not looking for scalps or for anything that designated surrender,' he said, but he needed an assurance that the people's will would not be frustrated. De Valera argued, on the other hand, that 'the disappearance of the party spirit would bring ample security'.[14]

'We had pleasant conversations, but they did not result in

anything,' Collins told the Dáil on 19 May.[15] De Valera had still not abandoned Document No. 2, the alternative that he had proposed during the Dáil debate on the Treaty, but Collins had little time for it. 'The English are ready to give us all that is contained in Document 2,' Collins had said.

'Why the deuce then don't you press them to do so?' the anti-Treaty deputy Seán T. O'Kelly asked. 'I have grown to interpret your attitude to Document No. 2 as one of complete indifference even distaste for its realisation as a thing of no advance on the Treaty.'[16]

Collins replied that he had 'no objection' to O'Kelly's assessment. 'I certainly would not ask any Irishman to risk his own life or take the life of a brother Irishman for the difference – the difference which was described by Mr de Valera himself as "only a shadow",' Collins insisted.[17]

With de Valera insisting that the new constitution should be consistent with Document No. 2, the talks appeared to have broken down on the night of 19 May. Griffith welcomed this news. 'The man who stood up at any time against the English government on the grounds of democracy and the right of the people, and that now, when English government is gone from the country or is going, would stand up to say to the people that they must not determine for themselves, is as great an enemy to the Irish people as any English government ever was,' Griffith argued. 'We would be poltroons of the worst kind if, after having stood up against England and painted her as a tyrant, which she was, we should now submit to a tyranny just as mean and less supportable.'[18]

That night John Chartres, who had been one of the senior secretaries with the Irish delegation during the Treaty negotiations, called at O'Kelly's home at 91 St Stephen's Green. Chartres had just had dinner with Collins at the nearby Shelbourne Hotel, and he urged O'Kelly to intervene with de Valera, as he was sure Collins was anxious to make a deal. O'Kelly's wife, Mary, called her sister Min, who was married to Dick Mulcahy, and a meeting was arranged between the two men for the morning. Afterwards Mulcahy brought O'Kelly to Collins and a further meeting was arranged with de Valera, this time at the Mansion House. While the two leaders were closeted together, O'Kelly suggested that he, Mulcahy and Harry Boland should join the meeting to try to help 'to bring about agreement'. As the Big Fellow and the Long Fellow were discussing proposals made by the Dáil peace committee, O'Kelly asked how far they had got.

'We haven't got past the first b— line,' Collins said.

'Well,' O'Kelly recalled, 'I suggested, let us now start with the last paragraph of that report and work backwards. I am going to act as chairman. Thus, we five started. There was heated argument, there was abuse, which sometimes almost led to violence.'[19] After about three hours of argument the two leaders signed a pact. In accordance with it, the two wings of Sinn Féin would put forward a united panel of candidates in ratio with their existing strength in the Dáil and, in the likely event the party was successful, they would form a kind of coalition government in which there would be a president elected as usual and a minister for defence selected by the army, and there would be five other pro-Treaty ministers and four anti-Treaty ministers. In short, the Treaty would not be an election issue at all between the members of Sinn Féin.

News of the election pact received a mixed reaction in England. 'On the surface it would seem that Mr Griffith and Mr Collins have only found peace by surrender of their position, and that the election in June will be little more than an empty form', *The Times* of London noted.[20] 'Under this agreement the June election will be more or less a farce,' the *Daily Herald* observed. 'But perhaps the great advantage of the plan lies precisely in its apparent weakness. It is not a settlement – it is a postponement – and what Ireland needs is precisely a postponement of the decisive struggle until it can take place in more peaceful conditions.'[21]

'We should welcome this agreement very heartily if it could be demonstrated to mean that at least de Valera had gained an inkling of the truth,' the *Daily News* commented. That unpalatable truth was that the whole island was being reduced 'to a state of chaos which may easily develop into a disastrous reign of terror', that newspaper explained. 'The perverted patriotism of those who to gratify their vanity or to satisfy their own conception of the logic of liberty are prepared to sacrifice its reality has been Ireland's worst enemy since the days of Greenwoodism and the Black and Tans.'[22]

None of the principals on any side were pleased with the election pact. Some members of the Provisional Government were unhappy when Collins presented them with the pact at Earlsfort Terrace. They saw it as a victory for de Valera, but the Long Fellow did not share that view. It is 'no victory', de Valera wrote. He thought it was more likely a 'slippery slope', because he did not believe Collins would insist on a republican constitution. Having always seen himself as primarily a propagandist, de Valera was in a weak position in which he really felt powerless and besieged. Only the previous week he complained that 'the propaganda against us is overwhelming. We haven't a single daily newspaper on our side, and but one or two weeklies. The morale of the people seems to be almost completely broken, but that was only to be expected when the leaders gave way.'[23]

Others saw the election pact as evidence of the Big Fellow's reluctance to break with de Valera, but friends of Collins thought he had little time for the Long Fellow. 'He had no great regret regarding the loss of de Valera's friendship, nor no great fear of the opposition he alone could offer,' Ó Muirthile noted. 'He did not worry too much either about parting company with others of his political colleagues.'[24]

Cracks were even developing in the relationship between Griffith and Collins, and these became more apparent during the negotiations on the pact. 'Griffith is up in arms,' Collins told Seán T. O'Kelly. 'He is really angry and a number of his pals are backing him in his opposition.' Seán Milroy and Seán McGarry were both backing the president.[25]

'You are running away,' O'Kelly said to Collins. 'Can't you be a man of your word. You are the Boss. You have signed the Pact. You have the power to force it through. Go back and do so.'

'To my great surprise Collins did not react,' O'Kelly recalled. 'I thought he would get real vexed and curse and damn as was his habit. Instead he took my words quietly.'[26]

When the cabinet met to discuss the pact, Griffith 'seemed to be under tremendous emotional stress', according to Ernest Blythe. 'He spent three whole minutes reflecting, pulling nervously at his tie and wiping his glasses. The other ministers waited in silence for his answer.' Then in his typical taciturn way, he said, 'I agree.' And he made no further comment.[27]

'I think the majority of us almost wished that he would say

no, in the hope that Collins would be forced to reconsider his support of the Pact,' Blythe later recalled. But Griffith showed his displeasure by henceforth addressing the Big Fellow as 'Mr Collins', instead of the more familiar 'Mick'.[28] Despite his own reservations, Griffith called on the Dáil to ratify the pact. In the circumstances it was readily approved, and the whole process took only ten minutes.

'Though the air was electric with rumours of big political happenings, few anticipated the dramatic announcement of the success achieved,' *The Freeman's Journal* reported.[29]

The Sinn Féin Ard-Fheis was reconvened on 23 May to approve the election pact and Collins hinted strongly that he was endorsing it, even if it endangered the Treaty. Although de Valera was hoping that there would be no contests in the election, Collins emphasised that the pact specifically allowed for all other groups to put forward their own candidates. To keep the spirit of party unity, de Valera asked that there be no further speeches at the Ard-Fheis on the pact. One person objected to this procedure, so the pact was ratified by a show of hands, with only four or five dissenting votes.

18

'Northern Rebellion'

The political and military manoeuvrings in Dublin had taken much of the spotlight off IRA activities in Northern Ireland. For months Collins had been surreptitiously co-operating with the Northern Command, which was instigating a military offensive in the six counties. Commanders of all five IRA northern divisions met in Clones on 21 April 1922 and decided to stage a major uprising in the north, beginning in early May. The aim was to embarrass and destabilise the Belfast government to compel it to be more accommodating with Dublin, while at the same time aiding the search for IRA unity in the twenty-six counties by enlisting the support of the northern IRA and neutralising the partition issue. But the planning of this Northern Offensive, which was variously styled as a 'Northern Rebellion' or the 'May Rising', went seriously awry.

Chief of Staff Eoin O'Duffy promised that GHQ would provide the needed arms, but when the 3rd Northern Division covering much of Counties Antrim and Down was unable to get the arms it was expecting, the operation was delayed. As the 2nd Northern Division, which covered Counties Derry and Tyrone, pleaded that it could not postpone its plans on such short notice, GHQ at Beggars Bush authorised it to go ahead.

Collins was implicated in these operations, which were financed by the Provisional Government, but he insisted that all the activities had to be in the name of the IRA. He had never made any secret of the fact that he saw the Treaty as a stepping-stone to the desired goal. His ultimate aim was still an Irish Republic. His involvement in the military and political talks leading to the election pact with de Valera not only helped to obscure his machinations in relation to the north, but also lent credibility to his efforts to avoid civil war in the twenty-six counties. Assisting beleaguered northern nationalists was an issue on which he could find substantive agreement within the IRB and leading members of the IRA Executive, such as Rory O'Connor and Liam Lynch.

Liam Lynch blamed the Beggars Bush garrison for the postponement, because all the promised weapons were not delivered, but the British were already wise to the exchange. General Macready, the commander-in-chief of British forces in Ireland, reported that an intercepted message from Lynch to Rory O'Connor indicated that a 'considerable quantity of arms and ammunition (30 Thompson Machine guns with 8,000 rounds (.45), 75 rifles and 10,000 rounds .303 ammunition)' were to be dispatched 'at the request of the Provisional Government from North County Cork area for use in the north of Ireland'. Macready thought it was significant to note not only that 'the Provisional Government were responsible for ordering the dispatch of arms to the north or at any rate northern border', but also that it could afford to spare so many arms.[1]

'Under present circumstances burning and destruction of property is the only way in which we can hit Belfast men,' Minister for Defence Richard Mulcahy had told members of the north-east advisory committee on 11 April 1922. But he had some reservations. 'I don't think you will get away from the fact that if property is destroyed in Belfast now if there is any settlement that we will probably have to pay for it … And it is simply taking money out of the pockets of the Irish people generally rather than out of the pockets of Belfast Capitalists.'[2]

As the weapons being sent by Beggars Bush to the No. 2 Battalion of the 3rd Northern Division would not arrive in Belfast until just two days before operations were due to begin, the local commandant went to Beggars Bush and personally got GHQ's approval for a postponement.

O'Duffy instructed Seamus Woods of the 3rd Northern Division not to move until after a meeting of the northern divisional commandants. 'This meeting was held at GHQ on 5 May and it was decided that each Division complete its plans and await instructions from GHQ,' Woods noted.[3] It was left to the chief of staff to determine the date, to be in the near future, on or after which every division would strike.

The 2nd Northern Division had planned to launch its offensive in early May and got permission to go ahead on its own. On 2 May its forces launched simultaneous attacks on police barracks at Bellaghy, Draperstown and Coalisland. Special Constable John Harvey was shot dead at Bellaghy and three colleagues were wounded, while two were wounded at Draperstown. Various bridges and railway lines were damaged, and the IRA engaged in an orgy of arson. A weaving mill was set ablaze in Limavady and a flax mill at Ballykelly. The IRA also attacked and set fire to the home of Special Constable William J. McClung at Annaghmore, near Coalisland. When colleagues tried to go to his rescue they were ambushed and Constable Robert J. Cardwell was shot dead.

The IRA ambushed and fatally wounded Special Constable William McKnight about six miles from Cookstown. In another ambush that night a Special Constabulary sergeant and two constables – Sergeant Frizelle and Constables Hunter and Heggarty – were killed at Ballyronan, County Derry. The IRA also attacked the Special Constabulary post at Elagh, three miles north of the city of Derry, where one sergeant was wounded. In addition, they fired on the home of Major R. L. Moore, about three miles south of the city, breaking all the windows. He was not only commandant of the local Special Constabulary, but also grand master of the Orange Order in the city of Derry.

Six Special Constabulary constables were killed in the first two days of the offensive. But the 2nd Northern Division was very much on its own. Although both the pro- and anti-Treaty wings of the old IRA were supposedly co-operating, the adjacent 1st Northern Division in County Donegal was embroiled in a vicious internal conflict. On 4 May forces from the Executive IRA raided a bank in Buncrana and got away with £800, but not before engaging with troops of the Provisional Government. A gunfight ensued and several people were wounded, including two innocent bystanders – nine-year-old Essie Fletcher and eighteen-year-old Mary Ellen Kavanagh, who both died of their wounds. Some hours later the Executive IRA ambushed the Provisional Government troops a short distance away near Newtowncunningham. Four of those attacked were fatally shot and two others seriously wounded. The 1st Northern Division of the IRA was so bitterly divided that it was no help to the 2nd Northern Division, which came under intense pressure in the following days as the loyalists retaliated with ferocity by killing innocent Catholics in what were clearly sectarian reprisals.

On 6 May six suspected members of the Special Constabulary took two men, Catholic teachers John M. Carolan and his nephew Michael Kilmartin, from a friend's house, about five miles from Dungiven. Although shot six times and dumped into a flax dam, Kilmartin managed to escape and make it to hospital, where he died hours later. The same day John McCracken, a publican from Dringate near Cookstown, was killed in his bar. The following week there was an outrage that was hauntingly similar to the McMahon massacre in Belfast. Men wearing police caps raided the McKeown home at Magherafelt and shot three sons in the house in front of their elderly parents. James McKeown was shot dead instantly, while his brother Francis survived with sixteen bullet wounds and Thomas survived four shots. As in the case of the McMahons, the McKeowns had no involvement in Sinn Féin; their crime was that they were Roman Catholics.

The intense pressure on the isolated 2nd Northern Division meant that by the time the 3rd Northern Division began its offensive later in month, the IRA in Derry and Tyrone had already virtually collapsed. When the north-east advisory committee met in Belfast on 15 May, a few days before the 3rd Northern's offensive, it advised that the Provisional Government should notify the British government that Craig had failed to carry out the terms of the March agreement. 'We further recommend that the army chief be asked to consider the advisability of carrying out a policy of destruction inside the six county area, removed from the border with a view to making government by Belfast parliament more expensive and difficult,' the committee advised. It recommended the destruction of roads, bridges, railways and property generally. These operations were 'to be carried out as soon as government think it most expedient'.[4]

In view of General Macready's report that the Provisional Government was engaged in supplying weapons to the IRA, Churchill balked on 16 May at a request from Collins for 10,000 extra rifles. The colonial secretary was not prepared to supply further arms until he was satisfied that the Provisional Government would use them against the Executive forces. For a man who tended to see such matters in stark simplistic terms, however, he was apparently not fully convinced of the Big Fellow's duplicity. Churchill reminded his cabinet colleagues, for instance, that 'the lives of members of the Provisional Government were in danger. They were faced with every kind of difficulty and he was anxious not to put upon them more than they could bear.'[5]

The 3rd Northern Division of the IRA began its delayed offensive on Thursday night, 17 May 1922, with a raid on the RIC barracks on Musgrave Street, Belfast. The aim was to seize weapons and military vehicles parked in the yard of the barracks. With inside help, the raiders managed to enter the police station dressed as police, but then things went badly wrong and the whole station was roused by the fatal shooting of Constable John Collins, who happened to be a Catholic. The raiders had to flee largely empty-handed and they captured none of the vehicles that they had planned to seize. The following day the division's brigades engaged in attacks on commercial property in Belfast as well as RIC barracks, stately homes and railways stations in different parts of Antrim and Down. The 4th Northern Division was also supposed to have taken to the offensive on 19 May, but for some unexplained reason it did not go into action.

Buildings destroyed in the IRA's arson attacks on the night of 17 May included Shane's Castle, the home of Lord O'Neill, the father of the speaker of the Stormont parliament; Oldcourt Mansion, Strangford; Crebilly Castle, along with the stationmaster's office, telegraph office and a railway bridge in Ballymena; and Glenmona House, the summer home of the diehard Westminster MP Ronald McNeill in Cushendun, where the Northern Bank was raided and £2,000 taken. The raiders then burned the bank to the ground. Reid's motor garage in Carnlough was raided and the owner's car was driven into the street and set on fire, while the garage and an adjoining stable with a valuable horse inside were torched. As this was going on some of the men raided the local post office, and a number of private houses in the Carnlough area were torched. There were also attacks on the police station at Martinstown and the nearby Rathkenny creamery, which was torched. A Special Constabulary patrol helped to put out the flames but was then ambushed by the IRA and Special Constable James O'Neill was killed. Trees were felled to block the road near Ballykinlar, and a military officer and his wife drove into one of them. She was killed and he was seriously injured. *The Irish Times* reported that there were no casualties in an attack on the police station at Castlewellan, but *The Freeman's Journal* reported that three raiders were killed, seven wounded and ten taken prisoner, and seven constables were reportedly wounded. There were also attacks that night on police stations at Cushendall, Cushendun, Ballycastle Barracks and the post offices at Cushendall, Carnlough, Ardglass and Ballymena. Several stations of the Midland Railway system were extensively damaged.

Next day loyalist gunmen retaliated. Two men entered the lumberyard of J. P. Corry in Belfast and enquired about the religion of various workers. On receiving responses from all the men, they shot and mortally wounded John Connolly, who identified himself as a Roman Catholic. Two teenage cattle drovers – Patrick McAuley, eighteen, and Thomas McGuigan, seventeen – were killed at the Midland Railway cattle pens while loading cattle into wagons for Stranraer. They were among fourteen people murdered in Belfast that day. Although the story of the Dáil's acceptance of the election pact featured prominently on the front page of the *Sunday Independent*, even more space was devoted to the dreadful news of a serious eruption of trouble in Northern Ireland.

Six more people were killed on Monday 22 May, including the first political assassination. The IRA killed William J. Twaddell, a unionist member of the Stormont parliament. He was shot dead in the street in broad daylight. President Arthur Griffith roundly denounced Twaddell's assassination. 'His murder strikes at the foundations of representative government,' he said. 'The honour of the Irish nation is concerned in this matter.'[6]

On Tuesday the northern government invoked the Special Powers Act to introduce internment without trial. The police rounded up and interned 350 suspected republicans, including many from the divisions, as the northern authorities had the captured documents from St Mary's Hall which gave the names of nearly all of the brigade officers in Belfast. Only twelve Protestants were interned, even though loyalists had been responsible for most of the killings.

If Collins had hoped that the offensive would put the focus firmly on Northern Ireland, he must have been disappointed, because his plans were again upstaged by outrageous incidents within his own jurisdiction. Three former RIC men and a former British soldier were shot dead in the twenty-six counties over the weekend of 20–21 May. Timothy O'Leary, a former RIC constable, was killed on Saturday 20 May on his way to visit his mother in Kilbrittan, near Bandon in County Cork. A former RIC sergeant, J. Walshe, was killed in the presence of his wife at their home in Newport, County Tipperary, while former Head Constable Joseph Ballantine, fifty, who was about to move with his family to Portadown in Northern Ireland, was killed in front of his wife at their home in Raphoe, County Donegal. The following night Patrick Galligan, an ex-soldier, was shot dead in Newport.

The IRA in the north was initially content with the progress of the offensive of the 3rd Northern Division. 'Each Brigade made a good start and the men were in great spirits, anxious to go ahead, but in a few days the enemy forces began to pour into our areas as no other Division was making a move,' James J. McCoy, the adjutant of the 3rd Northern Division noted. 'Things became so bad in No. 3 (East Down) Brigade where lorry loads of Specials were coming in from Newry (4th Divisional area).'[7] Although the initial plan was for the offensive to be staged throughout six counties, it began one division at a time, with the result that the northern authorities were able to rush reinforcements from the different areas to suppress the different divisions one at a time. McCoy called on O'Duffy on 24 May to order the 4th Northern Division into action. The chief of staff said he would do so immediately, but nothing happened. 'A week later, as nothing was happening in other areas, we found it necessary to disband the columns, and leave the men in groups of three or more to move about as best they could, in the hope of re-mobilising them when operations became general,' McCoy noted. 'Under such conditions it was natural to expect that the men would become demoralised.' In the following weeks, he wrote 'the demoralisation has practically completed its work'. He continued his report:

> The enemy soon felt the operations were not general and concentrating in great numbers in our area, they realised that it was not difficult to cope with the situation. They now believe that they have beaten the IRA, completely in Antrim and Down …
>
> There is a feeling among the civil population that we are not recognised by GHQ and that our orders came from the Executive. Most of the priests are under this impression also and some of them in fact have said from the pulpit that they will not give absolution to anyone who is a member of secret Military Organisation … They have refused to hear Fianna boys' confessions.
>
> The people who supported us feel they have been abandoned by Dáil Éireann, for our position to-day is more unbearable than it was in June 1921. Then the fight was a national one and our suffering was in common with all Ireland. Today the people feel that all their suffering has been in vain and cannot see any hope for the future.
>
> The people who did not support us are only too glad of the opportunity of assisting the enemy, and practically all over the Division the Police Barracks are stormed with letters giving all available information against the IRA and their supporters. We have captured some letters and in most cases suggestions are made to the Police as to how they could best cope with the situation. In some cases they regret they did not give this information two years ago.[8]

19

'I CAN'T LEAVE THESE PEOPLE UNPROTECTED'

During a Dáil discussion on the northern situation on 22 May 1922, there were complaints that the Dublin press had not been covering what was happening in the north properly. Collins, despite criticising *The Irish Times* on those grounds only weeks earlier, now said that authentic incidents were being published and the journalists had been helpful. He saw no justification for threats against newsmen and was obviously playing to the press gallery as he raised the spectre of the attack in which the IRA Executive from the Four Courts had wrecked the machinery of *The Freeman's Journal* at the end of March. He added that he was sorry to hear some in the hall that day threaten to go on suppressing the press.

'Certainly, if they don't do their duty,' one delegate shouted.

'If you are for that kind of freedom, I have no use for it,' Collins replied.

'You will get more value out of the Press by telling them what their duty is than by forcing them to adopt what you think is their duty,' Collins continued after some interruptions. 'That is the way we ask you to look upon it, and if the advice of one delegate from the body of the Hall were to be taken, that the papers were to be burned all over the country, what kind of stable conditions would you have?'[1]

He was engaged in a devious game, telling various people what they wished to hear. 'Unity at home was more important than any Treaty with the foreigner,' he told some anti-Treaty people. 'If unity could only be got at the expense of the Treaty – the Treaty would have to go.'[2] He was trying to reconcile the irreconcilable, in drafting a republican constitution that would be compatible with the Treaty. Mary MacSwiney questioned his sincerity in seeking such a constitution. 'If he is sincere in that, why is he risking civil war on the acceptance of the Treaty?' she asked. 'Collins is undoubtedly a clever man, and I am sorry to say an unscrupulous one but do you think for an instant that he can beat L. George in the game of duplicity?'[3]

Who was Collins really trying to deceive – Lloyd George, Churchill and the British, or de Valera and his followers, or Liam Lynch, Rory O'Connor and the more radical republicans?

Although privately scathing about the election pact, Churchill adopted a more reserved attitude in public. 'We have not yet been able to form any final conclusion in regard to it,' he said. 'We have, therefore, invited the Irish co-signatories of the Treaty to come to London and discuss these issues with the British signatories.'[4] In effect, the invitation was more like a summons. Collins initially balked. 'I learn from Mr Cope with great apprehension that you consider yourself unable to come,' Churchill wrote to Collins. 'Your absence would I fear be misunderstood. Certainly it would be deeply regretted.'[5]

In fact Collins delayed his visit to London because he was trying to deal with the mutiny in the Civic Guard. On 26 May, as President Griffith and two cabinet colleagues – Kevin O'Higgins and Ernest Blythe – were beginning their talks with the British in London, Collins was in Kildare, addressing the mutineers. 'A higher standard of discipline is required in a police force than in any other body,' he told them. 'It is your duty to enforce discipline on others, and to show by your example that you are fit persons to do so.' When they finished their training, they were going to be scattered throughout the country, away from the immediate control of their higher officers. Hence their training at this stage was important. 'It is up to you so to train and discipline yourselves that when you go out amongst the people your conduct will contrast favourably in every way with that of the force whose place you are filling.'[6]

Next day Collins went to London. He told Churchill the pact with de Valera was necessary as an election would otherwise be impossible. 'The idea was to try and get a non-party government so as to secure tranquillity in Ireland and at a later date stage a proper election on the main issue,' he explained.

'The two parties agree to simply monopolise power,' Churchill told his colleagues. 'The one inducement offered to the public to accept the agreement is the hope of escaping from anarchy.'[7]

'The story of the surrender of the government to Mr de Valera was one of the most pitiful, miserable, and cowardly stories in history,' Field Marshal Sir Henry Wilson declared. 'Now ... Mr de Valera had Mr Collins in his pocket, and it was another proof that, quite apart from the misery of the thing, the government had miscalculated every single element that went to make the Irish situation.'[8]

Ever since Wilson had been invited to advise the northern government on security matters, he had been highly critical of Collins and also of both the British and the Belfast governments for not standing up to the Big Fellow. Wilson essentially depicted the British government as propping up Collins, who was being manipulated by the radical republicans. 'What are our troops doing in Ireland?' he asked the House of Commons on 10 May. 'Are they there at the request of Mr Collins? If so, will the Government say so? Will Mr Collins say so?'[9]

'Have the Government not yet learnt their lesson about Ireland?' Wilson continued. 'Can they not yet see that a Provisional Government, which is not able to eject a small handful of men from the Four Courts in Dublin and Kilmainham Gaol, is totally unable to govern 3,500,000 souls in the 26 counties.'[10] After the signing of the pact between Collins and de Valera, Wilson warned that English public opinion would be manipulated by British propaganda into accepting the twenty-six counties as a republic, just as it had become accustomed to murders.

In Stormont Sir James Craig announced that he had anticipated for some time something like the arrangement agreed in Dublin. 'The pact means that between Mr Collins and Mr de Valera there is an understanding,' he said. 'Part of that understanding has been published to the world. How much has been arranged behind backs? We here in Ulster can afford to take no risks.[11]

'What we have now we hold against all combinations,' he said. 'We will not have any boundary commission under any circumstances whatever. I state that without equivocation or reservation.'[12] That was the agreed view of his cabinet.

Churchill was annoyed, because if the north could renounce the one aspect of the Treaty relating to it, then Craig would weaken Britain's position in dealing with Dublin. 'The effect of such a statement on your part is to make it far more difficult for the imperial government to give you the assistance you need, and also it robs the Ministers who will meet the Provisional Government representatives of any effective reproach against Mr Collins for the contemptuous manner in which he has spoken of the Treaty,' Churchill wrote to Craig.[13] Although the northern prime minister and his colleagues were highly suspicious of Collins, Churchill essentially dismissed their fears and went on to provide a strong endorsement of what he believed was the good faith of Collins and his colleagues. 'I do not believe that the members of the Provisional Government are acting in bad faith ... I do not believe, as has been repeatedly suggested, that they are working hand in glove with their republican opponents with the intent by an act of treachery to betray British confidence and Ireland's good name. I am sure they are not doing that.'[14]

'There is a very grave danger that the British Cabinet will come to the view that the pact between Mr Collins and Mr de Valera does not violate the Treaty,' Field Marshal Wilson told the Belfast correspondent of *The Irish Times*. 'Should that happen it will be not only a direct menace to Ulster, but, by establishing an independent republic within the Empire, it will be the beginning of Imperial disruption.'[15]

The Treaty stipulated that every member of the Provisional Government had to signify acceptance of it in writing. 'The cabinet will sign, and we will have these 4 as "extern" ministers,' Griffith said.[16] It was like de Valera's old idea of External Association. The four republicans would be externally associated with the cabinet, with the same status as minister.

'The idea is that they will not be members of the cabinet, but departmental heads,' Duggan explained.

'I believe that will be held to be a breach of the Treaty,' Churchill insisted.

'Are we to be debarred from doing our best for the Treaty?' Kevin O'Higgins asked. 'Does it matter if de Valera is in charge of education? Are we bound to take steps which would wreck the Treaty?'

'I did not say they would not sign,' Griffith argued. 'I did not discuss it with them. But in order to save their faces they may be unwilling.'[17] But his colleagues gave the distinct impression that de Valera and company would not sign.

'I realise your difficulties, and sympathise,' Churchill said, 'but I do not think they need all have arisen. You will find that we are just as tenacious on essential points – the crown, the British commonwealth, no republic – as de Valera and Rory O'Connor, and we intend to fight for our points.'[18]

Had the election proceeded without the pact, Churchill told the British cabinet, 'the republicans would have maddened England with a series of outrages'. While those people 'were fanatical republicans who were pure in motive though violent in method, behind them had gathered all the desperate elements of the population, who pursued rapine for private gain'.[19] The election pact afforded the opportunity of isolating criminal elements so that they could be tackled first and a climate could then be created for a proper free election. As things stood the Provisional Government would not be able to protect all the old RIC, especially in isolated areas.

'Things are serious – far more serious than any one at home thinks,' Collins wrote to Kitty Kiernan. 'In fact it is not too much to say that they are as serious as they were at the worst stage of the negotiations last year. And even while we are here there comes the news of two British soldiers being killed in Dublin and two ex-policemen in Boyle. Coming at such a time it is impossible to get away from the conclusion that they are done deliberately to make things more difficult for us in our task here. It is not very credible to those who are responsible for the actions themselves but it is simply disastrous for the name of Ireland.'[20]

The two British soldiers had been shot while riding a motorbike and sidecar on a busy street near College Green, Dublin, shortly after noon on Saturday. The same day James Grier, a retired RIC officer, was taken from his home and shot near Boyle, County Roscommon. The assassins then went to the home of his son Thomas, also a former RIC man. They ordered him to accompany them and when he refused to go, they killed him in his hallway, shooting him eleven times.

'Things are bad beyond words, and I am almost without hope of being able to do anything of permanent use,' Collins wrote to Kitty Kiernan on 30 May. 'It is really awful – to think of what I have to endure here owing to the way things are done by our opponents at home.'[21]

As offence is frequently the best form of defence, Collins obscured his problems by going on the attack. 'They had raised the question of Ulster at once,' Lloyd George told his cabinet. 'The tone of the interview throughout had been of great gravity and of menacing character – not that the language used was menacing but the nature of the discussion was so serious as to be menacing. They alleged that the murders in Belfast were part of a deliberate warfare on Catholics.'[22]

When Austen Chamberlain pressed him to disavow the IRA's

campaign, Collins replied that he could not 'hold the hands of the northern government when Catholics were being murdered'.

Lord Randolph Churchill, Winston's late father, had famously said to Prime Minister Gladstone, 'You call yourselves a government, whom do you govern?' Austen Chamberlain recalled the remark and then said to Griffith and Collins, 'You have handed over the government of Ireland to an Englishman, Erskine Childers.'

'You must let us govern in our own way,' Griffith and Collins insisted. 'The solution will depend on the maintenance of good feeling. We will get Ireland right.'

'They went on to argue that we were paying for the police in Ulster, and therefore we had responsibility there,' according to Chamberlain. 'They all alleged that the murders were committed by "Specials" in our pay. They urged that we had handed law and order over to Sir James Craig, and the responsibility, therefore rested with us.'

Collins gave the British a dossier with particulars of the killings in Northern Ireland. 'I can't leave these people unprotected with 48,000 Specials out against them,' he said.

'We could get Mr Collins to talk of nothing else,' Lloyd George said, 'and when we were able at last to point out that there had been 37 murders in the south, he replied that this was due to the excited state of feeling provoked by Belfast, and that unless something were done the whole of Ireland would get out of hand.' Two or three times Collins indicated, in frustration, that he was willing 'to give Ireland back' to the British 'as a present'.

'Collins was now manoeuvring us into a position where our case was weak,' Lloyd George told the cabinet. 'He had challenged us on Ulster. The first murders were the murders of Catholics – in the main the murder of members of the minority. No one had been punished, we had made no enquiry, we had armed 18,000 Protestants. It would be a bad case.'

The prime minister continued, 'If we broke on the issue of "Republic versus Monarchy" we could count on solid support, but if we broke on Ulster we should get into the same atmosphere of doubtful responsibility as in the case of reprisals.' He was in favour of a judicial inquiry and could not understand why Craig had objected. 'There had been 80 Catholics and 49 Protestants murdered and nobody had been punished or arrested,' he explained. 'It was our business to maintain a stern impartiality between all races and creeds.'[23]

Tom Jones told Lloyd George after the day's discussions that Henry Wilson and company in the north were stoking the Ulster issue 'in order embroil us on their side against the south and get us back into the pre-Treaty position'.[24]

Collins had 'become obsessed' with Northern Ireland, according to Lloyd George, who found himself in the unenviable position of trying to placate the volatile personalities of both the Big Fellow and Churchill. He felt 'there was a strain of lunacy in Churchill', and he said that 'Collins was just a wild animal – a mustang'. When someone suggested that negotiating with Collins was like trying to write on water, Lloyd George interjected, 'shallow and agitated water'.[25]

Éamonn Duggan tried privately to impress on the British that they should realise that Collins had been under enormous pressure. 'We ought to remember the life Collins had led during the last three years,' Jones noted. 'He was very highly strung, and over-wrought, and sometimes left their own meetings in a rage with his colleagues.'[26] Collins had enormous ministerial duties as chairman of the Provisional Government and minister for finance. He was faced with a serious deficit as revenue was expected to fall £10 million short of the £30 million that the government expected to spend, yet that was only a minor problem in comparison to difficulties in his other functions. He was chief propagandist for the Provisional Government as he travelled to speaking rallies around the country, often under the most trying conditions. He was also the person mainly responsible for conducting the thorny day-to-day negotiations with the British at the inter-governmental level and with both the republican and unionist minorities in Ireland, as well as being ultimately responsible for the drafting of the new constitution. Of course, Duggan would have known that Collins was also involved up to his neck in the conspiracy to destabilise Northern Ireland.

Any one of those functions was a full-time job, especially when each frequently involved trying to reconcile so many irreconcilables. In the process Collins left himself open to the charge of dealing in bad faith with everyone – the republicans, the unionists, the British and even some of his own colleagues. The Big Fellow had taken on too much for any one man.

On top of all these he was in love and was writing almost every day to Kitty Kiernan. 'It is almost heart breaking not to have heard a word from you,' he wrote to her from London on 31 May.[27] Later there were rumours that he was having an affair with Hazel Lavery, the wife of the painter Sir John Lavery. Sir John and Hazel actually drove Collins to Downing Street for one of the meetings. The three of them were photographed in the car and Hazel was described as his sweetheart in the caption of at least one of the published photographs. 'I can have all sorts of lovely libel actions,' Collins wrote to Kitty. 'Some of the correspondents recognised my friend but the story was too good.'[28]

20

'THIS GULF IS UNBRIDGEABLE'

Collins had certainly done a credible job in persuading Lloyd George that the twenty-six counties had a legitimate grievance against the north. Even though Churchill was personally critical of Craig's behaviour, especially in his dealings with Craig himself, the colonial secretary seemed ever ready to excuse that behaviour in discussions with his own cabinet colleagues. He told the cabinet on 30 May, for instance, that 'Craig had made a great effort to help, but after the de Valera–Collins pact he had gone over to this other side. Sir James Craig had been willing to go to great lengths and while he could not stand for unity he would resign rather than stand in its way.'[1]

This would have been absurd in the eyes of Collins, because Craig had done very little to implement either of their two agreements. No Catholics had been re-hired at the dockyards, even though those ousted included over 1,000 Catholics who had served in the British army during the First World War. No convicted IRA prisoners had been released, and Craig had refused to hold any investigation into the killing of Catholics in Belfast during the hours after the second agreement was signed. Moreover, when internment without trial was introduced on 23 May, the overwhelming majority of those rounded up were Catholic nationalists, even though loyalists had committed a clear majority of the murders. The whole thing made a mockery of any sense of justice.

'Had Collins taken strong steps and turned the Irregulars out of their Dublin strongholds the whole situation in Belfast would have improved,' Churchill argued, 'but having joined hands with avowed republicans we could hardly wonder that the north had gone back to its extreme and violent position. I think we have to give them assurances of help.'[2] The die-hard element in the north believed, of course, that Collins was behind the republican campaign there. They were right, but Churchill did not seem to suspect that the Big Fellow was so involved – not at this stage at any rate. It did not matter anyway, because he was siding with the loyalists.

Collins had, however, been able to mollify Churchill's attitude towards the election pact, or at least to persuade him to adopt a more understanding attitude towards the circumstances in which the pact was concluded. It 'would not be right' to say that an election held under the pact 'would be worthless', Churchill told the British cabinet afterwards. 'Some Labour and Independent candidates might be elected.'[3]

The Irish had presented the British with the Irish Free State's draft constitution on 27 May. Lionel Curtis provided the British government with a detailed critique of the document two days later, and Lloyd George sent Tom Jones to talk to Griffith and Collins on 30 May. 'Collins was in the most pugnacious mood,' Jones reported. 'This gulf is unbridgeable,' Collins reportedly said. He then 'talked on at a great rate in a picturesque way about going back to fight with his comrades'. Collins accused the British of being 'bent on war', because they were doing nothing about the situation in Belfast. Jones also noted that Collins went 'on and on at great length about the Ulster situation'.[4] Throughout the meeting Griffith said very little and Jones suspected that he had not seen the whole constitution.

Later Lloyd George and Austen Chamberlain discussed the constitution with Griffith and Collins for one and a half hours. The draft was an attempt to implement the External Relations idea in accordance with which Ireland would be associated with the British commonwealth but independent in theory as well as practice.

That night Churchill received an alarming telegram from Craig about a 'very grave incident which has occurred on the frontiers of Ulster. We are informed that the townships of Belleek and Pettigo have been seized and occupied by the Irish republican forces.'[5] This was supposedly a prelude to an attack on the city of Derry. Six days earlier Craig had sent a similar telegram. 'This is S.O.S on behalf of Derry City, which is in grave danger,' Craig warned Churchill on 24 May. 'I have reliable information that a force is mobilizing in Donegal to launch an attack when word is given from high authority.'[6] Churchill took both warnings very seriously. After the first telegram he ordered that Royal Navy ships be dispatched to Derry, and after the second he confronted Collins and his colleagues in London.

'We invited the representatives of the Irish Provisional Government, who were here in London, to visit us at Downing Street,' Churchill told parliament next day. 'We asked them, assuming that this was correct, had these forces any authority from them or were they in any degree responsible? They immediately gave us the most unqualified assurance that they were in no way responsible, that they repudiated the action of these forces in the strongest possible manner, and, of course, that they had no information.'[7]

Griffith, Collins and W. T. Cosgrave were sitting in the Distinguished Strangers Gallery while Churchill was speaking on 31 May. Speaking for about fifty minutes, he delivered a powerful address, which attracted considerable press attention. John H. Whitley, the speaker of the House of Commons, described Churchill's speech as the best he had ever heard. Collins, who was never the most patient of listeners, changed his position frequently. 'Sometimes he sat with folded arms, then he rested his head on his right hand. A few moments later his head was projected over the railings,' according to the correspondent of *The Freeman's Journal*.[8]

In the speech Churchill was very critical of the election pact between Collins and de Valera, because it denied the Irish electorate the opportunity to approve the Treaty. If a proper election was held, the Irish people would 'have been free to reject or accept our offer with their eyes open,' he said. 'Had they rejected it and returned a parliament pledged to set up a republic, an issue would immediately have been raised comparable to that which arose in the American Civil War between the States of the American Union and the seceding Confederate States.'[9] That conflict was not fought to end slavery, but to preserve the union, and Churchill was clearly indicating that the United Kingdom would go to war with Ireland on the same grounds, if the Irish people rejected the Treaty. His distorted concept of national freedom was blinded by his own imperialism.

If de Valera and his colleagues were included in a coalition government in line with the election pact, they would have to subscribe to the Treaty formally, in accordance with the terms of the Treaty itself. 'If they become members of the government without signing that declaration,' Churchill said, 'the Treaty is broken by that very fact at that very moment.' At that point the imperial government could reclaim all the powers transferred, or reoccupy the twenty-six counties. 'I must make it clear to the House,' he added, 'that we shall not in any circumstances agree to deviate from the Treaty either in the strict letter or the honest spirit.'[10]

If the pact led to a cessation of attacks on former servants of the crown and Protestants in the twenty-six counties, as well as the ending of incursions across the border into the six counties, those advantages could 'be set off against the disadvantages of increased delay in ascertaining the free will of the Irish people in respect of the Treaty', Churchill told parliament. 'If we are wrong, if we are deceived, the essential strength of the imperial position will in no wise be diminished, while the honour and the reputation of Ireland will be fatally aspersed … Let us on our part be very careful that we do all we have to do in scrupulous and meticulous good faith … By so doing we may yet succeed. But if we fail in spite of all our efforts and forbearance, then by these efforts and that very forbearance we shall have placed ourselves upon the strongest ground, and in the strongest position, and with the largest moral resources both throughout the Empire and throughout the world, to encounter whatever events may be coming towards us.'[11]

'The conditions in southern Ireland were degenerating so rapidly, that they had not got the power to hold a freely contested election,' Churchill contended. There would have been sporadic fighting, ballot boxes would have been burned, candidates would have been intimidated, and 'no coherent expression of the national will would have resulted from an election held in these circumstances'. Yet bad as things were in the south, he went on to admit that they were even worse in Northern Ireland. 'Far fewer persons have been killed and wounded throughout the whole of Southern Ireland in any given month since the Treaty was made than in the City of Belfast alone,' he said. The disturbances and the warfare between Catholics and Protestants 'have undoubtedly played their part in making the position of the Provisional Government in Ireland difficult, in exasperating the Catholic majority throughout Southern Ireland, and increasing the supporters of Mr de Valera and the extremists who follow him.'[12]

Churchill equated what was happening in Ireland with the events in Bolshevik Russia. 'Will the lesson be learned in time, and will the remedies be applied before it is too late? Or will Ireland, amid the stony indifference of the world – for that is what it would be – have to wander down those chasms which have already engulfed the great Russian people?' he asked. 'This is the question which the next few months will answer. Already there is a trickle – only a trickle – but it may broaden into a stream, from Ireland to this country, of refugees from the Loyalist or Unionist population.'[13]

Afterwards some of the unionists were highly critical. 'I never heard anything so pathetically hopeless as the statement of the Colonial Secretary this morning,' Colonel John Gretton said.[14] Churchill had said that Collins had nothing to do with the troops massing on the Donegal border with Derry. 'But I gravely doubt that,' Charles Craig said. 'I do not believe that all the people who are operating in Ulster are doing so against the express wishes and commands of Mr Collins. But, whoever is doing it, the fact remains that a most determined campaign is being pursued in Ulster, the object of which is to make the Government of Northern Ireland impossible.' Field Marshal Wilson suggested Churchill's speech was an admission from beginning to end 'that every single element of the Irish problem has been miscalculated'.[15]

During his speech Churchill had quoted a letter from the Provisional Government accepting 'financial liability' in the case of law-abiding Protestants who had been forced to leave Ireland.[16] Collins mentioned this to the press immediately afterwards. 'Although I think it was quite proper for him to quote what he did quote', Collins thought it would have been better if Churchill had read the full letter, because the Provisional Government had also raised the plight of those victims of Orange pogroms who 'had to flee from Belfast and other portions of Carsonia into the twenty-six counties, where they were maintained'. He added that the British government was financially responsible 'for the condition of affairs' in Northern Ireland.[17]

'My government feels assured that upon Mr Churchill's representation His Majesty's Government will accept financial liability for the provision of relief to the Catholic inhabitants of an area for the government of which the imperial government is immediately responsible and will allocate the necessary sum for this purpose,' Diarmuid O'Hegarty wrote on behalf of the Provisional Government. 'It is also the earnest hope of the Provisional Government that His Majesty's Government will take immediate steps to ensure that adequate protection is afforded to the Catholic inhabitants of that area, and that it will arrange for the speedy return of their homes and property to those refugees who have been driven therefrom.' Collins released a copy of this letter and *The Irish Times* – possibly still smarting over his earlier criticism – published it in full the following day.[18]

Afterwards Collins visited Churchill in his office. 'I mentioned to him amicably that if any part of the Irish Republican Army, either pro-Treaty or anti-Treaty, invaded northern soil, we would throw them out,' Churchill noted. 'He took it quite coolly, and seemed much more interested in the debate.'

'I am glad to have seen it,' Collins said, 'and how it is all done over here. I do not quarrel with your speech; we have got to make good or go under.'[19]

The extensive coverage of Churchill's speech in the British press was indicative of a political crisis. It was noted that Bonar Law was sitting directly behind Field Marshal Wilson in the House of Commons. Bonar Law had not only been close to the unionists in Northern Ireland, but he was already being seen as a real alternative to Lloyd George, whom he would actually replace later that year.

'Great Britain is in the presence of one of the gravest crises in her history. She is faced with an anarchic movement,' *The Times* of London declared in an editorial the next day. 'It threatens to hold the great part of Ireland in its grip, to promote internecine war between North and South, and, perhaps to involve this wearied and overburdened land in yet another struggle for the maintenance of its pledged honour and the basic principles of civilisation.'[20]

'There were certain verbal phrases in Mr Churchill's Irish pronouncement which he would have been well advised to omit,' the *Westminster Gazette* observed in an editorial. 'His reference to Russia invites the obvious retort that, just as the calamities in which Russia has been plunged are largely due to the stimulus given by himself to her civil wars, so those that threatened Ireland are in great part the legacy of a disastrous past, for which he and his colleagues, far more than any Irishmen, were responsible. This announcement that we may in certain circumstances "re-occupy" Ireland is even more objectionable.'[21] While questions may be asked about Churchill's early involvement in matters relating to Russia, it was ironic because he had talked, rather recklessly, during the early days of the Black and Tans in May 1920 about adopting Bolshevik policies in Ireland.

When the Black and Tans engaged in unofficial reprisals, Field Marshal Wilson had denounced these as being bad for moral discipline among British forces. He was opposed to the idea of the men being allowed to take the law into their own hands and said that Lloyd George's government should take responsibility for reprisals, that they should 'collect the names of Sinn Féiners by districts: proclaim them on church doors all over the country; and whenever a policeman is murdered, pick five by lot and shoot them!'[22] One could hardly imagine anything more likely to provoke the indignation of Irish people than defiling their churches in such a way. 'Somehow or other terror must be met by greater terror,' Wilson argued, according to the cabinet secretary.[23]

'You have been right all along,' Churchill had written to the field marshal in October 1920, 'the government must shoulder the responsibility for reprisals.'[24] By June 1922, however, Churchill seemed to be questioning Wilson's judgement, which, of course, questioned his own earlier judgement. On the day after the latest meeting with Collins, the colonial secretary told three Belfast Catholics who called on him that the election pact between Collins and de Valera had doubled the power of radicals like Wilson. 'You are being tortured by Wilson and de Valera,' Churchill told his visitors.[25]

If Dublin decided to violate the Treaty, Churchill argued, Britain should seize Irish ports and exert economic and financial pressure on the Provisional Government while leaving it in control of the Irish countryside. Lloyd George drew the colonial secretary out 'into the most vivid details, apparently in complete sympathy', according to Tom Jones.[26]

While Churchill was advocating that the British army clear republican forces out of Pettigo on 3 June, Collins was persuading his colleagues 'that a policy of peaceful obstruction should be adopted towards the Belfast government and that no troops from the twenty-six counties, either those under official control or attached to the Executive, should be permitted to invade the six-counties'.[27] In other words the offensive was being called off in favour of a more passive approach.

Collins obviously realised that the British suspected the Provisional Government's involvement in the Northern Offensive. It is not clear at what point Churchill suspected that Collins was involved, but Craig's people were eventually able to convince him with captured documents that the local IRA operations were being orchestrated from the south. Craig was thus able to persuade Churchill to act in relation to Pettigo, which was on the Donegal side of the border, while Belleek was in Northern Ireland.[28]

When British Intelligence investigated the alarmist warnings about republican troops supposedly massing on the Donegal borders for assaults on Derry city and Strabane, they realised that they were grossly exaggerated. 'Many of these scares are started and kept up by the Ulster Press in order to deliberately affect public opinion at home,' Intelligence warned its officers on 6 June. 'Others owe their origin to "windy individuals", sometimes the police, sometimes prominent civilians with no military knowledge.'[29] But in the interim Churchill's impetuosity had led to British forces invading Pettigo in what was undoubtedly the most serious incident between the armies of the British and Irish governments since the Truce of 1921. Strangely the incident has been largely overlooked by history.

21

'WORSE THAN ARMENIAN ATROCITIES'

With Churchill convinced that the IRA in Donegal was planning an incursion into Northern Ireland, he had British soldiers cross the border and seize the town of Pettigo on 4 June 1922. In the process they killed seven soldiers and arrested, or essentially kidnapped, fifteen others, including Commandant Michael O'Farrell. All were in the uniform of the army of the Provisional Government.

With the British troops poised to move on the village of Belleek, Andy Cope reported from Dublin Castle that the Provisional Government claimed to have information that the British planned to destroy some barracks or buildings on the Donegal side of the border. Belleek Fort was on a hill in Donegal overlooking the village. If the British planned on attacking the fort and other buildings in Donegal, Cope warned, it would create a very critical situation.

'Collins is most anxious that no untoward incident should take place particularly in view of the conflicting reports as to Pettigo,' Cope telegraphed Churchill. 'He states that a repetition of Pettigo at Belleek might easily be disastrous and he states that he relies on you to give directions to our troops to take no further action pending Griffith's meeting with you when the situation can be fully discussed. He fears that the firing of a single shot by an irresponsible would have most serious results. He requests your immediate attention as it is rumoured that our troops are taking action almost at once.'[1]

Churchill summoned the cabinet committee he was chairing next morning and read the appeal from Collins. The secretary of state for war, Sir Laming Worthington-Evans, pointed out that he had already telegraphed that 'the attack on Belleek should be postponed'. Churchill regretted that the assault had been called off, as he was clearly so annoyed at the Big Fellow that he wished to teach him a lesson. He had hoped to be able to reply to Collins 'that the operations were now complete'. He believed the Belleek operation would have 'a salutary effect' by showing the Free State leaders 'that His Majesty's government were ready to act'. If the attack was to take place, Cope suggested that London should 'warn Mr Collins that a continuation of the raiding and firing into Ulster from the Free State could not be tolerated'.[2]

The territory of Northern Ireland 'must be cleared of the raiders from the Free State', Churchill insisted. The cabinet committee approved a telegram to Collins. In it, Churchill stated 'that Belleek village would be occupied and that if any shots were fired from the fort on Free State territory on British troops in the village the necessary steps would be taken to silence the fire'. The telegram went on to indicate that operations would cease with the occupation of Belleek, 'unless further provocation is given by fire or raid from your side of the border'.[3]

Churchill had 'no difficulty in justifying the action of the troops. Ulster territory had been invaded, general alarm had been caused in the border districts, shops had been looted and our patrols had been fired upon'. He was obviously seething that Collins had apparently lied to him the previous week. 'You told us that these forces were not your forces,' Churchill reminded him a few days later, 'you disclaimed any responsibility for them. I announced this in parliament in your presence the same afternoon. It is with surprise that I received in the communiqué issued from GHQ Beggars Bush that there were "no other Irish troops", other than "our troops", i.e. Free State Troops, "in the district now or then" and I shall be glad if you will explain the discrepancy,' Churchill wrote.[4]

He was now determined to clear any intruders from Belleek, but Lloyd George was decidedly uneasy. He sent the assistant cabinet secretary, Tom Jones, to find out what Churchill planned. Things got somewhat heated between them.

Having finally settled the Home Rule issue with the Treaty and having got it through parliament, Jones felt it was vital to ensure that it was supported. 'We had put ourselves right and the important thing was to be absolutely fair as between the north and south. Why was not pressure brought on Craig to deal with the murderers in Belfast?' he asked.

Churchill replied that 'he was doing so and thus he had to try to retain the confidence of the Ulster people in him and he had to watch our parliamentary position, that he could not face parliament on Monday if he were unable to say what the position in a British village was,' according to Jones.

'I recognised fully the great patience he had shewn [sic] up to the present in dealing with the Irish situation, but,' Jones continued, 'I was very nervous about impulsive action with the troops.'

'If the P.M. were going to butt in,' Churchill warned, according to Jones, 'he could take the business on himself and have his resignation.'[5]

Churchill dictated a message for Jones to take to Lloyd George. 'The troops, having taken Pettigo, are now preparing to move forward on Belleek village,' Churchill stated. 'This is wholly in our territory, and we certainly cannot allow it to remain in the hands of raiders.' Before the troops moved in, he explained that they would send an armoured car or other reconnoitring vehicle with a British officer to determine the exact situation in Belleek. If it was not being held, it could be reoccupied easily without fighting. 'If, however, our reconnoitring party is driven back, the orders which have been issued to reoccupy the village by force will hold good and will be executed by the troops at their earliest convenience.'[6]

'I'm profoundly disquieted by the development on the Ulster border,' Lloyd George replied. 'We are not merely being rushed into a conflict, but we are gradually being manoeuvred into giving battle on the very worst grounds which could possible be chosen for the struggle. I cannot say whether Henry Wilson and de Valera are behind this but if they are their strategy is very skilful. They both want a break and they both want to fight a battle on this ground. I am not convinced that a break is inevitable. On the contrary, with patience, with the adroitness of which you have such command, I believe we can get through in the end.'[7]

Even if he were wrong, Lloyd George still felt it was necessary to avoid a conflict on the Ulster issue, because it was the weakest ground on which the British could fight. International opinion, and even opinion in the dominions, would not support Britain on the issue. Opinion in Britain itself would be divided. Hence he was concentrating on the issue of the Free State constitution. 'If the Free Staters insist upon a constitution which repudiated crown and empire and practically set up a republic, we should carry the whole world with us in any action we took,' the prime minister argued. 'That is why the Anti-Treatyites are forcing the issue on Ulster,' he emphasised.

'Our Ulster case is not a good one. In two years 400 Catholics have been killed and 1,200 have been wounded without a single person being brought to justice,' he continued. 'Several Protestants have also been murdered, but the murder of Catholics went on at a rate of three or four to one for some time before Catholic reprisals attained their present dimensions; and even now the proportions are two Catholics murdered to one Protestant although the population is two Protestants to one Catholic.'[8]

The prime minister was obviously not impressed by the reports he was getting about events in the Pettigo area. The previous day the British army command in Ireland had reported that there was a distinct outbreak of 'nerves' following the introduction of internment in Northern Ireland the previous week. Reprisals were feared both within Northern Ireland and from across the border. 'It was only necessary for small collections of IRA to appear on the Free State side of the western border to raise the cry of "invasion" and "Derry will be attacked and looted",' Colonel John Brind noted in the absence of General Macready.[9]

'It was reported to us on the authority, I believe, of the Ulster government that there were concentrations of Free State troops against Londonderry, Strabane and the Pettigo salient and a serious invasion was predicted,' Lloyd George wrote to

Churchill on 8 June. 'On investigation it was discovered that there were no troops massing against either Londonderry or Strabane and when we got to the Pettigo salient and threatened it by an elaborate manoeuvre with two brigades of infantry and one battery of artillery we found twenty-three Free Staters on Free State territory in Pettigo of whom seven were killed and fifteen captured. If war comes out of this, will it not make us look rather ridiculous?' He therefore warned Churchill against any further action over Belleek, especially when he believed that Seán MacEoin was involved on the Free State side.[10]

'Now I understand, we are marching against a rotten barrack at Belleek garrisoned by a friendly blacksmith and a handful of his associates with an equally formidable force.' The prime minister was particularly perturbed that a British colonel had ordered, 'The operation is to be carried out as a military operation by Imperial troops only and in such a manner as to inflict the greatest possible loss on the enemy.'

Had Belleek been a German stronghold during the world war, the colonel's tone would have been apt, but it was not appropriate in relation to what was actually happening. They mistakenly believed that Seán MacEoin – who the prime minister considered 'a strong Treaty man and has publicly denounced de Valera and the Pact' – was implicated in the seizure of Belleek. 'If he should be killed at Belleek it would be a disaster to the cause of reconciliation with the Irish race,' Lloyd George continued. 'Quite frankly, if we force an issue with these facts we shall be hopelessly beaten,' he continued. The diehard element might give a shout of approval, but there would be no public opinion behind them to carry on a costly campaign. 'Let us keep on the high ground of the Treaty, the Crown, and the Empire. They are unassailable. But if you come down from those heights and fight in the swamps of Lough Erne you will be overwhelmed,' Lloyd George wrote to Churchill.[11]

'I beg you not to be tempted into squandering what you have already gained by a precipitate action, however alluring the prospects may be. We have surely done everything that Ulster can possibly expect to ensure its security. Fifty-seven thousand armed men ought to be equal to the protection of so small a territory … It is our business as a great empire to be strictly impartial in our attitude towards all creeds. We have more creeds assembled under our flag than any empire in the world and our prestige depends upon maintaining a stern impartiality in our attitude towards them.'[12]

Churchill insisted on having his way. 'Belleek village and fort were occupied today by strong forces,' Churchill reported to Lloyd George that evening. 'About 20 shells and 400 rounds were fired. On one shell bursting near the fort its garrison of forty fled without loss of any kind.' MacEoin was not in the area.

'As far as we know the "battle" has been almost bloodless,' he continued. 'One soldier has been slightly wounded and no enemy casualties have been found or prisoners taken. I am issuing a communiqué explaining that the operations are at an end, that our troops will advance no further, that no further fighting will take place unless they are attacked, that communications are being made to the Provisional Government with a view to establishing peaceful conditions on this part of the border, and that as soon as we are assured there will be no further incursions, the British forces will be withdrawn wholly within the Ulster border-line.'[13]

Lloyd George broke out the champagne to celebrate the victory at 'the great bloodless Battle of Belleek'.[14]

'The results of the operation which threaded its way so narrowly between tragedy and ridicule were salutary,' Churchill later wrote. 'Ulster felt that if it came to actual invasion they would certainly be defended. The Irish Republican Army realised that we should not hesitate to levy open war, and the Free State government knew that at any rate one line was drawn which could not be transgressed. Not the slightest ill will was manifested by those Free State with whom we are in relation. On the contrary, they seemed fortified in spirit for the very serious crisis which was soon to supervene.'[15]

On the following day, 10 June, the *Daily Mail* and the Manchester *Guardian* carried reports that showed the so-called Battle of Belleek in a very different light. The *Daily Mail* correspondent witnessed the whole thing from the Donegal side of the border, where Belleek Fort was situated on the brow of a hill in County Donegal, about 200 yards above the village of Belleek, which was in County Fermanagh. 'A battle I suppose it will be called, but, from my own observation, I am bound to say that the attack was unprovoked,' the *Daily Mail* correspondent reported. Instead of the forty IRA men who supposedly fled the fort when the shelling began, there were four men, all Executive IRA, in the fort when Commandant McGowan arrived with the reporter. The commandant warned them that they were likely to be attacked and he advised them not to return fire as this might be regarded as an excuse for turning artillery on the fort. The first shots seemed to be fired at McGowan and the reporter, who were both unarmed. The reporter was prepared to testify that the British had opened fire without provocation.[16]

That day Collins was attending a political rally at Dublin's Mansion House, where he shared the platform with Mulcahy, Boland, Stack and de Valera, who opened the meeting. 'This was not a time to take on a war with the north-east of Ireland and with the British Empire as well,' Collins told the gathering. Within the past week, he explained, a critical situation had developed on the Fermanagh–Donegal border with British troops being called in to support the northern government. They had crossed a certain distance into Donegal, which was a move that could reignite the Anglo-Irish war. There was no essential difference along the border, he argued. The differences were in Belfast, and 'the sensible course was to meet the trouble from the seat of the trouble'.[17]

In an interview with Clyde A. Beales, the Dublin correspondent of the *New York Herald*, Collins contended that the attack on the Free State forces in Pettigo and the area around Belleek had been unprovoked. Churchill had informed him about 'certain spasmodic irregularities committed by unofficial and irresponsible forces, chiefly along the Belleek sector of the border', but he had not said anything to him or anybody else in the Provisional Government of his suspicions about Pettigo. 'We were placed in an extremely awkward position when the attack occurred, as we were completely in the dark as to whether it was Sir James Craig's government or the British government who were responsible for the extraordinary proceedings,' Collins explained. 'Those drastic operations were not directed against Irregular forces, but against official Irish troops, who were in quiet and legitimate occupation of their barracks in the Co. Donegal town of Pettigo, and who were quite unprepared for a sudden and unwarranted attack.'[18]

Collins was insisting that 'impartial investigators' should examine what happened in Pettigo and Belleek. 'It is, for instance, asserted and universally believed that British troops, who have hesitated with commendable patience for months to take any actions against the savage anti-Catholic mobs in Belfast, have shown an astonishing readiness to become involved with our troops on the six county boundary line,' Collins said. 'The attacks would appear to have been entirely unprovoked,' he added. The lack of British casualties was proof that the Irish forces had no aggressive intent.[19]

'These unprovoked attacks, by whomsoever ordered, are carrying out directly the policy of Sir Henry Wilson and other prominent advisers of Sir James Craig,' Collins insisted. 'The men, quite avowedly, want to destroy the position created by the Treaty, and want to pave the way through a Boundary situation on the northern-eastern border, for the return of the British troops, and thence the ultimate reconquest of Ireland.'[20]

'Their policy is manifest,' Collins continued. 'At the moment imperial British troops are in occupation of some square miles of our territory in Co. Donegal.' Under British protection the Orange Specials were provoking a reaction that would allow the British troops to advance still further into the twenty-six counties. 'I have seen this coming for some time past,' he said. 'The whole object of the Belfast government and their advisers was to deflect world attention from the worse than Armenian atrocities that are of daily occurrence in Belfast, and concentrate it on their order in the hope that the situation would arise such as may confront us day by day now. In this design they were largely assisted by certain powerful British influences and unconsciously by some of our own people.'[21]

In some undated notes among his personal papers, Collins gave an insight into his thinking on the northern issue:

> An interval was given to north-east Ulster to allow them graciously to acquiesce in what, in fact, is an inevitable necessity if they are economically to survive.
>
> How have we used that interval? Not in doing our best to create a strong, promising, stable and united Ireland inviting in its promises of prosperity. We have allowed the merging of a divided National Ireland, an economically sick and dying Ireland, which would be no inducement for anybody to join it …
>
> We all know only too well the hopes and aims of Orange north-east Ulster. They are well expressed to the world in a light veiled brutality in the language of Sir Henry Wilson. They want their ascendancy restored. They want their privileges secured. They want the British back.[22]

The Freeman's Journal warmly endorsed the call for an inquiry into the operations in Belleek and Pettigo. 'The whole unwarranted occupation of southern territory, was part and parcel of the plot concocted by Sir Henry Wilson to embroil British and Irish troops in a border quarrel, in the hope of precipitating an outbreak that would divert attention from the horrors of Belfast and might pave the way for a new attempt to re-conquer Ireland, by force of arms.'[23]

Next day Collins visited London and met with Churchill. 'We argued a little about Pettigo and Belleek and about Belfast atrocities,' the colonial secretary noted.

'I shall not last long; my life is forfeit, but I shall do my best,'

Collins told him. 'After I am gone it will be easier for others. You will find they will be able to do more than I can do.'

'I never saw him again,' Churchill concluded.[24]

22

'COLLINS MIGHT APPOINT A CHARWOMAN'

Having denied calls by Collins for inquiries into the Clones Affray, and both the McMahon and the Arnon Street killings, the British obviously felt pressured to concede in the face of the latest demand in relation to the events at Pettigo and Belleek. Lloyd George clearly had serious reservations about what happened at Pettigo. Collins had managed to convince Lloyd George that he had a case, and the British decided to appoint a leading civil servant to investigate the collapse of the second Collins–Craig Pact. Maybe it was just to take pressure off the Pettigo situation that Churchill called for an investigation into the Belfast killings. 'Such an inquiry would be of real value,' Churchill wrote to Craig. 'Having supplied you with arms and financial aid for your own police forces, I feel entitled in the general interest to make this request to you, and to make it seriously and definitely.'[1] But he was not prepared to go so far as enquiring into the conduct of British soldiers at Pettigo and Belleek.

'It is not intended to institute any such inquiry,' Churchill told the House of Commons. 'His Majesty's government believe themselves to be fully informed as to the facts, and accept full responsibility for the action which the military authorities took by their express direction.'[2] This, of course, undermined his request for the other investigation, especially after Dawson Bates, the minister for home affairs at Stormont, objected strenuously. 'It is impossible to agree to Mr Churchill's suggestion without gravely weakening the Government of Northern Ireland,' Bates warned. 'To set up an outside tribunal to inquire into the action which is found necessary from hour to hour, and to justify or condemn it would strike at the very roots of government.'[3]

Craig met Churchill that day and suggested that a public official should conduct a preliminary inquiry at least. The British cabinet appointed Colonel Stephen Tallents, private secretary to the lord lieutenant, to evaluate the implementation of the second Collins–Craig Pact. Tallents considered that the pact was a virtual invitation to Collins to act as the representative of the northern minority, and it encouraged the latter in refusing to recognise the legitimacy of the northern government, much to the exasperation of the unionist population. Moreover he thought that the failure to implement the clause of the pact calling for a cessation of IRA activities in the north was a major cause of the failure of the agreement, and this was largely the responsibility of the Provisional Government. The northern government had documentary evidence that the Provisional Government was fully aware of the 'active co-operation between the members of the IRA inside the six counties with members of that force outside the six counties who are undoubtedly representatives of the Provisional Government'.[4]

On the other hand Tallents was highly critical of the Special Constabulary, especially the B Specials. He described their behaviour as disquieting and disgusting. He was also critical of Minister for Home Affairs Dawson Bates, whom he considered an asset to the republicans. 'If I had to choose a precise wish for immediate fulfilment in Northern Ireland,' Tallents wrote, 'my first selection would be the kindly removal of the present Minister of Home Affairs to a less responsible ministry.'[5] While Tallents thought that a judicial inquiry into the events in Belfast might have been feasible at one point, it was no longer appropriate because it would not have any advantage and it would revive matters best forgotten. Moreover, it would encourage Collins to interfere in northern affairs and he needed no such encouragement.

June 1922 was a particularly hectic month for Collins. The British balked at the draft constitution, and he was involved in a general election campaign, while things took another sinister turn in Northern Ireland. Any one of those items would have taxed the most proficient of politicians, but he had to deal with all of them at the same time. Most of the negotiations in relation to the constitution were left to President Griffith and Hugh Kennedy, who was the attorney general of the Provisional Government. The British felt that the draft constitution conflicted on six different points with the existing British monarchical system and thus with the provisions of the Treaty:

(1) In Canada the governor-general acted on the advice of the Canadian ministers, but the crown was the symbolic source of all authority, whereas the king's representative in the Irish Free State would be reduced to little more than a kind of commissioner in the draft constitution.

(2) The Irish Free State was claiming the right to make her own treaties with countries outside the British Commonwealth, whereas Britain retained that right in regard to the dominions,

which had the right to be consulted and had to consent to any decision affecting them.

(3) The Supreme Court in the Free State would be the court of final appeal, thus the right of appeal to the Judicial Committee of the Privy Council was being eliminated.

(4) The British objected that the Treaty-oath was omitted from the draft constitution.

(5) All Irish ministers were not being compelled to subscribe in writing to the provisions of the Treaty.

(6) There was no recognition of the position of Northern Ireland in the Treaty.

In public the British played down the difficulties with the draft constitution from the outset, because, as Lloyd George explained to his cabinet, it would put the Irish representatives in 'an impossible position if it leaked out that they had come over with one constitution and gone back to Ireland with another'.[6] If those six issues were not changed, however, the British decided that they would consider the Treaty as having been violated. Lloyd George formally outlined the British objections in a letter handed to Griffith at 6 p.m. on 1 June, and it was arranged that Griffith and Collins should see him thirty minutes later and they would deliver a formal reply the following afternoon. Collins immediately complained that the British were adopting 'the attitude of Shylocks' by demanding the fulfilment of the last letter of the Treaty.[7] Lloyd George essentially asked the same question he had asked at the end of the Treaty negotiations the previous December – were the Irish representatives prepared to come within the British Commonwealth of Nations? Both Griffith and Collins replied that they stood by the Treaty and stressed that they were within the Empire. But Collins insisted 'that the position of Ireland in regard to the crown must be identical with that of Canada'.[8]

The prime minister informed the cabinet afterwards that 'Collins had laid great stress on the strong feeling prevailing in Ireland against allowing appeals to the Judicial Committee of the Privy Council, in view of the fact that three of the Judges were men who had publicly taken up a very hostile attitude to the Irish Free State.' Collins was referring to the law lords Carson, Sumner and Cave. Where they had taken part in controversies that might come before the Privy Council, they would stand aside, Lloyd George replied. 'The participation of these Judges in political questions was a great misfortune, and its effect would extend beyond Ireland,' the prime minister told the cabinet. He added that 'Collins had repeatedly raised the question of the Ulster situation and of our responsibility for it, in view of the fact that we were at any rate in part paying the cost of the "Specials", and pressed for an impartial Enquiry into the events in Belfast.'[9]

Every member of the committee that drew up the draft constitution was a supporter of the Treaty, Griffith explained in his formal response. The crown would be the same in the Irish Free State as in the dominions in all 'constitutionally effective' matters, and Ireland would accept the same treaty-making powers as Canada. The Treaty stipulated that all members of the Free State parliament should subscribe to the Treaty-oath, but that did not necessarily mean it had to be included in the constitution. A case for excluding the oath from the constitution could certainly be made, as the provisions of the Treaty could be covered by ordinary legislation, but Griffith had no intention of defending the republican symbols of the draft constitution to the point of breaking with the British. He therefore wrote that the inclusion of the Treaty-oath 'does not present any difficulty', and the members of the Provisional Government would be required to sign the declaration subscribing to the provisions of the Treaty. He essentially conceded on every point, though he did state that 'there are in Ireland particular reasons for the objection widely entertained to the idea of taking appeals to the Judicial Committee'.[10] While the British cabinet felt that 'further elucidation would be necessary' on the position of the crown and the issue of appeal to the Privy Council, it was content to move ahead, and officials from both sides engaged in intense discussions behind the scenes.

The draft constitution incorporated a clause stipulating that 'the legislative, executive and judicial authority of Ireland shall be derived solely from the Irish people'. There was also a clause stipulating that only the Free State parliament could declare war on behalf of the country. If the British parliament ratified such a constitution for the Irish Free State, it would be tantamount to acknowledging the right to neutrality – that prized right which de Valera had contended would make 'a clean sweep' of the whole defence question during the Treaty negotiations.[11]

The British disliked the way that the role of the king was played down in the draft constitution. Although the functions of the crown were not defined in Canada, or even Britain, Lloyd George noted that it was of 'a greater potential force' than other aspects of the everyday government of a dominion. This was what de Valera had been warning. Tom Jones suggested that 'Collins might appoint a charwoman' to the post of governor-general. 'I see no great objection if she's a good one,' Jones added, 'but others may take a different view of what is fitting.'[12]

Griffith and Kennedy agreed to incorporate the oath and the Treaty in the constitution, with the stipulation that in any conflict between the Treaty and the constitution, the Treaty would take precedence.

The text of the agreed constitution was released on the eve of the election, which met the strict conditions of the Ard-Fheis agreement, but the Irish people did not have a chance to examine it properly, as it was only published in the daily newspapers on the day of the election.

Collins hoped the electorate would be presented with an opportunity to support pro-Treaty candidates from other parties, as well as independents. But some republicans engaged in a strong campaign of intimidation to prevent other parties contesting the election. In the days leading up to the close of nominations, Godfrey J. Green, who had been selected as a Farmers' Party candidate in the East Tipperary and Waterford constituency, withdrew after eight or nine men fired shots into his home and wounded him in the arm. Daniel Morrissey of the Labour Party refused to succumb to the intimidation in the other Tipperary constituency. The Kilkenny home of Denis Gorey, another Farmers' Party candidate, was also attacked, but he fought back and refused to withdraw. In the Mayo North and West constituency, the Farmers' candidate, Bernard Egan, came under intense pressure. The night before nominations closed, two armed men had tried to persuade him to withdraw his candidacy. He refused, but the next day the man delivering his nomination papers was kidnapped and Egan duly withdrew that day. There were also late withdrawals of Farmers' Party candidates in Kerry-West Limerick, in Clare, in Leitrim, in North Roscommon, in South Mayo and in South Roscommon, so there were no contests in those six constituencies, or in Donegal.

In the other nineteen constituencies the Sinn Féin panel was opposed by forty-seven other candidates – eighteen from the Labour Party, twelve representing the Farmers' Party and seventeen independents, almost all of whom were avowedly pro-Treaty. Collins told the British that many pro-Treaty independents and Farmers' Party and Labour Party candidates would undoubtedly replace some of those on the anti-Treaty Sinn Féin panel.

It was not only political candidates who were being intimidated. There was also considerable intimidation of business people and former policemen. In the Loughrea area of Galway there was a report that armed men had kidnapped a former RIC sergeant, John Kelly, from his home on Friday 9 June. He had recently purchased a local public house for £2,400. The same night as he was kidnapped, shots were fired through the windows of the Athenry homes of eight former members of the RIC. Four of these were married men with children, and all found it necessary to move. In Ballinasloe two former constables were wounded and another said that he had been given twenty-four hours to leave, much to the indignation of the local priest, who denounced such intimidation from the pulpit. Former policemen in the Nenagh area were also ordered to leave and shots were fired into the home of the wife of a former RIC sergeant.

The Sinn Féin factions held a joint rally at the Mansion House,

Dublin, on that Friday night. In his address Collins appealed for unity and decried the growing unrest throughout the country. He complained in particular about communist activities. In recent weeks there had been reports that workers at seven Cleeve factories – which specialised in dairy products in Counties Cork, Tipperary and Limerick – had 'attempted to establish Soviet rule'. The red flag was hoisted over the factory in Clonmel. The following day Collins referred to Soviet activities after workers from the Clonmel factory picketed shops that did not stock Cleeve's butter. The men and women picketers refused to move for the republican police and the IRA, even after the troops threatened to open fire if the street was not cleared. The picketers held their ground and the IRA withdrew. A local priest and the president of the Trades Council then succeeded in getting the crowd to disperse quietly.[13]

The thatched roof of Denis Carroll's home was torched in Ballywilliam, near Nenagh, in the early hours of the morning of Monday 12 June. Once the fire began, his son Patrick rushed from the house and was shot dead. Another son, John, a fourteen-year veteran of the RIC, had been shot dead in February 1921 after a visit home. He was part of a convoy that was spending the night in Nenagh en route from Dublin to Cork. He left his colleagues to visit his parents but was seized the following morning and killed as he tried to return to Nenagh. There was no explanation for the subsequent shooting of his brother Paddy. 'People in the neighbourhood who knew the deceased personally informed our representative that he was one of the most harmless and inoffensive young men in the parish and that the foul deed met with the strongest condemnation from the people of the parish,' reported the *Nenagh Guardian*. 'They have my two sons shot now, and they were good sons,' Denis Carroll told the inquest in tears. 'I have neither family nor home now.' The coroner, James O'Brien, told the inquest that he had never before been called upon to investigate such a harrowing and heart-rending case.[14]

Shots were fired in Ballinasloe on Monday into the home of a Protestant businessman who had been warned to leave town, apparently because he was a Protestant. A local Guinness representative, who happened to be a Protestant living in Cleaghmore with his wife and family, was also given a final notice to quit, as was a Protestant widow living with her teenage daughter. They were ordered to get out, as their home was supposedly needed for Belfast Catholics. A local linesman and the stationmaster, both Protestants, were also warned to leave. Fr P. J. Heenan condemned the outrageous intimidation as uncharitable, un-Christian, and un-Irish. The same day there were attacks on Protestant-owned businesses in Mullingar – Porter & Son, grocers, Hutchinson's two business houses, Connolly's drapery, Carson's boot shop, and Loftus's saddlery. They and other Protestants had received notices ordering them to get out of town.

On Tuesday men stoned a Methodist church in Cork, smashing windows and doing some internal damage. Two Protestants in the Listowel area of County Kerry were given ultimatums to leave the vicinity, as were several Protestants in the Athlone area. Moore's Hotel, nine miles from Mullingar, was raided and looted on Tuesday night. There were also attacks on Protestants in Athy and the windows of the Methodist church there were smashed.

It was an attack on another Protestant, Darrell Figgis, the main architect of the draft constitution, which attracted most attention. A former national secretary of Sinn Féin, Figgis was critical of the election pact because it allowed the anti-Treaty people to pretend that the Treaty was not an election issue. Over the weekend he wrote to the press about the 'powerful plea for loyalty to the government' that Collins made at the Mansion House rally on Friday evening. Although he endorsed what Collins had said, he was critical of those who were pretending that the Treaty was not an election issue, when it was really the main issue. 'Not all the words in the world can mask this plain and honest issue,' Figgis argued. 'Not to have a plain understanding on it is to sow the seeds of a harvest of future trouble; nothing is more certain than this, that if we sow confusion we shall reap confusion. The country desires above all things to settle the Treaty finally, to have no more words about it, to establish the Free State, to be loyal to the government of that Free State and to begin the practical, hard work of construction and development.'[15]

On the night of the publication of his letter in both *The Irish Times* and the *Irish Independent*, three young men forced their way into his home and cut his beard. The main reason given for the attack was his refusal to withdraw as an independent candidate for elections. The young men were obviously distressed. 'They had themselves stated that they strongly objected to the orders they had received and disliked the work that had been committed to them,' Figgis told the press afterwards. 'The offence lay not with these boys but with the men who had charged them and finally with the leaders of those who opposed the Treaty.'[16] The attack got enormous publicity, and was even reported in *The New York Times*. There is little doubt that it enhanced his election campaign.

Even though he had little empathy with Figgis, Collins, on his return from London, called on him and his wife and gave them a pistol for protection. Figgis did not wish to keep it, as he did not believe in the use of firearms, but he said his wife, Millie, 'felt greater safety and comfort in her mind knowing that the revolver was in the house'. In the circumstances they decided to keep the weapon, but this was to have unfortunate consequences some months later when she shot and killed herself in a taxi. She left a suicide note explaining that she was using the gun given to them by Collins.[17]

While Collins did not comment publicly on the attack on Figgis during the election campaign, he did take exception to an advertisement in which Cumann na Poblachta, the anti-Treaty organisation, intimated that non-party candidates who contested the election were acting against the national interest. Collins emphasised that the pact agreement with de Valera specifically stipulated 'that any and every interest is free to go up and contest the election equally with the national Sinn Féin Panel'.[18]

23

'YOU UNDERSTAND FULLY
WHAT YOU HAVE TO DO'

Following his return from London on the night of 13 June, Collins headed for Cork late the following afternoon with J. J. Walsh. They arrived around 9 p.m. No arrangements had been made for any speeches, but as there was a large group to greet him, Collins delivered an impromptu address from a window of Turner's Hotel. He spoke 'while a downpour of rain drenched his audience, but did not disperse them'.[1]

'You are facing an election here on Friday, and I am not hampered now by being on a platform where there are coalitionists, and I can make a straight appeal to the citizens of Cork to vote for the candidates they think best of – to vote for the candidates whom the electors of Cork think will best carry on in the future the work that they want carried on,' he said. 'When I spoke in Dublin I put it as gravely as I could that the country was facing a very serious situation, and if that situation is to be met as it should be met, the country must have the representatives that it wants. You understand fully what you have to do and I will depend on you to do it.'[2]

Although it was probably the most significant speech of the whole campaign, it only attracted passing attention initially. *The Irish Times,* which was an avowedly unionist newspaper at the time, recognised that its readers had little real choice in much of the twenty-six counties. 'We know that many members of the southern minority are so heartily disgusted with the present state of things that they are tempted to surrender themselves to apathy or despair,' the newspaper noted in its lead editorial on the eve of the election. 'The Collins–de Valera pact has turned them into political cynics.'[3]

Collins had not elaborated on how people should vote, but *The Irish Times* advised its pro-Treaty readers on this subject. 'Darrell Figgis stands in County Dublin on the sole issue of the Treaty and on that sole issue is entitled to the fullest measure of support,' the newspaper noted in an editorial. 'Under the system of proportional representation every voter has as many choices as there are candidates. We advise our readers, when they have exhausted the independent candidates, to give their next choices to those members of the "Coalition" panel who are supporters of the Treaty.'[4]

The newspaper also had a separate article using, as an example, the Dublin County constituency, where there were nine pro-Treaty people among the ten candidates running for the six seats. Readers were advised to vote in the order of choice for all nine of those candidates.

Collins spent the next two days canvassing throughout west Cork and even went to Rathmore in County Kerry. He called on the people to support the pact agreement in the spirit in which it was made in order to establish a government that could secure order and stable conditions. 'Their duty was to vote for the people they thought would carry out their policy for whatever the life of the new parliament might be,' he told a crowd in Clonakilty on the eve of polling. 'Whatever government was brought into power they must deal with criminal acts as criminal acts. They must be dealt with, no matter under what name those criminal acts were done.' Things had been happening in the name of freedom, labour and the Irish republic that could not be tolerated. 'Let that be clearly understood,' he insisted. 'The things that have disgraced our nation for the past six months must be put an end to.'[5]

On election day, 16 June, *The Freeman's Journal* called on readers to heed the voting advice of Collins and reproduced his remarks from the window of Turner's Hotel at the head of a double-column editorial. Collins toured his constituency during the day, visiting Rosscarbery, Leap, Skibbereen, Bandon, Ballineen, Dunmanway, Macroom, Millstreet and Kanturk. The *Irish Independent* predicted that he would win 17,000 votes, and he actually got 17,188, which was the highest vote in the country and well over twice that of the second candidate elected in his constituency, Michael Bradley of the Labour Party.

Before any of the votes were counted there was a series of outrageous incidents in Northern Ireland. These latest incidents were largely in response to the killing of Patrick Creegan of Bessbrook and Thomas Crawley of Whitecross on 14 June, while those murders were, in turn, seen as retaliation for the murder ten days earlier of J. Woulfe Flanagan, a Catholic resident magistrate, who had been shot dead by the IRA in Newry as he left Sunday Mass at the Roman Catholic cathedral. In the early hours of 17 June, three teams of IRA under the command of Frank Aiken committed a series of horrific killings in the Newry area. Thomas Crozier, sixty-seven, and his wife, Elizabeth, were shot at Altnaveigh. She was hit in the arm and bled to death.

John Heaslip and his nineteen-year-old son, Robert, were shot at Lisdrumliskea. Mrs Heaslip witnessed the proceedings and pleaded for mercy for her husband and son. 'Belfast Catholics got no mercy,' one of men replied, before firing more shots into the two on the ground. William Lockhart was shot, after which his home was torched and his twenty-one-year-old son James was escorted away with Edward Little, a young neighbour. They were told not to speak, but Lockhart's mother followed pleading with the men and Lockhart turned to say something to his mother. 'You did not do what you were told,' one of the men said and shot the young man dead. Edward Little was then released.

'We have never hesitated to condemn the brutal and unchristian methods adopted against the Catholic population of the six counties,' the *Irish Independent* proclaimed in an editorial, 'nor can we now remain silent when a small section of our own people appears to be entering into a competition in crime with the fanatical element across the border.' Regardless of the provocation, the editorial concluded, 'a wrong cannot be undone by inflicting further wrongs'.[6] The killings provoked a wave of revulsion throughout the whole island, though this was swamped by news of the election returns in the twenty-six counties.

'The election was *declared* to be one in which the Treaty issue was not being decided,' Collins wrote. 'The people have chosen to *declare* otherwise.'[7] It took over a week to complete the count in his Cork constituency, but it was clear from very early that the electorate had voted decisively in favour of the Treaty. Of the sixty-five pro-Treaty Sinn Féin candidates, fifty-eight were elected, while only thirty-five of the anti-Treaty people were successful. But even that exaggerated the anti-Treaty support, because sixteen of them were returned without opposition; where the seats were contested, forty-one of forty-eight pro-Treaty Sinn Féin candidates were successful, while only nineteen of forty-one anti-Treaty candidates were elected.

The popular vote painted an even bleaker picture for the anti-Treaty side, which received less than twenty-two per cent of the first preference votes cast. No anti-Treaty candidate topped the poll in any constituency and Sligo-Mayo East was the only constituency in the whole country in which a majority of voters supported anti-Treaty candidates. Had the Labour Party, which was pro-Treaty, run more candidates, it might have surpassed the anti-Treaty Sinn Féin vote, seeing that the total vote of Labour's eighteen candidates was only 1,353 votes short of the combined total of the forty-one anti-Treaty candidates who faced opposition. Labour candidates won seventeen of the eighteen seats that they contested, and the party's only unsuccessful candidate lost out by a mere thirteen votes.

Anti-Treaty candidates fared dismally in Dublin, winning only one of the eighteen seats in the four constituencies. The losers included Kathleen Clarke, the widow of Thomas Clarke, one of the leaders of the Easter Rising. She finished last of the seven candidates standing for the four seats in Mid-Dublin. Countess Markievicz was fourth of the seven candidates on the first count in Dublin South, but she failed to hold her position on subsequent counts and ended up over 800 votes behind the fourth and final successful candidate. Margaret Pearse, the mother of Patrick Pearse, one of the leaders of the Easter Rising and first president of the Irish republic, also failed to retain her seat in County Dublin, even though she was the only anti-Treaty candidate running in the six-seat constituency. Seán T. O'Kelly was the only successful anti-Treaty candidate in Dublin; he managed to win the final seat in Mid-Dublin. Other notable anti-Treaty losers elsewhere in the country included Liam Mellows in Galway and Dan Breen in the East Tipperary and Waterford constituency. His colleagues Seamus Robinson, who lost out in Tipperary, Dr Jim Ryan and Erskine Childers also failed to retain their seats. Childers finished last of the ten candidates with a pathetic vote in the Kildare and Wicklow constituency.

Denis Gorey, the Farmers' candidate who stood up to the intimidation in Carlow-Kilkenny, was comfortably elected, while Darrell Figgis headed the poll in County Dublin, with over 15,000 votes, more than double the quota. His electoral appeal was probably enhanced by the outrageous republican attack on him. Thomas Johnson, the Labour leader, came in second, comfortably over the quota, and Daniel Morrissey won a seat on the first count in Tipperary.

'The rejection of so many anti-Treaty candidates, in spite of the protection afforded to them by the panel' could only be interpreted in one way, according to Collins. The Irish people were protesting against the anti-Treaty campaign of the past six months. 'They accept the Treaty as the best terms to be got *now*,' Collins wrote. 'They wish to garner the fruits of the recent struggle, and … they see in an era of peace and reconstruction … the best means by which the nation can grow strong to complete the march to freedom.'[8]

'We are hopelessly beaten, and if it weren't for the Pact it would have been much worse,' de Valera admitted.[9] 'Labour and Treaty sweep the country,' Harry Boland noted in his diary.[10]

Yet those who called themselves republicans had no intention of accepting the popular verdict. Two days after the election, the anti-Treaty IRA held another convention at which it was proposed to give the British government seventy-two hours' notice of their intention to terminate the Truce. Although twelve of the sixteen-man executive supported the motion, Chief of Staff Liam Lynch and Cathal Brugha vigorously opposed the proposal, which was narrowly defeated by 118 to 103 votes. Rory O'Connor and other hardliners refused to accept the decision. They returned to the Four Courts, where they locked out those who had voted against their motion. The twelve dissident members of the executive repudiated Lynch and elected a new chief of staff of their own, Joe McKelvey.

De Valera played no part in the machinations of those in the Four Courts. He concentrated instead on political matters, denouncing the decision of the people. 'These results seem indeed, a triumph for the imperial methods of pacification,' he contended in a statement issued on 21 June. As far as he was concerned, the Irish people were intimidated into voting as the British desired by the threat of war, 'but their hearts and their aspirations are unchanged,' he added. 'Ireland unfree will never be at rest, or genuinely reconciled with England.'[11]

De Valera still confidently expected to be a member of the new cabinet in line with the election pact. General Macready concluded that it was possible that 'Collins cleverly agreed to the pact in order to get a fairly open election and then to find some excuse to declare the agreement null and void on gaining a large pro-Treaty majority.'[12] It was suggested that Collins had abrogated the election pact by his speech from Turner's Hotel, but this overlooked the whole series of violations by the other side. 'Any and every interest or organisation would be free to contest the election,' Collins had insisted from the very outset. 'Labour and Farmers candidates were threatened to compel them to abstain from the contest. Thus, the pact was violated on its fundamental provision and Collins had to declare the pact abrogated by the action of the anti-Treaty forces.'[13] Members of the IRA Executive made it easy for him to turn his back on the pact with their conduct after the election.[14]

In fairness there was no suggestion that de Valera had personally violated the pact, other than by his silence in the midst of such intimidation. It later became apparent that he really had no control over Rory O'Connor and his followers. The Long Fellow made it clear, however, that he would oppose ratification of the new constitution. 'It will exclude from public service and disenfranchise every honest republican,' he contended. 'Dáil Éireann will not dishonour itself by passing it.'[15]

The Roman Catholic hierarchy called upon the people to insist that the government prevent Ireland being rushed headlong into the abyss.

24

'THE SAFETY OF THE NATION IS THE FIRST LAW'

The already tense political climate in Ireland was further strained on 22 June 1922 by the assassination of Sir Henry Wilson in London by two Londoners with strong Irish connections – Richard Dunne and Reginald O'Sullivan. Both were in their mid-twenties, born and raised in London, and each had served and was wounded in the First World War, in which O'Sullivan had lost a leg in 1918. Each was living with his parents at the time and both were members of the IRB. They were captured after a short chase. The killing sparked a chain of events that was to have tragic consequences for the nation.

'Documents have been found upon the murderers of Field Marshal Sir Henry Wilson which clearly connect the assassins with the Irish Republican Army, and which further reveal the existence of a definite conspiracy against the peace and order of this country,' Lloyd George wrote to Collins. 'The ambiguous position of the Irish Republican Army can no longer be ignored by the British government. Still less can Mr Rory O'Connor be permitted to remain with his followers and his arsenal in open rebellion in the heart of Dublin in possession of the courts of justice, organising and sending out from this centre enterprises of murder not only in the area of your government but also in the six northern counties and in Great Britain.'[1] The British assumed those in the Four Courts were behind the killing.

Before the Truce Dunne and O'Sullivan had reported to Rory O'Connor, who was in charge of IRA activities in England for a time, but some of those closest to Collins later stated that it was the Big Fellow himself who ordered the hit on Wilson, without telling his government colleagues. The British Special Branch actually concluded that Dunne and O'Sullivan operated independently. 'We have no evidence at all to connect them, so far as the murder is concerned, with any instructions from any organised body,' the home secretary informed Lloyd George. 'They were both undoubtedly members of the IRA, but that was not known until their arrest.'[2] Of course, there is no proof of this any more than there is hard evidence that Collins ordered the Squad to kill various detectives in 1919. History must rely on the word of people like Liam Tobin, Frank Thornton, Joe Dolan and Joe Sweeney.

Collins actually met Joe Sweeney within hours of the killing. 'How do we stand about the shooting of Wilson?' Sweeney asked.

'It was two of our men did it,' Collins replied, looking very pleased with himself.[3]

When Liam Tobin told Richard Mulcahy that Collins was behind the killing, Mulcahy was so annoyed that he threatened to resign. It would seem that Collins had allowed his weakness for intrigue and his turbulent nationalism to get the better of his judgement in the midst of a barrage of crises.

De Valera had no involvement: 'I do not know who they were who shot Sir Henry Wilson, or why they shot him,' he told the press. 'I do not approve but I must not pretend to misunderstand.'[4]

Later he contended that the killing of Wilson more 'than any other single happening' was responsible for the breakdown of the uneasy peace. He also said that a virtual ultimatum from the British had prompted the Provisional Government to attack the Four Courts.

'Now you are supported by the declared will of the Irish people in favour of the Treaty,' Lloyd George warned Collins, it was the view of the British government that 'they have a right to expect that the necessary action will be taken by your government without delay'.[5] The British offered to furnish artillery for an attack on the Four Courts and when the Provisional Government did not move, the British government ordered Macready to use British troops to attack the complex. Macready believed that Churchill's 'feverish impetuosity' had led to the decision. 'Panic and a desire to do something, no matter what, by those whose ignorance of the Irish situation blinded them to possible results, was at the root of this scheme,' Macready noted. He concluded that the impetuous move was a mistake and he sent his adjutant to London to argue that the British should give the Provisional Government more time to act, so the attack planned for 26 June was postponed. 'I have never ceased to congratulate myself on having been instrumental in staving off what would have been a disaster from every point of view,' Macready wrote in his memoirs.[6]

Churchill gave vent to his frustration. British Intelligence had finally concluded that the Provisional Government was deeply implicated in the Northern Offensive. On 23 June Lionel Curtis had written to Churchill saying there was evidence that 'it was scarcely possible to doubt that the IRA headquarters in Dublin under General Mulcahy' was 'responsible' for organising the IRA in Northern Ireland.[7]

'Hitherto we have been dealing with a Government, weak because it has formed no contact with the people. Hitherto we have been anxious to do nothing to compromise the clear expression of Irish opinion. But now this Provisional Government is greatly strengthened ... It is its duty to give effect to the Treaty in the letter and in the spirit ... without delay,' Churchill told the House of Commons on 26 June 1922. He went on to accuse publicly those in the Four Courts of encouraging 'murderous outrages' not only in Ireland but also in Great Britain, which was an obvious reference to the recent killing of Wilson.[8]

'The time has come when it is not unfair, not premature, and not impatient for us to make to this strengthened Irish Government and new Irish Parliament a request, in express terms, that this sort of thing must come to an end. If it does not come to an end, if either from weakness, from want of courage, or for some other even less creditable reasons, it is not brought to an end, and a speedy end, then it is my duty to say, on behalf of His Majesty's Government, that we shall regard the Treaty as having been formally violated, that we shall take no steps to carry out or legalise its further stages, and that we shall resume full liberty of action in any direction that may seem proper ...'[9]

'Let Churchill come over and do his own dirty work,' was the Big Fellow's initial reaction.[10]

'There must be no suggestion that Collins is prompted to take action at the request of British Government,' Assistant Under-Secretary Cope telegraphed from Dublin. 'Such a suggestion would do infinite harm.'[11]

It was Ireland's great misfortune at this time that the man at the helm of Irish affairs in Britain was someone as volatile and tempestuous as Churchill, who prided himself as a man of action, but whose judgement on Irish matters was distinctly suspect. In some respects he was actually behaving like Collins. On the following day, for instance, Churchill told the House of Commons that he was in contact with the Provisional Government about the holding of people who had been kidnapped in Northern Ireland. 'Some were taken in the raid at Belcoo and others were taken in different forays on the frontier,' he said. 'We have proof that some of them are being held at present at Athlone.'[12]

'What steps exactly are the British Government taking in order to recover them?' Viscount Curzon asked.

'I am addressing the Provisional Government on the whole matter, and meanwhile we are holding the fifteen other persons who are in our possession,' Churchill replied.

Did he think the Provisional Government was treating his inquiries with contempt? Churchill was asked. 'No, I do not think so at all,' he replied. 'I think they are very anxious to get back their own fifteen men of the Free State forces whom we are at present holding.'[13] (These were fifteen prisoners taken at Pettigo, who had been brought across the border and were being held in Northern Ireland.) Churchill was essentially admitting that the British were holding them hostage to secure the release of the policemen taken at Belcoo, who had been held since March.

That same day, in Dublin, forces from the Four Courts raided the car dealership of Harry Ferguson in Baggot Street, where they seized sixteen cars. Commandant Leo Henderson, director of the Belfast boycott at the Four Courts, led the raid. Troops of the Provisional Government surrounded the garage while the raid was in progress, compelling the raiders to evacuate the building, and Henderson was arrested. At 11.15 p.m. that night Lieutenant General J. J. 'Ginger' O'Connell, the assistant chief of staff at Beggars Bush, was kidnapped by forces from the Four Courts after he had seen his girlfriend home following a night at the theatre. He was held hostage for the release of Henderson and five men arrested in Drogheda the previous day.

Collins had by this time already decided to attack the Four Courts. 'The action which my government is now compelled to take has been rendered absolutely necessary by the recent commission of grave offences against the fundamental rights of our citizens, involving attacks on their persons and their property,' Collins explained in a statement issued to the International News Service later that day. 'We have borne with extreme patience the illegal and improper conduct of certain elements in our midst since the signature of the Treaty with Great Britain and its endorsement by the Supreme Authority of the nation – Dáil Éireann.'[14]

Those in the Four Courts had refused to accept the democratic verdict of the people. Instead, they brought things to a climax 'by the raiding and plundering' of Ferguson's garage. 'We were obliged to arrest the ringleader of this armed gang, and he is at present in custody awaiting trial on a number of counts.' The kidnapping of General O'Connell compounded the assault on the garage. 'It is now obvious that we could no longer tolerate glaring outrages of this nature against the people and the people's government, and so the Irish troops were ordered on Monday last to take measures to protect the life and property of our citizens and to disperse unauthorised and irregular assemblies,' Collins said. 'The safety of the nation is the first law, and henceforth we shall not rest until we have established the authority of the people of Ireland in every square mile under their jurisdiction.'[15]

Those occupying the Four Courts were given an ultimatum at 3.40 a.m. to vacate the buildings by 4 a.m. on 28 June. When they failed to do so, the army of the Provisional Government opened up a bombardment, with weapons provided by the British, at around 4.15 a.m. In view of Churchill's comments in the House of Commons hours earlier, republicans concluded that the attack was launched at the bidding of the British. Henceforth this was considered the start of the Irish Civil War.

Collins was anxious to stress that the decision to attack the Four Courts was made before word of Churchill's speech at the House of Commons reached Dublin. If that were so, then the decision was also taken before he learned of the kidnapping of General O'Connell, but it did make it easier to press ahead with the decision. Hugh Martin of the *Daily News* reported on the night of 27 June, hours before the attack, that 'it is a matter of the first importance to realise that the Irish Government had acted of its own volition and not in response to the crack of the whip in London'.[16] But the British had already sent a virtual ultimatum when Lloyd George wrote to Collins demanding that he clear out the Four Courts. Indeed, within twenty-four hours of Macready persuading his government to postpone ordering an attack on the Four Courts, Collins ordered his own forces to do so.

Curiously, no evidence of any communication has been unearthed in relation to the hostages in Athlone, but it is known that an informal channel of communication had been set up with Collins. In April 1922 Collins had placed his own man within the remnants of the British administration at Dublin Castle. Thomas

Markham, who went under the cover name of Tom Donovan, was not a conventional spy. Collins introduced him to Alfred Cope, who then placed Markham at the centre of the residual British administration. Rather than a spy, he was really a conduit to pass on sensitive information that the British wished Collins to know without leaving a paper trail of their own. Markham was allowed to see correspondence between Churchill and Cope, but it must be assumed that the bulk of this material related to matters the British were happy to share, 'or even actively wanted Collins to have'.[17]

Churchill had indicated that he was in touch with the Provisional Government in relation to the hostages in Athlone, so one can only speculate that Markham passed on this information. A fortnight later Churchill was particularly defensive when he was challenged about holding those arrested at Pettigo as hostages. 'I have never admitted that they were being held as hostages,' he said. 'They are being held.'

'If they are not being held as hostages, why is the right hon. Gentleman keeping them?' Colonel Wilfrid Ashley asked.

'I am keeping them because I hope that their release will synchronise with the release of other persons,' Churchill replied.[18]

'According to the latest information I have received, these eleven constables, who are believed to be confined at Athlone, have not yet been released,' Churchill said. 'I am assured that steps are being taken by the Provisional Government in response to the continued representations I have made to them to secure the release of these and other inhabitants of Northern Ireland who are being detained in the South.'

'Is not Athlone in the hands of the Free State authorities, and what difficulty can Mr Collins have in obtaining the release of these men?' asked Captain Charles Craig.

'I suppose the difficulty of the strain and stress under which that Government is labouring at the present time,' the colonial secretary replied.[19]

After four days of shelling, the Four Courts surrendered; by then much of the complex, which contained the Public Record Office and some irreplaceable documents, was in ruins. Churchill was delighted. 'If I refrain from congratulations it is only because I do not wish to embarrass you,' he wrote to Collins. 'The archives of the Four Courts may be scattered but the title-deeds of Ireland are safe.'[20]

As it was, Churchill had already said too much in parliament. When Collins was asked about Churchill's speech, he replied that he would reserve comment on it and other matters until the new Dáil met. But he did not live to see the convening of the new Dáil.

De Valera condemned the pro-Treaty forces for attacking their former comrades in arms 'at the bidding of the English'. Those in the Four Courts 'would most loyally have obeyed the will of the Irish people freely expressed', he had contended, but they had instead shown contempt for the will of the people and de Valera had shown contempt for the truth in the way he supported them. He soon came to regret 'Rory O'Connor's unfortunate repudiation of the Dáil, which I was so foolish as to defend, even to a straining of my own views in order to avoid the appearance of a split'.[21] Yet at the time de Valera asked the Irish people to rally to their assistance: 'Irish citizens, give them support! Irish soldiers, bring them aid!'[22]

De Valera joined the republicans occupying the Hammam

Hotel on Dublin's O'Connell Street. A couple of days following the outbreak of hostilities, J. F. Homan, a senior member of the St John's Ambulance Brigade, sought to mediate an end to the assault on the hotel. 'They and their leaders are at liberty to march out and go to their homes unmolested,' Collins told him, 'if only they will deposit their weapons in the national armoury, there to remain until and unless in the whirl of politics these men become a majority in the country in which case they will have control of them.' He was careful to use the words 'deposit their weapon' rather than 'surrender' them.[23]

Homan found that de Valera 'was anxious for an immediate peace', but was insisting that the republicans should be allowed to keep their arms. 'He told me he would be prepared to recommend to the insurgents, and was confident he could get them to agree, to go home, each man carrying his weapon with him,' but Collins insisted that they had to lay down their arms.[24]

As the men would not surrender or give up their weapons, 'There is no use negotiating with Mr Collins,' Cathal Brugha told Homan. 'The most they would agree to would be to leave this place with their arms and go and join our men fighting elsewhere,' Brugha said. 'And, for my part, I would oppose even that. You are wasting your time. We are here to fight to the death.'[25]

The Provisional Government was prepared to be reasonable, Collins assured the Catholic archbishop of Dublin, the lord mayor and Cathal O'Shannon of the Labour Party. 'We don't want any humiliating surrender,' he emphasised.[26] But it was necessary for the government to restore order.

25

'KEEP OPEN SOME AVENUE OR AVENUES TO PEACE'

The second Dáil was supposed to meet on 1 July 1922 to dissolve formally so that the new Dáil could come into existence, but the Provisional Government announced that it should 'stand prorogued to Saturday, the 15th day of July next'. It would have been irresponsible to convene the Dáil amid the heavy fighting that continued at the Four Courts. The postponement announcement was accompanied by the names of Collins and Diarmuid O'Hegarty.[1] However, the Dáil was supreme, so Collins and his colleague had no legal authority to postpone it. 'Professions of faith in the people's will are empty phrases when the people's representatives are treated with contempt,' Labour leader Thomas Johnson complained.[2]

While pro-Treaty candidates had won ninety-two seats in the general election, Sinn Féin won only fifty-eight of those. Labour and anti-Treaty Sinn Féin had fifty-three seats between them, with the result that seventeen independent deputies held the balance of power. This undoubtedly helped to explain the Provisional Government's reluctance to convene the Dáil.

'What really happened was that the executive usurped the government of the country and by a *coup d'état* established a new government,' de Valera later contended. 'It was really in consequence of that that I felt that I could consistently and constitutionally take up arms and fight for the constitution.'[3]

If Collins had upheld the election pact, it would have been a violation of the Treaty. He admitted as much after the election when a reporter of the *Sunday Express* asked whether de Valera would be excluded from the cabinet. 'Acceptance of the Treaty by members of the Provisional Government is a clause of the Treaty,' Collins replied.[4] Whether he or his opponents had first violated the election pact may be debatable, but Collins certainly made no effort to uphold his end of that agreement afterwards.

De Valera and others slipped out of Dublin and headed for Munster, which was a republican stronghold. De Valera served for a time as adjutant to Seán Moylan, the director of operations, at IRA headquarters in Clonmel, but the republican operations were a shambles. As early as the second week in July, Erskine Childers was writing that 'Dev says we should surrender while we are strong'.[5]

'It may be well to keep open some avenue or avenues to peace,' Collins wrote to his librarian friend Thomas Gay. 'We don't wish for any surrender of their principles.' Yet it was necessary for his opponents to accept the verdict of the people in favour of the Treaty. The government had shown its determination to uphold the people's rights, and it had 'answered the challenge to governmental authority by the recovery of General O'Connell' and by clearing out the occupied buildings in Dublin. 'Every constitutional way is open to them to win the people to their side, and we will meet them in every way if only they will obey the people's will and accept the authority of [the] government of the people,' Collins insisted. 'That alone is our concern.'[6] The opponents of the Treaty had been taught a lesson, and he was confident that the Provisional Government would be in a strong position so long as the Irish people were aware that it was prepared to be reasonable. Having gained an important advantage by the surrender of O'Connor and Mellows at the Four Courts, he was anxious not to make the mistake of building sympathy for them by taking 'resolute action beyond what is required'.[7]

One of those killed in the fighting in Dublin was Cathal Brugha, who was mortally wounded at the Hamman Hotel on O'Connell Street. Despite Brugha's animosity towards him, Collins still recognised Brugha's sincerity. 'Many would not have forgiven had they been in my place,' Collins wrote. 'Yet I would forgive him anything. Because of his sincerity I would forgive him anything … At worst he was a fanatic – though in what has been a noble cause,' he continued. 'At best I numbered him among the very few who would have given their all that this country – now torn by civil war – should have its freedom.'[8]

Collins decided to devote all his energies to ending the Civil War by asking the cabinet to appoint him commander-in-chief. He essentially wrote his own terms for taking over the army. 'It would be well, I think, if the government issue a sort of official instruction to me nominating the War Council of Three, and appointing me to act by special order of the government as commander-in-chief during the period of hostilities,' he wrote to Griffith.[9] He asked for a general address to be issued calling on him to carry on the fight for Irish freedom, this time against the armed minority who were trying to establish a dictatorship without regard to the wishes of the people.

The government promptly responded with an address to

the public signed by Griffith and all the other members of the cabinet. It was really a piece of propaganda designed to dramatise the determination of both Collins and the government to end the fighting as quickly as possible. 'You have been entrusted with supreme command of the National Army, and with General Mulcahy and General O'Duffy you have been constituted a War Council to direct the military operations now in progress,' the address began. 'The Irregular's method of warfare is utterly destructive of the economic life of the nation. Sheer brigandage is a fair term to apply to it. Wherever they go they burn and wreck property, destroy roads, railways and bridges; seize food, clothing, and supplies even from the poorest people; conscript men into their ranks, and use forced labour. In short they are doing their best to ruin and demoralise the country.'[10]

Other senior army appointments included Joe McGrath as director of intelligence with the rank of major general, Kevin O'Higgins as assistant adjutant general with the rank of commandant general, and Diarmuid O'Hegarty with the rank of commandant general on the general staff. In a technical sense it appeared that Collins was firmly establishing the principle of civilian control and taking his orders from Griffith and the Provisional Government, but the reality was somewhat different.

W. T. Cosgrave took over as acting chairman of the Provisional Government. Some later suggested that this amounted to a *coup d'état* in which Collins was ousted, but it was done at his request. De Valera suggested it was a tactical move so that Collins could ingratiate himself with the soldiers, who were mistrustful of all politicians. It was a way of building up rapport with the men to prosecute the war more effectively. Peter Young, for many years the army archivist, argues that it was an astute move to bolster army morale. 'Putting him in uniform, at the head of an army defending the existence of the new state, and with a press that was largely pro-Treaty, raised his stature to heroic proportions,' Young argued. 'The army as well as the general population required a sense of identity. Without the appointment of Collins as commander-in-chief, it is only too likely that it would have been beset by the local rivalries and animosities.'[11] As leader he exuded an authority and control that nobody else could have commanded. Collins was obviously aware of that, seeing that he spent so much time in the following weeks visiting army units on tours of inspection.

Collins and Cosgrave got on well together, even though they were very different characters. Cosgrave saw himself as primarily a politician. He had first been elected as a Sinn Féin candidate to Dublin Corporation in 1909. He was greatly underestimated by many of his contemporaries. De Valera dismissed him as 'a ninny' and Kevin O'Higgins reportedly sneered at him as 'a Dublin corporator'. Collins was reputed to have sworn in exasperation 'at the clerical susceptibility of Cosgrave's personality', but they had an easy relationship with each other. Cosgrave later recalled how Oliver St John Gogarty and the Big Fellow used to call out to his home and deliberately shock him. Collins would roar with laughter at Cosgrave's stunned expression as Gogarty made irreverent remarks. 'I often thought that pair of rascals took more delight in shocking me than in talking serious business when they came out to tea,' Cosgrave recalled.[12]

Cosgrave wrote to Collins 'that the government should be kept in constant touch with the military situation throughout the country', and that the army authorities should report regularly to him 'as acting chairman, similar to those reports which were formerly supplied to you'.[13] The nature of the subsequent correspondence, however, was more like Collins informing the government about what he had decided to do, rather than seeking permission to do it. Cosgrave seemed to be consulting him, rather than the other way around.

'The government have a vague war policy but absolutely no civil policy,' Churchill noted. 'Individual members of the administration all wait on Mr Collins.'[14]

When Collins decided to postpone the Dáil for another two weeks until the end of July, he instructed Kathleen McKenna of the publicity department to emphasise that he hoped the struggle would be ended in two to three weeks. 'We suggest once more that the government would act wisely in explaining to the country the nature and extent of the resistance that remains to be overcome,' Collins advised. 'A perfectly frank statement on the subject would define the army's goal and would secure not merely the whole-hearted, but the intelligent co-operation of the Irish people.'[15]

The Cork Harbour Commission – which was sympathetic to the republicans – wrote complaining about the suspension of the Dáil. Collins was careful to reply openly in a reasonable manner. This was not the brash, arrogant young man who had announced back in April 1919 that they were going to initiate the War of Independence whether people wanted it or not.[16] 'Even now it is a simple matter to end hostilities if those who are opposing the people's will but turn from their resistance and give the people the chance they desire,' Collins replied. 'No member of the government wishes to prolong the struggle, but equally, no member of the government, and, I am certain, no right thinking man in the whole of Ireland can contemplate without a shudder, the triumph of an armed minority over the people.'[17]

Collins was still waging a somewhat reluctant war and he was anxious for peace on moderate terms. When Thomas Gay wrote complaining about the hardline approach being taken by the Provisional Government, Collins seemed to agree. 'Generally speaking, what you say represents to a very large degree my own feelings about the main situation,' Collins replied. 'Anybody who is out for blood or scalps is of little use to the country; equally, of course, the real issue cannot be departed from.'[18]

'Our Press Organs should be very reticent in their tone about both active Irregular and Political Opponents,' Collins warned Cosgrave. 'Much of the criticism lately has been inclined towards abuse. This is not good from our point of view, and it is not the best way to tackle them.' He did not doubt that many of them deserved to be abused, but they were not 'the real driving force' on the irregular side. 'The men who are prepared to go to the extreme limit are misguided, but practically all of them are sincere,' he continued. 'Our propaganda should be on a more solid and permanent basis even if what may look to be advantages have to be sacrificed.'[19]

De Valera, who had always functioned primarily as a propagandist, was despondent about the press coverage from the republican standpoint. 'The newspapers are as usual more deadly to our cause than the machine guns,' he wrote.[20]

The convening of the new Dáil on 26 July was postponed for a third time until 12 August 1922. 'No one knows when the Dáil will assemble,' Churchill noted. 'I think it came to be taken for granted that the opening will be delayed as long as possible.'[21]

Collins demonstrated a keen awareness of the situation. 'We are in a strong position,' he wrote to Mulcahy. 'The opponents have shown themselves entirely without an objective.' They had no cohesive plans, immediate or long term. 'These leaders are waiting for something to turn up. When the Four Courts were attacked they said "the people are coming round to us" – but the people have resolutely refused to come round to them, and they must realise that without the people they have no hope.' Collins was anxious to avoid recrimination. It was pointless placing blame, he warned Mulcahy. 'What matters is not the past six months but the present position and the future six months and after the future six months, the entire future.'[22]

Collins was perceptive about the government's public image and agreed with Desmond Fitzgerald that censorship should be kept on broad, general lines. 'It should be very nominal,' he advised Mulcahy. 'We might get more good from a communication to the press giving them general lines to go on rather [than] relying on the public spirit to omit certain things.'[23] He was anxious for the government to take responsibility for decisions, while the cabinet seemed quite content to leave things to him. 'It was decided that the government will support the military authorities in whatever steps they may consider necessary to restore order in districts where military operations have ceased, but in which outbreaks of violence still continue,' he wrote to Mulcahy. 'I am afraid it is not very helpful to us, and we shall therefore have to frame proposals to be sanctioned by government.'[24]

He asked the government to introduce an element of martial

law by deeming certain areas liable to military searches and demanding that all arms should be surrendered by a specified date. He was calling the shots but he was anxious to avoid any appearance of military dictatorship. 'When the military effort is ended with the defeat of the hostile forces, peace can be said to have been restored. But peace will have to be maintained!' He wanted local committees to promote confidence so that the people would 'become actively interested in the new life of the nation'.[25]

Some members of the government were more militant than their military counterparts. Cosgrave wrote to Collins on 27 July, suggesting that the government should issue a proclamation warning all concerned that 'the troops have orders to shoot persons found sniping, ambushing or in possession of bombs, or interfering with railway or road communications, in areas in which military operations have ceased'.[26] Fearing that this would be tantamount to giving soldiers the right to execute people in cold blood, Collins objected. He was mindful that there were friends of his on the other side. Before responding to Cosgrave, he wrote to Harry Boland:

> Harry – It has come to this! Of all things it has come to this.
>
> It is my power to arrest and destroy you. This I cannot do. If you will think over the influence which has dominated you it should change your ideal.
>
> You are walking under false colours. If no word of mine will change your attitude then you are beyond all hope – my hope.[27]

Next day Collins replied to Cosgrave saying that the decision on the kind of proclamation suggested would be a matter for the government and the army would loyally implement it, but he was opposed to the idea. Drastic actions were needed, but allowing them to engage in summary executions was going too far. It was necessary to be mindful that there would be exceptions such as 'a man who deliberately shoots a soldier and then throws down his rifle and puts up his hands'.[28]

Ironically, the following day there were serious questions about the circumstances in which Harry Boland was shot and mortally wounded supposedly 'trying to escape'. Collins was 'grief-stricken' at a cabinet meeting some hours later. 'He spoke bitterly but movingly of his former comrade,' according to Ernest Blythe. 'The man who shot him must come forward and say he did it,' Collins declared. 'We are a government now and we cannot have any more of the business of shooting a man and running away.'[29]

'Last night I passed Vincent's Hospital and saw a small crowd outside,' Collins wrote to Kitty Kiernan. 'My mind went in to him laying dead there and I thought of the times together, and, whatever good there is in any wish of mine, he certainly had it. Although the gap of 8 or 9 months was not forgotten – of course no one can ever forget it – I only thought of him with the friendship of the days of 1918 and 1919.'[30]

Collins was told that on his deathbed Boland asked his sister Kathleen, 'Have they got Mick Collins yet?'

'I don't believe it so far as I'm concerned and, if he did say it, there is no necessity to believe it,' Collins wrote to Kitty Kiernan. 'I'd send a wreath but I suppose they'd return it torn up.'[31]

Kitty was obviously very upset when she replied. 'I have lost a good friend in Harry – and no matter what, I'll always believe in his genuineness, that I was the one and only. I think you have also lost a friend. I am sure you are sorry after him.'[32]

The three of them had been involved in a love triangle. Boland had wished to marry Kitty before her relationship blossomed with Collins. Maybe her remarks hit a sore spot, because he was apparently not as sympathetic about Boland as he might have been when he and Kitty had lunch together in a private room at the Shelbourne Hotel that day. He later asked Kitty not to misunderstand whatever he had said about Boland. 'You'll also appreciate my feelings about the splendid men we have lost on our side, and the losses they are and the bitterness they cause, and the anguish. There is no one who feels it all more than I do. My condemnation is all for those who would put themselves up as paragons of Irish nationality, and all the others as being not worthy of concern.'[33]

26

'DOGGING THE FORTUNES OF IRELAND'

'You need never have any fear that I will not appreciate any effort that is calculated to make things go in the right direction,' Collins wrote to his friend Thomas Gay on 1 August 1922. 'If people had a little more forbearance, and a little truer appreciation of the other people's opinion, we might never have got into this present morass.'[1]

A group calling itself the People's Rights Association of Cork (PRAC), had been trying to arrange peace for some days. Liam Lynch, the chief of staff of the IRA, had told PRAC that forces would lay down their arms 'when the Provisional Government cease their attack on us'.[2] He added that his forces would have no difficulty giving allegiance to the second Dáil, or the third Dáil once it met. On 1 August, therefore, Michael Ó Cuill of PRAC wrote to Collins asking:

1. Do you agree to arrange for such a cessation of hostilities as General Liam Lynch intimates he is prepared to accept?

2. Do you agree to call forthwith a meeting of the Second Dáil, to be followed by a meeting of the Third Dáil, as previously arranged, and to allow the sovereign assembly of the people to decide on the necessity or policy of a bitter and prolonged civil war?[3]

Collins replied promptly that the letter should really have been sent to the government, not to him as commander-in-chief of the army, seeing that he was just implementing government policy, which was insisting that the anti-Treatyites should submit to the rule of the people in the form of the duly elected government. Of course, this was not the true nature of his relationship with the government and he seemed to betray this by answering the questions anyway. 'When the irregulars – leaders and men – see fit to obey the wishes of the people, as expressed through their elected representatives; when they will give up their arms and cease their depredations on the persons and property of Irish citizens, then there will be no longer need for hostilities,' he explained. If his opponents wished to end the conflict, all they had to do was stop fighting. To secure their freedom all the arrested irregulars had to do was merely sign the following statement:

> I promise that I will not use arms against the parliament elected by the Irish people, or the government for the time being responsible to that parliament, and that I will not support, in any way, any such action. Nor will I interfere with the property or the persons of others.[4]

Most anti-Treaty prisoners refused to sign such a pledge, so Collins concluded that they obviously intended to take up arms again against the government. 'If this is the spirit which animates Liam Lynch, then I am sure your body will agree it is very little good endeavouring to talk about terms,' Collins wrote. 'Look facts squarely in the face. The time for face-saving is passed. Irregular leaders, political and military, got an opportunity of doing this over a period of seven or eight months. The issue now is very clear. The choice is definitely between the return of the British and the irregulars sending in their arms to the people's government, to be held in trust for the people.'[5]

Collins had already decided to put the partition question on the back burner for the duration of the Civil War in the twenty-six counties. 'My attitude towards Ulster, which is the attitude of all of us in the government, is not understood,' he had told the *Daily Mail.* 'There can be no question of forcing Ulster into union with the twenty-six counties. I am absolutely against coercion of the kind. If Ulster is to join us it must be voluntarily. Union is our final goal, that is all.'[6]

Following the May offensive the IRA in Belfast had resorted to attacking economic targets during June. The Big Fellow's interview with the *Daily Mail* at the end of June might have given the impression of a more conciliatory policy towards the northern loyalists, but there had always been some blatant contradictions between his public and private remarks in relation to Northern Ireland. As a public figure he was not likely to get away with such naked deception for long. He seemed to be lying to everyone to the point of becoming dangerously delusional. He was not only publicly contradicting the policy he had been pursuing behind the scenes, but there was a contradiction in the policy he was advocating within government. Even his colleagues could not have known where he really stood.

Having taken over as acting chairman of the Provisional Government, Cosgrave decided to stop paying northern elements, such as the Catholic teachers and nationalist local authorities that were refusing to recognise the Stormont regime. 'The question of payments in the six-county area is in a pretty chaotic condition,' Cosgrave wrote to Collins on just his second full day in the new job. 'There was no authority to spend money raised by taxing the south in the north,' he added. 'The northern government may be enabled to avoid its own proper liabilities and this is done in such a manner that the Free State tax payer cannot tell that his money is being spent in this way.'[7]

'The people were for a peace policy and for a recognition of the northern government,' Mulcahy wrote to Collins on 24 July. 'They are even giving information to the Specials. Our officers seem to realise there is no other policy for the north but a peace policy of some kind, but the situation for peace or war has gone beyond them, none of them feel they are able to face the policy of one kind or the other.'[8]

'I have scarcely a moment for any business other than the urgent business of restoring peace and settled conditions to the country,' Collins wrote to Churchill the next day. But he had no intention of forgetting the partition issue. 'Believe me,' he added, 'this all-important question is never far removed from my thoughts and were it not for my new obligations and commitments I would be devoting all available time and energy towards its solution.'[9]

Collins had protested to Churchill on 28 June about the Craig government's plans to abolish proportional representation in Northern Ireland, which had been introduced by the British to protect the nationalist minority. This amounted to a naked invitation to gerrymandering. It was more than a month before Churchill replied. 'The Bill has been exhaustively examined by His Majesty's Government. As a result it appears very doubtful whether under the system of proportional representation, which the Bill abolishes, the Catholic minority in the six northern counties would obtain a more adequate representation on the county councils and other municipal and local bodies than they may expect to obtain under the system by which under the Bill proportional representation is replaced.' It was politically possible for Craig to push through the changes with the south preoccupied with the Civil War. 'In any event,' Churchill continued, in what was a thinly disguised attack on the policies adopted by Collins, 'I feel bound to observe that the continuing refusal of the Catholic minority to recognise the northern government robs of much of their substance and possible validity the arguments urged in your letter against the passage of the Bill.'[10]

'It is a sentence of death or expulsion on every Catholic in the north,' Collins wrote on the first page of the letter.[11] 'The civil war will be over in a few weeks and then we can resume in the north,' he told an IRA group that he met from the north at Portobello Barracks on 1 August. He added that in the interim those men would get 'intensive training'.[12] On the following day he met men from the various northern divisions and again stressed that he could not devote the attention he would like to Northern Ireland. 'With this civil war on my hands, I cannot give you men the help I wish to give and mean to give,' he emphasised. 'I now propose to call off hostilities in the north and to use the political arm against Craig so long as it is of use. If that fails the Treaty can go to hell and we all will start again.'[13]

'I am forced to the conclusion that we have yet to fight the British in the north-east,' Collins warned Cosgrave on 3 August 1922. 'We must by forceful action make them understand that we will not tolerate this carelessness with the lives of our people.'[14]

Yet he took time to send a further lengthy protest to Churchill about the abolition of proportional representation, which he stressed would 'prejudice the Catholic and nationalist position in the whole of the north-eastern counties'. The move would further inflame sectarian bitterness and was a major cause of the violence that erupted in Northern Ireland almost half a century later. 'Do you not see, or have His Majesty's advisers not disclosed, the true meaning of all this?' Collins asked Churchill on 9 August. 'Not merely is it intended to oust the Catholic and nationalist people of the six counties from their rightful share in local administration, but it is, beyond all question, intended to paint the Counties of Tyrone and Fermanagh with a deep Orange tint in anticipation of the operation of the "Ulster Month" and the boundary commission, and so, to try to defraud these people of the benefits of the Treaty.'[15]

The war was going well for the Provisional Government, with the landing of troops near Tralee on 2 August 1922. The largest town in the south-west fell in an afternoon to government troops led by Major General Paddy O'Daly. The following day troops landed at Tarbert in north Kerry, and then at Kenmare in the southern part of the country on 11 August. Meanwhile troops under Major General Emmet Dalton landed at Passage West on 8 August and took control of Cork city within a matter of days. The war was turning into a procession of victories for the Provisional Government.

Collins wrote to Cosgrave suggesting a further postponement of the Dáil, this time until 24 August. His motivation seemed as much military as political: 'We would have occupied sufficient additional posts in the south to dominate entirely the positions, and would be able to indicate so definitely our ability to deal with the military problem there, that no parliamentary criticism of any kind could seriously interfere with that ability,' he wrote. He wished to 'confirm to the general public our determination to clean up the matter definitely', so the IRA in Munster would not conclude that the government forces had hesitated and convened the Dáil out of weakness, because they were reluctant to confront the IRA boldly. If this happened, it could lead to a 'rise in morale' in the IRA, and this could then have serious consequences.[16]

Collins realised that it was necessary to establish an efficient police force if peace and security were to be properly restored in the area already taken. 'The nucleus must be the civic guard organisation,' he wrote to Cosgrave on 6 August. 'The matter is one on which we ought to hasten slowly.' He did not want a casual force but one that was properly trained. 'It is not necessary for me to illustrate this by pointing to the wretched Irish republican police system, and to the awful personnel that was attracted to its ranks,' Collins continued. 'The lack of construction and the lack of control in this force have been responsible for many of the outrageous things that have occurred throughout Ireland.'[17]

There was a grim reminder of the awful consequences of the struggle when Collins and other army leaders joined members of the government at a funeral Mass at Portobello Barracks on 8 August for nine soldiers killed in Kerry. 'The scenes at the Mass yesterday were really heartbreaking,' he wrote to Kitty. 'The poor women weeping and almost shrieking (some of them) for their dead sons. Sisters and one wife were there too, and a few small children. It makes one feel, I tell you.'[18]

Up to this point Collins had been stressing the necessity for moderation in the treatment of Civil War opponents, but it was significant that he wrote to Joe McGrath, the director of intelligence, on the day after the funeral stipulating that 'any man caught looting or destroying should be shot on sight'.[19] But when Dunne and O'Sullivan were convicted of the murder of Field Marshal Wilson on 18 July and were sentenced to be hanged on 16 August 1922, Collins wrote to Cosgrave as 'acting chairman' of the Provisional Government to intercede with the British government on behalf of the two men. 'I am of opinion that we must now make an official representation that mercy be extended to these men,' he wrote. 'Please let me know what is being done in the matter.'[20] Dunne and O'Sullivan were hanged. If the Big Fellow had given the order to kill Wilson, then the two men took the secret to the grave with them.

Collins was in Tralee on 12 August, when he got word of the sudden death of Arthur Griffith from a brain haemorrhage in Dublin. 'There seems to be a malignant fate dogging the fortunes of Ireland, for at every critical period in her story the man whom the country trusts and follows is taken from her,' Collins told reporters in Tralee. 'It was so with Thomas Davis and Parnell, and now with Arthur Griffith. Only those who have worked with him know what Arthur Griffith has done for Ireland; only they can realise how he has spent himself in his country's cause,' Collins continued, adding that he had 'no shadow of doubt' that the president's untimely death had been hastened by mental anguish as a result of the Civil War.[21]

'Is it possible that the death of Mr Arthur Griffith may unite the nation?' a reporter asked.

'At the moment I am a soldier, but I think I can promise that if those who are against us will, even now, come forward and accept the terms offered by the government, our differences can be composed. I must not be misunderstood on this point. Militarily, our position warrants us in our belief that our opponents are in a hopeless position. Look at the map: see where our troops are, what they have achieved, and where the armed forces of the other side have been driven. But, even so, it is not too late for de Valera and those who are with him to honour the passing of a great patriot by now achieving what that patriot has given his life for – a united Ireland, and Irish nation.'[22]

Collins related how Griffith likened the de Valera party to Dermot McMurrough. 'He was the man who first brought the British to Ireland,' Collins continued. De Valera and his followers were really trying 'to bring the British back as conquerors, and what true Irish patriot can wish for that?' he asked.[23] In reality de Valera had very little influence at the time, but he was widely attributed with leadership of the republican forces because of the way the media and pro-Treaty spokesmen railed against him.

Collins was convinced that the Civil War was coming to a close. 'The military situation is entirely satisfactory,' he told reporters in Limerick on his way to Dublin for Griffith's funeral. The main military operations would be completed within the next fortnight, he said. 'I can advise the government that, as far as the military situation is concerned, the new parliament can meet at any time,' he added. 'Whether it will be further postponed out of respect to the late President Griffith I do not know.'[24]

At Griffith's funeral on 16 August, Collins marched in uniform at the front of the headquarters staff officers, with Mulcahy by his side. It was his first public appearance in the uniform of commander-in-chief. They marched at a funeral pace through the city, and spectators got a good look at him. 'I marched just behind him in the ranks, and heard the murmurs of admiration which rose from people on the route,' Piaras Béaslaí wrote. 'The people looked to him with confidence as the one man who could get the nation out of the morass into which it had sunk.'[25]

Although Collins had been saying privately at the start of the month that the Civil War was almost over, he was more guarded in his public comments. 'The attempt to fix a date for our finishing this job is as ridiculous as it is futile,' he told the journalist Hayden Talbot. 'No man can do more than hope for a speedy termination of this senseless campaign of robbery, arson and murder.' Rather than a forecast, he suggested that the prediction of an early end to the war would be better called 'an official hope'. 'It is no easy job we have undertaken – and it is not going to be accomplished quickly,' he added. He stressed that the fighting ability of the other side should not be underestimated. 'They have a commander of exceptional ability,' he said.[26]

Talbot assumed Collins was talking about Liam Lynch, but he was quickly disabused of the idea. 'It's a lad named Liam Deasy,' Collins said. 'He is every inch a natural-born general. I like him immensely, and anything I may say about the rest of them does not apply to him. He is worth all the rest of their leaders put together. If we had him with us, instead of against us, our job would be fifty per cent easier.'[27]

On the day after Griffith's funeral, the Provisional Government finally took control of the whole of Dublin Castle. It was handed over to the Civic Guard without fanfare, but then Collins had exploited the supposed handover in January as 'the surrender of Dublin Castle'.[28]

27

'WHAT MATTER IF FOR IRELAND DEAR WE FALL'

On 18 August 1922, Collins met the playwright George Bernard Shaw for the first and only time. Shaw, who was visiting Ireland, was sanguine. 'Ireland is obviously on the point of losing its temper savagely,' he told the press after the meeting:

> When the explosion comes, General Collins will be able to let himself go in earnest, and the difficulty of the overcrowded jail and the disbanded irregular who take to the road again the moment the troops have passed will be solved, because there will be no prisoners; the strain will be on the cemeteries.
>
> General Collins beat Sir Hamar Greenwood at the wrecking game because he had the people with him. What chance against him has Mr de Valera without military aptitude or any of Sir Hamar Greenwood's enormous material resources? Of course he can enjoy the luxury of dying for Ireland after doing Ireland all the damage he can. 'What matter if for Ireland dear we fall' is still the idiot's battle song. The idiocy is sanctified by the memories of a time when there was really nothing to be done for Irish freedom but to die for it; but the time has now come for Irishmen to learn to live for their country. Instead of which they start runaway engines down the lines, blow up bridges, burn homesteads and factories, and gain

nothing by it except such amusements as making my train from Waterford to Rosslare several hours late. Ireland would be just as free at this moment if I had arrived punctually. You see, the cause of Ireland is always dogged by the ridicule which we have such a fatal gift of provoking, and such a futile gift of expressing.

I suppose it will have to be settled, as usual, by another massacre of Irishmen by Irishmen. If Mr de Valera had any political genius he might avert it. But with the strongest sentimental bias in his favour I cannot persuade myself that he has any political faculty at all …

I cannot stand the stale romance that passes for politics in Ireland. I cannot imagine why people bother so much about us; I am sure we don't deserve it … But what matter if for Ireland dear we fall! It is too silly: I must hurry back to London. The lunatics there are comparatively harmless.[1]

After Collins was dropped in Greystones, his car was involved in an ambush near Stillorgan on returning to Dublin. To his disappointment, the incident was not reported. 'I recounted the incident to the government meeting last night, but apparently it was not of sufficient interest for publication,' he wrote to the director of publicity. 'The commander-in-chief's car was ambushed on Friday at 1 p.m. about one mile the Dublin side of Stillorgan, on its way from Greystones. 2nd Driver Rafter was wounded on hip and is now in Baggot Street Hospital. One bomb and between 20 and 30 rifles shots fired. Fire was returned, casualties of attackers unknown. The car is badly damaged.'[2]

The morning after the Stillorgan ambush Collins visited the Foxrock home of Sir Henry Robinson, who had been put through a frightening ordeal the previous evening when his home was robbed at gunpoint. After the withdrawal of the RIC and British army, Robinson noted that officials like himself 'were left at the mercy of any thugs that happened to take a dislike to us'. Those who had started the War of Independence had not been able to call it off at the stroke of a pen. 'The habit of taking what you want at the end of a revolver is not got rid of as easily as that and, Treaty or no Treaty, there were a whole heap of private vendettas to be settled up, and there was quite a lot of loot available for bandits without any police to interfere with them,' Robinson's son wrote.[3]

Collins had told them that 'the new government were in no position to protect anybody. We had much better clear out, and come back later on when things had settled down a bit.' The following day they learned the raiders 'were not republicans at all but just local hooligans, led by a very bad hat, who luckily was not there on the night of the raid'.[4]

'I find myself in far more danger since the peace came than ever I did in the war,' Collins joked in an interview published in a London newspaper on 19 August.[5] The danger was closer than he probably realised. That evening he was in a touring car that was involved in an accident in Dun Laoghaire when it collided with a military tender carrying troops. 'The crowd which collected round the damaged vehicles recognised the general and cheered him,' according to *The Irish Times*.[6]

Next day the Stillorgan ambush was plastered across a seven-column headline as the lead story in the *Sunday Independent*. It was also fully reported on Monday in *The Irish Times,* which went on to mention that it had learned 'on good authority' that Collins was not actually in the car at the time.[7] General Macready, who noted that Collins was not in the car, reported to the cabinet in London that 'this attack was probably intended to avenge the death of Harry Boland'. He noted that republican propagandists were holding Collins responsible for Boland's 'so-called murder'.[8]

Collins did not attend the cabinet meeting on Monday morning when it took a momentous decision on the north. Ernest Blythe, who had been vocal in favour of a militant policy in the south before the arrival of the Black and Tans, warned the cabinet that the aggressive policy towards the six counties was counter-productive. He advocated that the pro-Treaty IRA be disbanded in the north. The Provisional Government formally adopted this 'peace policy', but it is significant that it only did so subject to 'the approval of the commander-in-chief'. As he began his fatal tour of the south, it was obvious that members of the cabinet still looked to Collins as the man in charge.[9]

As was the case with Shaw, the Irish public still tended to see the conflict as a kind of contest between Collins and de Valera. The latter had actually become preoccupied with the thought of arranging peace. 'In Fermoy, Mallow, and other towns, the people looked at us sullenly, as if we had belonged to a hostile invading army,' recalled Robert Brennan, who sometimes acted as secretary for the Long Fellow. 'Dev had seen all this, as had I, and that was one of the reasons he was so desperately trying for peace while he still had some bargaining power.'[10]

'The people must be won to the cause before any successful fighting can be done,' de Valera believed.[11] Like Collins, he appreciated the value of propaganda, but the republicans had no newspapers on their side and they were badly organised. De Valera was trying to persuade them to give up the fight. 'Dev passing through your area talking peace,' Liam Lynch wrote to his deputy chief of staff, Liam Deasy. 'Give him no encouragement.'[12]

'Dev's mission is to try to bring the war to an end,' Deasy told his men, adding that they were 'on no account to give Dev any encouragement as his arguments don't stand up'.[13]

De Valera met Deasy in Gurranereagh, County Cork, on 21 August. 'We discussed the war situation far into the night,' Deasy recalled. 'His main argument was that, having made our protest in arms and as we could not now hope to achieve a military success, the honourable course was for us to withdraw.' Deasy agreed to an extent but pointed out that the majority of the IRA 'would not agree to an unconditional cease fire'.[14]

Having arrived in Cork on the evening of 20 August, the following morning Collins visited some local banks in an effort to trace republican funds lodged during their occupation of the city. During July the IRA had collected £100,000 in customs revenue and hidden this money in the accounts of sympathisers. Collins got the bank directors to identify suspicious accounts. He concluded that 'three first-class independent men' were needed to conduct a forensic investigation of the banks and the Customs and Excise in Cork. He asked Cosgrave to consider three people 'but don't announce anything until I return'.[15] At the end of a long day the Big Fellow strode into the lobby of the Imperial Hotel in Cork to find the two hotel guards sleeping on duty. He grabbed them and banged their heads together.

The next day Collins set out early with a small escort convoy which consisted of a motorbike outrider, Lieutenant Smith, followed by an open Crossley tender with two officers, two machine gunners with a Lewis gun and eight riflemen. A Leyland Thomas touring car with Collins and Emmet Dalton in the back seat, and two drivers in front followed this. An armoured car brought up the rear of the convoy. Collins noted in his pocket diary that they departed at 6.15 a.m. He planned to go to Macroom first, where he had promised the Lewis gun to the local captain. Only a few miles outside Cork they ran into difficulties as the retreating republicans had destroyed a number of bridges in the area.

Shortly before 8 a.m. they reached Macroom, where he met Florrie O'Donoghue. Although O'Donoghue had been very prominent in the IRA, he was taking a neutral stand in the Civil War. He recalled that the Big Fellow was acting like he believed his opponents were afraid of him. 'I've been all over this bloody country but no one has said a bloody word to me,' Collins said.

As a bridge on the main road to Bandon had been blown up, the Collins convoy had to take a back road. On the way they passed through Béalnabláth at around 9 a.m. The locality was a hive of republican activity. Volunteers retreating from Limerick, Kilmallock and Buttevant as well as from Cork city were all in the general area. They planned to have a staff meeting at Béalnabláth that day. Denis Long, who was on guard duty there, gave Lt Smith, the motorcycle outrider, directions to Bandon. He noticed Collins in the convoy as it passed.

It was just after nine o'clock when de Valera and Deasy reached Béalnabláth and were told that Collins and a small military convoy had passed through only minutes earlier. Deasy remarked that the IRA should prepare an ambush in case Collins returned by the same route later that day. 'De Valera then remarked that it would be a great pity if Collins were killed because he might be succeeded by a weaker man,' according to Deasy.[16]

The republicans were determined to respond to what they considered his audacious challenge. They placed a mine in a metal tin with sticks of gelignite and buried it in the road near Béalnabláth. They then commandeered a four-wheel dray, driven by Stephen Griffith, who was told to take his horse to a local farm and await further developments. They took one of the wheels off the dray, propped it up on boxes of bottles and then waited throughout the remainder of the day. The number lying in wait fluctuated from twenty-five, estimated by Deasy, to much more, depending on who was telling the story.

Having reached Bandon, Collins and his party went on to Clonakilty. They had a good deal of trouble with the touring car, possibly caused by dirty petrol. They had to push it on a number of occasions, especially up some of the steeper hills. Although Collins was commander-in-chief, he was always ready to lend a hand with the pushing. 'It was a beautiful August day,' Dalton recalled. 'Because there were still daily ambushes, I was in trepidation of what could happen, but Collins saw no danger.'[17] They were both confident that the Civil War could not last much longer.

'It's almost over,' Collins said. In a sense it was a prophetic remark.

The group stopped for a meal at Clonakilty, and Collins met some old friends. Afterwards they went to Rosscarbery and then on to Skibbereen, where Collins and Dalton had a brief exchange with the famous writer Edith Sommerville, before heading back for Cork shortly after 4.30 p.m.

On reaching Sam's Cross, the convoy stopped off at the pub of Collins' cousin, Jeremiah. The Big Fellow bought two pints of Clonakilty Wrastler for each of his crew. While there he met his brother Johnny, and two of Johnny's daughters – Mary and Kitty – as well as his first cousin Michael O'Brien. He told them that his main goal was to end the Civil War and then he would be re-dedicating himself to the task of securing full national freedom. He was not about to be content with the Treaty settlement but would get further concessions from the British government once peace was restored. He seemed in good form, according to Johnny, but this was probably because his spirits were lifted in the midst of his family and friends, not to mention that he had consumed a fair bit of alcohol that day.

'I hope you are travelling in the armoured car, Mick, because there is still danger around,' Johnny said.

'Not at all, this is my bus,' Michael replied motioning towards the open touring car.

He crossed the road for a brief visit to his aunt and some other people in the neighbourhood. 'Take care Michael,' one of them said to him, according to Johnny, 'take good care of yourself.'

'They will never shoot me in my own country,' he replied.[18]

The convoy moved on to Bandon and from there back by the same route through Béalnabláth, where the republicans had been waiting to ambush him throughout the day. As the convoy had not returned by 7 p.m. they assumed that he had either taken a different route or was not coming back that night, and the ambush was called off. Seven men were left to dismantle the mine and clear the road. With the light failing, around 7.15 the Free State convoy approached the ambush site. It was surrounded by hills and when the first shot was fired Dalton realised it was an ideal spot for an ambush. 'Drive like hell!' Dalton shouted, but Collins put a hand on the driver's shoulder.

'Stop!' he ordered. 'We'll fight them.'[19]

Collins got to his feet and went over behind the armoured car to use it for cover as he fired some shots. 'Come on boys!' Collins shouted, apparently believing the ambushers were on the run. He left the protection of the car and moved about fifteen yards up the road. He dropped into the prone firing position and opened up on the retreating republicans. A few minutes had elapsed when Commandant O'Connell came running up the road under fire and threw himself down beside Dalton asking, 'Where is the Big Fellow?'[20]

'He's round the corner,' Dalton replied.[21] They could hear Collins shooting. At one point he was standing up on the road firing as if he was daring somebody to shoot him. It seemed an amazingly foolish thing to do. Had the drink dulled his senses, or was he incredibly naïve when it came to an ambush situation?

'Next moment,' Dalton said later, 'I caught a faint cry: Emmet I'm hit.'[22]

Dalton and O'Connell found Collins lying on the road, still clutching his rifle. He had a gaping wound at the base of the skull behind his right ear. 'It was quite obvious to me with the experience I had of a ricochet bullet, it could only have been a ricochet or a "dum-dum",' Dalton recalled.[23]

O'Connell dragged Collins behind the armoured car. 'I bandaged the wound and O'Connell said an "Act of Contrition" to him,' Dalton said. 'He was dying if not already dead.'[24] The body was placed in the armoured car and moved down the road out of danger and it was then transferred to the touring car. They asked a local man, Ted Murphy, to guide them to the nearest priest. He got into the tender.

'This is a night that will be remembered,' one of the soldiers remarked.

'Why?' Murphy asked.

'The night Michael Collins was killed.'[25]

They drove about two miles to house of Fr Timothy Murphy in Cloughduv. A soldier asked him to come out to the car. The soldier was carrying an old carbide lamp that was providing very bad light. At the car the body of Collins was propped up with his head lying against Dalton's shoulder.

'I was crying and so was O'Connell,' Dalton recalled.[26]

The priest realised they were looking for the last rites for their dead comrade, so he turned to go back into the house for the necessary oils. They thought he was refusing to anoint Collins' body. O'Connell raised his rifle to shoot the priest. 'Only that I struck up the barrel the priest would have been shot,' Dalton explained later. 'The bullet was actually discharged.' They then drove off, incensed at what they considered the unchristian behaviour of the priest. 'This incident left a grim impression on the minds of the entire party,' Dalton added.[27]

As with the assassination of President John F. Kennedy over forty years later, the question of who actually shot Michael Collins has become more complicated with the years. Only seven men initially formed the remnants of the ambush party, but one or two others joined during the shooting. Afterwards the remnants of the ambush retired to Bill Murray's kitchen for tea.

'Fifteen minutes earlier and the lot would have been wiped out,' one of the men remarked.

Sonny Neill said he 'dropped one man'. This was war. He did not know who the man was.

When the men had finished eating Seán O'Galvin arrived with the news that 'Michael Collins was shot'. Anne White, the priest's housekeeper, had sent word to him.

One of the men jumped up and said, 'There's another traitor gone.'

'He's dead,' Neill said, rising from the table. 'May the Lord have mercy on his soul.' With that he walked out of the house.[28]

28

'HANG UP YOUR BRIGHTEST COLOURS'

Béalnabláth was only nineteen miles from Cork city, but the convoy with the body of Collins had a nightmare journey. 'We were forced to take to the back roads because of trees felled and trenches cut across the main roads,' Dalton recalled. 'At one point we had to drive through a farm haggard over a shallow ditch and cut through a paddock gate.'[1]

He also said, 'So long as I live the memory of that nightmare ride will haunt me.'[2]

It was the early hours of the following morning before news reached army headquarters in Dublin. A telegraph operator handed the message to Adjutant General Gearóid O'Sullivan, who went to wake Emmet Dalton's brother, Charlie, with the news. 'Charlie,' he said as he broke down in tears, 'the Big Fella is dead.' The grief was palpable. Tom Cullen and Joe O'Reilly, two of the men who had been particularly close to Collins over the years, went to inform Cosgrave in the morning. He brought them in to tell the cabinet. When they saw the faces of the ministers, O'Reilly and Cullen suddenly broke down and wept uncontrollably. 'This is a nice way for soldiers to behave,' Cosgrave exclaimed.[3]

'Ireland's greatest leader since Shane O'Neill has died at the hands of his own countrymen,' Pat McCartan wrote to Joe doubt that de Valera was some miles away from Béalnabláth when the ambush took place. He certainly took no direct part and it is most unlikely that he had any input whatever, because Deasy had no time for his military views.

Later the conspiracy theories would be taken further with Seán Feehan's suggestion that Emmet Dalton may have killed Collins. Dalton had served in the British army in the First World War, but like many others he came home to fight in the War of Independence. Most of those closest to Collins became disillusioned with the Free State authorities after his death. Dalton resigned from the army as a major general and tried his hand at a number of different ventures. During the Second World War he worked for British Intelligence in MI6 and hence the conspiracy theorists suspected that he might have been a British agent all along and that he killed the Big Fellow.

There is no real evidence to support any of these theories. The likely truth is that Collins was probably shot by one of the republicans who did not even recognise him. It was war and the men on both sides were shooting at the enemy. But the conspiracy theories that surround the death of Collins grew, just like the speculation about the death of President John F. Kennedy would four decades years later. Ironically there was another parallel in relatively similar posthumous speculation about their love lives. In the first full-length biography of Collins published in 1926, Piaras Béaslaí, who knew Collins well, depicted him as having little interest in the opposite sex. 'The society of girls had apparently no attraction for him,' Béaslaí wrote. 'He preferred the company of young men, and never paid any attention to the girls belonging to the Branch, not even to the sisters and friends of his male companions.'[11]

A second biography by Frank O'Connor, initially published in 1937 in America under the title *Death in Dublin*, was later published under the title *The Big Fellow*. It is a highly readable account, which shows Collins as a contradictory conglomeration of various characteristics – a buoyant, warm-hearted, fun-loving individual with a thoughtful, generous nature, but also a selfish, ruthless, ill-mannered bully. While other young men were looking for sex, he was more inclined to go looking for 'a piece of ear'. He would burst into a room, jump on a colleague, wrestle him to the floor and begin biting the unfortunate friend's ear forcing him to surrender, often with blood streaming from his head. It is the portrait of a rather strange fellow.

From the early biographies one grandnephew of Collins came to the conclusion that the Big Fellow was homosexual. He actually said this to his grandfather, Michael's eldest brother Johnny. The latter just laughed and said that if Michael had a 'problem', it was certainly not that he was not fond of women. Within his immediate family this would have been known, but they probably did not talk much about it.

At the time of his death, Collins and Kitty Kiernan were engaged to be married, but this was not even mentioned by either Béaslaí or O'Connor. She was later inclined to play the part of the grieving widow, which did not go down well with some of the Big Fellow's sisters. When Kitty later married, there were suggestions that her husband felt he was competing with the ghost of Collins. It was not until 1983 – long after her death and that of her husband – that her correspondence with Collins was published. By then Béaslaí's depiction of the misogynistic Mick had been well and truly demolished. Meanwhile rumours of his amorous activities had taken on a life of their own.

For his biography published in 1958, Rex Taylor had the advantage of a cache of sixteen letters that Collins wrote to 'John O'Kane' during the Treaty negotiations in London, but it seems that this may have been a pseudonym, because nobody else appears to have heard of O'Kane. Many of the Big Fellow's contemporaries were still around, but none of them knew O'Kane. There seems to be no reason to question that Collins actually wrote those letters, as there is evidence elsewhere to suggest that the views expressed in them were very much in line with his views and there has been speculation that John O'Kane was a pseudonym for Moya Llewelyn-Davies.

Since the early 1960s biographers have looked deeper into the background of Collins and new light has been thrown on his relations with many young women. Tim Pat Coogan was able to show in his biography that Collins had a close relationship with Susan Killeen while they were both in London before 1916, and they corresponded with each other following her return to Dublin. Their correspondence was of an affectionate nature.

Many of the people who worked for Collins – passing information on to him from within the British civil service, or doing direct secretarial work for him – were young women who obviously admired him. They included his cousin Nancy O'Brien, who later married his elder brother Johnny after the death of his first wife; Jenny Mason, who worked as one of his secretaries; Lily Merlin, who worked as a typist for the British army; and Eileen McGrane, who stored documents for him. There was also Dilly Dicker, the piano player who lived near him in Mountjoy Street, and there was Moya Llewelyn-Davies, whom he had known in London as

Moya O'Connor when she was friendly with his sister Hannie. Moya later married Compton Llewelyn-Davies, who was a solicitor friend of David Lloyd George. Like Eileen McGrane, Moya stored material for Collins at her house, Furry Park, on the Howth Road, Killester. This was also apparently one of his safe houses.

In his 1997 book, *Michael Collins and the Brotherhood*, Vincent MacDowell suggests that Collins was amorously involved with three married women while he was in London during the Treaty negotiations – with Moya Llewelyn-Davies, Lady Edith Londonderry and Hazel Lavery, the wife of painter Sir John Lavery. MacDowell actually suggests that Hazel Lavery was involved with Lloyd George in blackmailing Collins into signing the Treaty by threatening to disclose that Collins was the father of Moya's son Richard, who was born in 1912.[12] But on the basis of the evidence produced, Collins could just as easily have been the father of any of the children born in London from 1907 to 1916!

***

The record of some of those closest to Collins makes disturbing reading after his death. On 8 September 1922, men under Dalton's command tortured and killed Timothy Kennefick near Coachford, County Cork. A coroner's inquest returned a verdict of murder. The killers were former members of Collins' Squad serving under Dalton's command. Commandant Peter Conlon protested to Dalton that there would be mutiny if it happened again.

Even worse incidents took place in Kerry, including the blowing up of eight republican prisoners who were strapped to a mine at Ballyseedy. Major General Paddy O'Daly, who had been in charge of the Squad during the War of Independence, was in command of the Free State forces in Kerry where the worst atrocities were committed during the Civil War. He subsequently chaired the army inquiry, which was a proverbial whitewash. It was believed by many that he had actually ordered the outrage at Ballyseedy. Whether or not this was true, there was no doubt that he covered up the killings.

In 1924 the Free State government decided to cut drastically the size of the army, much to the disapproval of some of those who had been closest to Collins. General Liam Tobin and Colonel Charlie Dalton issued an ultimatum to the government to halt the demobilisation. They and their backers had followed Collins in accepting the Treaty as a stepping-stone to full freedom, but now it seemed that the government was happy with the Irish Free State as an end in itself. They therefore insisted that the goals of Collins be implemented. The army mutiny posed a real threat to democracy in Ireland. Mulcahy opposed the mutiny and loyally stood up to his former comrades. The mutineers were forced out of the army, but Mulcahy was compelled to resign from the government. He went quietly. By having the courage to accept his humiliation, he 'forestalled a really serious crisis', according to historian Joe Lee.[13]

When the boundary commission finally met in 1925, Lloyd George was long gone from power. The commission essentially decided on only minimal changes to the boundary – giving the Free State a bit of Northern Ireland here and giving Northern Ireland a bit of the Free State there. Since such changes would add insult to the outrage that was likely to be provoked by the surprise failure to transfer Counties Fermanagh and Tyrone to the Free State, the London, Dublin and Belfast governments all agreed to scrap the findings. As a sweetener the British agreed to absolve the Free State from any responsibility to contribute towards the British national debt. De Valera was later able to claim that this absolved the Free State from having to pay land annuities to Britain, but the Cosgrave government did not realise this at the time. 'In the long and sorry story of departure from undertakings and the spirit of assurances given by British Ministers there was never a more flagrant breach of faith by them than the cynical fiasco perpetrated at the time of the boundary commission,' in the opinion of Seán MacEoin.[14]

De Valera wished to exploit the political unrest, but Sinn Féin refused to take their seats in the Dáil, so he broke with the party, severed all connections with the IRA and founded Fianna Fáil (The Republican Party), which promptly became the main opposition party. In the days before Fianna Fáil came to power, Johnny Collins, Michael's eldest brother, was particularly anxious. In 1932 he had a young family and had only a temporary civil service job and his brother's political enemies were coming to power. Before the change of government he made frantic efforts to have his appointment made permanent, but he was unsuccessful. In desperation his wife explained their plight to the wife of a prominent Fianna Fáil politician. A few days later de Valera sent word that the appointment was being extended for six years and that he could keep the job as long as he was able to do it.

There was subsequently a controversy over blocking supporters of Collins from erecting a large headstone over his grave. The real issue was that the headstone was larger than the specifications allowed for everybody else. Maybe it was small of de Valera not to use his influence to allow the Big Fellow to have a bigger headstone, but then there were the families of others also to be considered. By contrast, de Valera – who was later buried with his wife, Sinéad, and their son, Brian – has a small headstone.

Fianna Fáil won more seats than any other party in the general election of 1932, with the result that de Valera was able to form a minority government with the help of the Labour Party. Eoin O'Duffy tried to get the army to join with him and the Garda Síochána in staging a *coup d'état*, but neither was prepared to support him. Nevertheless Cosgrave's party, Cumann na Gaedheal, soon joined with the Centre Party and the neo-fascist Blueshirts to form the United Ireland (Fine Gael) Party under O'Duffy, whose fascist tendencies proved so embarrassing that he was quickly removed as leader. But Fine Gael tried to frustrate de Valera's efforts to dismantle the 1921 Treaty by using the stepping-stone approach to full freedom advocated by Collins.

It was largely at the secret instigation of Cosgrave and his party that the British initiated the Economic War against the Irish Free State in 1932 over de Valera's refusal to pay land annuities to Britain. De Valera contended that the Free State did not owe the money. Chancellor of the Exchequer Neville Chamberlain admitted in March 1932 that de Valera had 'an arguable point', because the wording of the boundary commission agreement absolved the Dublin government 'from liability for the service of the Public Debt of the United Kingdom, and that the Irish annuities form part of the Public Debt'.[15]

The Irish people endorsed de Valera's stand in a snap general election in 1933 by returning Fianna Fáil with the first overall majority since the Treaty split. His government then systematically dismantled the objectionable aspects of the Treaty by abolishing the oath, introducing a new constitution, replacing the governor general with a popularly elected president, and securing both the handover of the Treaty ports and the abrogation of Britain's rights to Irish defence facilities in times of war. This paved the way for Ireland to stay out of the Second World War, which was the ultimate proof of independence. It is one of the great ironies of history that it was de Valera who proved that Collins was right – the Treaty was a stepping-stone to the desired independence.

Some critics blamed the Treaty for partition, but partition had already been introduced before the Treaty negotiations even began. De Valera subsequently pretended that he had opposed the Treaty because of partition, but this was a gross distortion. The partition clauses of the Treaty were essentially in line with what he had previously advocated in the Dáil, and he included those verbatim in his proposed alternative to the Treaty, Document No. 2. Collins and de Valera both stated publicly that they did not wish to coerce the unionists or loyalists into a united Ireland. Collins did, to an extent, try to win them over with the two pacts with Craig, but behind the scenes he encouraged a militant policy to coerce them. De Valera, on the other hand, did neither.

When he was negotiating to abrogate the defence clauses of the Treaty and end the Economic War in 1938, he tried to persuade the government of Neville Chamberlain to agree to a united Ireland behind the backs of the unionists. Seán MacEntee, who was a member of de Valera's negotiating team, wrote a strong letter disapproving of Fianna Fáil's attitude towards the northern question: 'In regard to partition we have never had a policy,' he wrote. Some of their colleagues had been 'subordinating reason to prejudice', he warned. As a government they had done nothing to try to win over the northern Protestants. 'With our connivance every bigot and killjoy, ecclesiastical and lay, is doing his damnedest here to keep them out.'[16]

People in the Republic of Ireland remained sublimely ignorant about aspects of the partition issue, and the role that Michael Collins had secretly encouraged. The mistakes of the Northern Offensive of 1922 were repeated to a lesser degree during the border campaign of the 1950s, but on that occasion the government of Éamon de Valera introduced internment to hamper the IRA. As minister for justice in the early 1960s, Charles Haughey was one of those who cracked down on the republicans and compelled the IRA to call off the campaign, yet, like his father before him, he became involved in efforts to support another campaign before the end of the decade.

'It is now necessary to harness all opinion in the State in a concerted drive towards achieving the aim of unification,' Captain James J. Kelly wrote on 23 August 1969 as he was organising the attempted gun-running that led to the Arms Crisis of 1970. 'This means accepting the possibility of armed action of some sort, as the ultimate solution.' At the time the arms were depicted as a means of helping the northern nationalists to protect themselves against armed loyalists, but Captain Kelly had a much more ambitious motive. He was trying to end partition. 'If civil war embracing the area was to result because of unwillingness to accept that war is the continuation of politics by other means,' he added, 'it would be a far greater evil for the Irish nation.'[17] Whether he was a mover or a mere conduit in the subsequent events is another question.

The events subsequent to 1922 are really beyond the scope of this book. But there were events in 1922 that history has largely ignored, and there is scope for suggesting that because of ignorance of that history the mistakes of 1922 were repeated again and again.

NOTES

1 'WE WILL NOW CALL ON THE IRISH PEOPLE TO RALLY TO US'

1   For an in-depth analysis of the Treaty negotiation, see T. Ryle Dwyer, '*I Signed My Death Warrant': Michael Collins & the Treaty* (Cork, 2007).

2   Dáil Éireann, *Official Report: Debate on the Treaty between Great Britain and Ireland* (Dublin, 1922), S2 (7 January 1922), p. 347.

3   *Irish Independent*, 7 December 1921.

4   Dwyer, *I Signed My Death Warrant*, pp. 42–44, 224, 229.

5   *The Freeman's Journal*, 9 January 1922.

6   Childers, Minutes of meeting of 8 January 1922, Childers Papers, TCD.

7   *Ibid.*

8   Dáil Éireann, *Debate on the Treaty*, S2 (9 January 1922), p. 349.

9   *Ibid.*

10 *Ibid.*

11 *Ibid.*, p. 351.

12 *Ibid.*, pp. 352–3.

13 *Ibid.*, p. 356.

14 *Ibid.*, p. 357.

15 *Ibid.*, p. 376.

16 *Ibid.*

17 *Ibid.*, p. 380.

18 Dáil Éireann, *Private Sessions of Second Dáil* (Dublin, nd), 23 August 1921, pp. 54–5.

19 Dáil Éireann, *Debate on the Treaty*, S2 (10 January 1922), p. 399.

20 *Ibid.*, p. 410.

21 *Ibid.*

2 'YOU ARE A TRAITOR'

1   De Vere White, T. *Kevin O'Higgins* (Tralee, 1966), p. 84.

2   Greenwood, memo, 9 January 1922, CP 3605, CAB24/132, TNAGB.

3   See Erskine Childers, diary, 14 January 1922, MS 7819, Childers Papers, TCD.

4   Béaslaí, Piaras, *Michael Collins and the Making of a New Ireland*, Vol. 2 (Dublin, 1926), p. 369.

5   Hopkinson, Michael, *Green Against Green: The Irish Civil War* (Dublin, 1988), p. 37.

6   O'Malley, Ernie *The Singing Flame: A Memoir of the Civil War, 1922–24* (Dublin, 1978), p. 53.

7   Hopkinson, *Green Against Green*, p. 59; Coogan, Tim Pat, *Michael Collins: A Biography* (London, 1990), p. 311.

3 CHAIRMAN OF THE PROVISIONAL GOVERNMENT

1   Collins to James K. Maguire, 18 January 1922, Collins Papers.

2   Macready, General Sir Nevil, *Annals of an Active Life*, Vol. 2 (London, 1924), pp. 602–3.

3   *Ibid.*, p. 603.

4   Douglas, James G., *Memoirs of Senator James G. Douglas: Concerned Citizen*, ed. by J. Anthony Gaughan (Dublin, 1998), p. 78.

5   Dwyer, T. Ryle, *Big Fellow, Long Fellow: A Joint Biography of Collins and de Valera* (Dublin, 1998) p. 262.

6   Douglas, *Memoirs*, p. 78.

7   Conference with Irish Minister, 5 February 1922, CAB43/6, TNAGB.

8   Minutes of Provisional Government, 27 January 1922, G1/2, NAI.

9   Dáil Éireann, *Official Report: Debate on the Treaty between Great Britain and Ireland* (Dublin, 1922), S2 (28 February 1922), p. 121.

10 Dwyer, T. Ryle, *Tans, Terror and Troubles: Kerry's Real Fighting Story* (Cork, 2001), pp. 80–1.

11 Collins, address in Naas, 16 April 1922, quoted in the *Kildare Observer*, 22 April 1922.

4 'Coercion-of-Ulster is unthinkable'

1 De Valera to Patrick McCartan, 7 February 1918, Devoy Papers, NLI.

2 De Valera to Lloyd George 10 August 1921, in Dáil Éireann, *Official Correspondence relating to Peace Negotiations, June–September, 1921*.

3 Dáil Éireann, *Official Report: Debate on the Treaty between Great Britain and Ireland* (Dublin, 1922), S2 (11 August 1921), pp. 29–31.

4 Clause 12 of the Anglo-Irish Treaty, in Dáil Éireann, *Private Sessions of Second Dáil* (Dublin, nd), 1921, Appendix 16, pp. 312–16.

5 Shakespeare, Sir Geoffrey, *Let Candles Be Brought In* (London, 1949), pp. 89–90.

6 Craig to Lloyd George, 14 December 1921, SFB 42, CAB43/2, TNAGB.

7 *Ibid.*

8 Craig to Bonar Law, 13 December 1921, in Canning, Paul, *British Policy Towards Ireland 1921–1941* (Oxford, 1985), p. 55.

9 *Ibid.*, p. 56.

10 Cabinet conclusion, 15 December 1919, CAB23/18, TNAGB.

11 *The Freeman's Journal*, 11 January 1922.

12 Dáil Éireann, *Private Sessions*, p. 153.

13 Seán MacEoin to me, 20 March 1970.

14 Ernest Blythe to me, 3 July 1970.

15 Birkenhead to Balfour, 3 March 1922, quoted in *The Times* (London), 8 September 1924.

16 Ernest Blythe to me, 4 May 1970.

17 *Ibid.*

18 Collins, Notes on meeting with Lloyd George, 5 December 1921, in Dáil Éireann, *Private Sessions*, Appendix 13, pp. 304–6.

19 Cabinet 90 (21), 6 December 1921, CAB23/27, TNAGB.

5 'There was no Ulster Question'

1 Aiken interview with Ernie O'Malley, O'Malley Papers, UCDA.

2 For details of the killing, see Dwyer, T. Ryle, *The Squad and the Intelligence Operations of Michael Collins* (Cork, 2005), pp. 117–20.

3 Lynch, Robert, *The Northern IRA and the Early Years of Partition, 1920–22*, p. 78.

4 *The New York Times*, 6 September 1921.

5 Collins address in Armagh, *Irish Independent*, 5 September 1921.

6 *Ibid.*

7 James McCoy, Report of 3rd Northern Division, 27 July 1922, Mulcahy Papers, P7/B/ 77, UCDA.

8 Lynch, *Northern IRA*, p. 151.

9 Craig, address to Ulster Unionist Council, Belfast, 27 January 1922, quoted in *The Irish Times*, 28 January 1922.

10 Profile of Craig by Nichevo (R. M. Smyllie), *The Irish Times*, 28 January 1922.

11 Canning, Paul, *British Policy Towards Ireland 1921–1941* (Oxford, 1985), p. 54.

12 Collins report on meeting with Craig, Minutes of Provisional Government, 2 February 1922, NAI.

13 Minutes of Provisional Government, 23 January 1922, G1/2, NAI.

14 Collins–Craig agreement, 23 January 1922, S.1801A, NAI.

15 Dáil Éireann, *Official Report: Debate on the Treaty between Great Britain*

and Ireland (Dublin, 1922), S2 (6 August 1920), pp. 192–4.

16   Coogan, Tim Pat, *Michael Collins: A Biography* (London, 1990), p. 338.

17   Dáil Éireann, *Debate on the Treaty*, S2 (16 December 1921), pp. 192–4.

18   Provisional Government Minutes, 1 February 1922, G1/1, NAI.

19   *Ibid.*

20   *Ibid.*, 30 January 1922, G1/1, NAI.

21   Clause 2 of Collins–Craig Agreement, 21 January 1922, S.1801A, NAI.

22   Collins to John O'Kane, in Taylor, Rex, *Michael Collins* (London, 1958), p. 173.

6 THE COLLINS–CRAIG PACT

1   Greenwood, memo for week ending 23 January 1922, 192, CP 3658, TNAGB.

2   *The Cork Examiner*, 23 January 1922.

3   Macready, report for week ending 28 January 1922, CAB24/132, TNAGB.

4   Craig, address to Ulster Unionist Council, Belfast, *The Irish Times*, 28 January 1922.

5   *Ibid.*

6   Collins, statement, 3 February 1922, S.1801A, NAI.

7   Hopkinson, Michael, 'The Craig–Collins Pacts of 1922', *Irish Historical Studies*, 27 (1990), p. 149.

8   Provisional Government Minutes, 30 January 1922, G1/1, NAI.

9   Statement, issued on 1 February 1922, S.1801A, NAI.

10   *Ibid.*; *The Freeman's Journal* and *The Irish Times*, 2 February 1922.

11   Collins to Craig, 26 January 1922, in Coogan, Tim Pat, *Michael Collins: A Biography* (London, 1990), p. 343.

12   Craig to Collins, 27 January 1922, *ibid.*

13   Provisional Government Minutes, 1 February 1922, G1/1, NAI.

14   Provisional Government Minutes, 2

February 1922; Statement, 2 February, S.1801A, NAI.

15   *The Irish Times*, 4 February 1922.

16   Craig, P.A. interview, 3 February 1922, S.1801A, NAI.

17   *Ibid.*

18   Collins interview, 3 February 1922, quoted in *The Freeman's Journal*, 4 February 1922.

19   Capt. C. C. Craig, address, 3 February 1922, S.1801A, NAI.

20   Hopkinson, 'The Craig–Collins Pacts of 1922', p. 149.

21   W. S. Churchill to Clementine Churchill, 4 February 1922, in Gilbert, Martin, *Winston S. Churchill: World in Torment*, Vol. 4 (London, 1975), p. 1752.

22   Collins, statement, 3 February 1922, S.1801A, NAI.

23   Collins, P. A. interview, 3 February 1922, S.1801A, NAI.

24   Healy, T. M., *Letters and Leaders of My Day* (London, 1928), 2, p. 652.

7 TAKING HOSTAGES

1   *The Freeman's Journal*, 6 February 1922.

2   *Irish Independent*, 4 February 1922.

3   Collins, press statement, 6 February 1922, S.1801A, NAI.

4   *The Irish Times*, 7 February 1922.

5   Collins told the story to Fr Paddy Doyle, WS 807, BMH, NAI.

6   Eoin O'Duffy to Collins, 30 January 1922, in McGarry, Fearghal, *Eoin O'Duffy: A Self-Made Hero* (Oxford, 2005), p. 99.

7   *Ibid.*

8   Dwyer, T. Ryle, *Michael Collins: The Man Who Won the War* (Cork, 2008), p. 93.

9   *The Irish Times*, 9 February 1922.

10   *The Irish Times*, 10 February 1922.

11   *Ibid.*

12   Greenwood, weekly survey for week ending 12 February 1922, CP 3747, CAB24/133, TNAGB.

13 Cope to Thomas Jones, 8 February 1922, in Coogan, Tim Pat, *Michael Collins: A Biography* (London, 1990), p. 345.
14 Macready, report dated 8 February 1921, CP 2568, CAB24/119, TNAGB.
15 Dwyer, T. Ryle, *Big Fellow, Long Fellow: A Joint Biography of Collins and de Valera* (Dublin, 1998), p. 289.
16 Conference of Ministers with Griffith, 9 February 1922, CAB21/254, TNAGB.
17 Dwyer, *Big Fellow, Long Fellow*, p. 289.
18 Collins to Lloyd George, 9 February 1922, in Hopkinson, Michael, *Green Against Green: The Irish Civil War* (Dublin, 1988), p. 80.
19 Hopkinson, *Green Against Green*, p. 80.
20 *Ibid.*
21 Hansard (House of Commons), *Debates*, 150 (9 February 1922), cols. 457–8.
22 Jones, Thomas, *Whitehall Diary*. Vol. III: *Ireland, 1918–25* (London, 1971), p. 194.
23 *The Irish Times*, 9 February 1922.
24 W. S. Churchill to Clementine Churchill, 11 February 1922, in Gilbert, Martin, *Winston S. Churchill: World in Torment*, Vol. 4 (London, 1975), p. 1758.

8 CLONES AFFRAY

1 Greenwood, weekly survey for week ending 12 February 1922, CP 3747, CAB24/133, TNAGB.
2 Dwyer, T. Ryle, *Big Fellow, Long Fellow: A Joint Biography of Collins and de Valera* (Dublin, 1998), p. 290.
3 Hansard (House of Commons), *Debates*, 150 (13 February 1922), cols 591–2.
4 Macready, report for week ending 13 February 1922, CP 3769, CAB24/133, TNAGB.
5 *Daily Telegraph, Morning Post* and *The*

Irish Times, 10 February 1922.
6 Hansard (House of Commons), *Debates*, 150 (13 February 1922), col. 595.
7 *The Irish Times*, 14 February 1922.
8 Hansard (House of Lords), *Debates*, 49 (15 February 1922), col. 156.
9 Collins to Churchill, telegram, 16 February 1922, quoted in *The Irish Times*, 17 February 1922.
10 Cabinet 10 (22), 16 February 1922, CAB23/29, TNAGB.
11 Churchill to Collins, 14 February 1922, in Hopkinson, Michael, *Green Against Green: The Irish Civil War* (Dublin, 1988), p. 81.
12 Hopkinson, Michael, *Green Against Green*, p. 81.
13 Collins to Churchill, telegram, 16 February 1922, quoted in *The Irish Times*, 17 February 1922.
14 Collins to Churchill, telegram, 18 February 1922, quoted in *The Irish Times*, 22 February 1922.
15 Joe Dolan, WS 900, BMH, Army Archives.
16 *Ibid.*
17 *Ibid.*
18 Dwyer, *Big Fellow, Long Fellow*, p. 289.
19 Griffith to Collins, 15 February 1922, S.1801A, NAI.

9 'THE RATS LEAVING THE SHIP'

1 *The Irish Times*, 2 February 1922.
2 *Ibid.*
3 Dwyer, T. Ryle, *Big Fellow, Long Fellow: A Joint Biography of Collins and de Valera* (Dublin, 1998), p. 268.
4 *Ibid.*
5 *Ibid.*
6 *Ibid.*
7 *The Irish Times*, 20 February 1922.
8 *Ibid.*
9 *Poblacht na h-Éireann*, 28 February 1922.
10 *Ibid.*
11 *Ibid.*

12   *Ibid.*

13   *The Irish Times*, 10 February 1922.

14   *The Freeman's Journal*, 22 February 1922.

15   *Ibid.*

16   Béaslaí, Piaras, *Michael Collins and the Making of a New Ireland*, Vol. 2 (Dublin, 1926), p. 338.

17   Hopkinson, Michael, *Green Against Green: The Irish Civil War* (Dublin, 1988), p. 56.

18   *The Irish Times*, 22 February 1922.

19   *The Irish Times*, 23 February 1922.

20   *The Freeman's Journal*, 6 March 1922.

21   *Ibid.*

22   *Ibid.*

23   Ó Ruairc, Pádraig, *Military History of the Irish Civil War: The Battle for Limerick City* (Cork, 2010), p. 41.

24   Valiulis, Maryann Gialanella, *Portrait of a Revolutionary: General Richard Mulcahy and the Founding of the Irish Free State* (Dublin, 1992), p. 132.

25   Ó Ruairc, *Battle for Limerick City*, p. 42.

26   Younger, Calton, *Ireland's Civil War* (London, 1968), p. 244.

27   Churchill to Collins, 14 March 1922, in Churchill, Winston S., *The Aftermath* (London, 1929), pp. 322–3.

10 'LET THE BASTARD GO'

1   Greenwood, report for week ending 13 March 1922, CAB24/134, TNAGB.

2   Cork *Evening Echo*, 13 March 1922.

3   Collins, interview, 13 March 1922, *The Freeman's Journal*, 14 February 1922.

4   *Ibid.*

5   *Poblacht na h-Éireann*, 29 March 1922.

6   Collins speech, Cork, 12 March 1922, in Collins, Michael, *Arguments for the Treaty* (Dublin, 1922), pp. 18–24.

7   Collins to Mulcahy, 14 March 1922, S.1322, NAI.

8   Collins, interview, 13 March 1922, *The Freeman's Journal*, 14 March 1922.

9   *The Irish Times*, 13 March 1922.

10   Borgonovo, John, *Military History of the Irish Civil War: The Battle for Cork* (Cork, 2011), p. 32.

11   Coogan, Tim Pat, *Michael Collins: A Biography* (London, 1990), pp. 316–17.

12   De Valera to Griffith, 10 March 1922, quoted in *Irish Independent*, 16 March 1922.

13   Dwyer, T. Ryle, *Big Fellow, Long Fellow: A Joint Biography of Collins and de Valera* (Dublin, 1998), p. 275.

14   *Irish Independent*, 17 March 1922.

15   Dwyer, *Big Fellow, Long Fellow*, pp. 275–6.

16   De Valera, Éamon, *Speeches and Statements by Éamon de Valera, 1917–1973*, ed. M. Moynihan (Dublin, 1980), p. 98.

17   *Irish Independent*, 20 March 1922.

18   *The Irish Times*, 20 March 1922.

19   Dáil Éireann, *Official Report: Debate on the Treaty between Great Britain and Ireland* (9 January 1922), p. 379.

20   *The Times* (London), quoted in *The Irish Times*, 21 March 1922.

21   De Valera to *Irish Independent*, 23 March 1922.

22   *The Irish Times*, 30 March 1922

23   *The Irish Times*, 23 March 1922.

24   *Ibid.*

25   *Ibid.*

26   Macardle, Dorothy *The Irish Republic* (London, 1968), pp. 677–8.

11 'SOME OF YOU KNOW NOTHING ABOUT FREEDOM'

1   *The Irish Times*, 27 March 1922.

2   *Ibid.*

3   de Valera to Cathal Ó Murchadha, 13 September 1922, quoted in *The Freeman's Journal*, 16 October 1922.

4   Cabinet conclusion, 8 March 1922, CAB23/29, TNAGB.

5   Churchill to Collins, 14 March 1922, in Churchill, Winston S., *The Aftermath* (London, 1929), pp. 322–3.

6   *The Irish Times*, 15 March 1922.

7   *Ibid.*

8   *Ibid.*

9   *Ibid.*

10 Craig quoted in Memo by Provisional Government of Ireland Committee, CP 3873 CAB24/134, TNAGB.

11 Memo by Provisional Government of Ireland Committee, CP 3873 CAB24/134, TNAGB.

12 Macready, report for week ending 18 March 1922, CAB24/134, TNAGB.

13 Wilson to Craig, 17 March 1922, quoted in *The Irish Times*, 20 March 1922.

14 Collins to Churchill, 24 March 1922, CAB24/134, TNAGB.

15 Craig quoted in Collins to Churchill, 21 March 1922, CAB24/134, TNAGB.

16 Collins to Churchill, 24 March 1922, CAB24/134, TNAGB.

17 Collins to Fitzgerald, 20 March 1922, Seán MacEoin Papers P151/96, UCDA.

18 *Belfast Telegraph*, 20 March 1922.

19 Craig to Churchill, 21 March 1922, in Lynch, Robert, *The Northern IRA and the Early Years of Partition* (Oxford, 2006), p. 119.

20 Collins to *The Times* (London), 24 March 1922.

12 'THREE OF THE MOST DELIGHTFUL HOURS'

1   Gilbert, Martin, *Winston S. Churchill: World in Torment*, Vol. 4 (London, 1975), p. 698.

2   Dwyer, T. Ryle, *Big Fellow, Long Fellow: A Joint Biography of Collins and de Valera* (Dublin, 1998), p. 290.

3   Hansard (House of Commons), *Debates*, 152 (28 March 1922), col. 1291.

4   Lynch, Robert, *The Northern IRA and the Early Years of Partition* (Oxford, 2006), p. 194.

5   Hansard (House of Commons), *Debates*, 152 (28 March 1922), col. 1291.

6   *Ibid.*, cols 1291–2.

7   Collins statement, 27 March 1922, quoted in *The Irish Times*, 29 March 1922.

8   *Irish Independent*, 29 March 1922.

9   *Ibid.*, 28 March 1922, S.1801A, NAI.

10 *Ibid.*

11 McCoole, Sinéad, *Hazel: A Life of Lady Lavery, 1880–1935* (Dublin, 1996), p. 86.

12 Heads of Agreement, 31 March 1922, S.1801A, NAI.

13 Collins to Kitty Kiernan, 31 March 1922, quoted in *Irish Independent*, 18 May 1996.

14 *Ibid.*

15 *Westmeath Examiner*, editorial, 1 April 1922.

16 *Irish Independent*, 3 April 1922.

17 O'Farrell, Padraic, *The Seán MacEoin Story* (Cork, 1981), p. 78.

18 *Irish Independent*, 3 April 1922.

19 Craig to Collins, 4 April 1922, S.1801, NAI.

20 Collins to Craig, 5 April 1922, *ibid.*

21 Craig to Collins, 5 April 1922, *ibid.*

22 Collins to Craig, 5 April 1922, *ibid.*

23 Craig to Collins, 6 April 1922, *ibid.*

24 Collins to Craig, 8 April 1922, *ibid.*

25 *Connaught Telegraph*, 8 April 1922.

26 *Ibid.*

27 *Ibid.*

13 'CIVIL WAR CAN ONLY BE AVERTED BY A MIRACLE'

1   *Irish Independent*, 7 April 1922; MacManus, M. J., *Éamon de Valera* (Dublin, 1944), p. 198.

2   De Valera interview, 11 April 1922, in Macardle, Dorothy, *The Irish Republic* (London, 1968), p. 700.

3   *The Freeman's Journal*, 10 April 1922.

4   *Ibid.*

5   Coogan, Tim Pat, *Michael Collins: A Biography* (London, 1990), p. 341.

6   *The Irish Times*, 18 March 1922.

7   Collins to Kitty Kiernan, 14 April 1922, in Ó Broin, Leon, *In Great Haste: The Letters of Michael Collins and Kitty Kiernan* (Dublin, 1983), pp. 151–2.

8   Molly Childers to de Valera, 28 November 1940, Childers Papers, MS 7848-299, TCD.

9   O'Farrell, J. T., speech given to the Irish Senate, *Senate Debates*, 20, 16 January 1936, p. 1876.

10   *Ibid.*

11   Dáil Éireann, *Official Report: Debate on the Treaty between Great Britain and Ireland* (Dublin, 1922), S2, 40 (14 October 1931), p. 56.

12   Proclamation issued by de Valera on Easter Sunday, 16 April 1922, quoted in *Gaelic-American* (New York), 22 April 1922.

13   *Gaelic-American*, 22 April 1922.

14   *Kildare Observer*, 22 April 1922.

15   *Irish Independent*, 17 April 1922.

16   *The Irish Times*, 18 April 1922.

17   Durney, James, *The Civil War in Kildare* (Cork, 2011), p. 68.

18   *Irish Independent*, 25 April 1922.

19   O'Brien, William, *Forth the Banners Go* (Dublin, 1969), pp. 219–20.

14 'WE WILL CO-OPERATE IN NOTHING'

1   *Irish Independent*, 25 April 1922.

2   Younger, Calton, *Ireland's Civil War* (London, 1968), pp. 275–6.

3   *Irish Independent*, 25 April 1922.

4   *Kerry Leader*, 21 April 1922.

5   *Irish Independent*, 25 April 1922.

6   Dwyer, T. Ryle, *'I Signed My Death Warrant': Michael Collins & the Treaty* (Cork, 2007), pp. 194–204.

7   *Irish Independent*, 25 April 1922.

8   Dwyer, T. Ryle, *Tans, Terror and Troubles: Kerry's Real Fighting Story* (Cork, 2001), pp. 230–5.

9   *Irish Independent*, 25 April 1922.

10   Hopkinson, Michael, *Green Against Green: The Irish Civil War* (Dublin, 1988), p. 40.

11   MacSwiney to Mulcahy, 24 April 1922, Childers Papers, MS 7835, TCD.

12   *The Freeman's Journal*, 27 April 1922.

13   *Irish Independent*, 7 April 1922; Dwyer, T. Ryle, *De Valera: The Man and the Myths* (Dublin, 1991), pp. 107–8.

14   Cabinet conclusions, Cabinet 32(22), 2 June 1922, CAB23/30, TNAGB.

15   Collins to 'A Chara', 8 March 1922, S.1011, NAI.

16   Meeting of North East Advisory Committee, 11 April 1922, S.1011, NAI.

17   Londonderry to Collins, 5 April 1922, S.1011, NAI.

18   Londonderry to Collins, 7 April 1922, *ibid.*

19   Collins to Craig, 11 April 1922, *ibid.*

20   Craig to Collins, 15 April 1922, S.1801A, NAI.

21   Wilson, diary, in Gilbert, Martin, *Winston S. Churchill: World in Torment*, Vol. 4 (London, 1975), p. 709.

22   Wilson, diary, 12 April 1922, in Callwell, C. E., *Field-Marshal Sir Henry Wilson: His Life and Diaries*, Vol. 2 (London, 1927), p. 236.

23   Churchill to Collins, 12 April 1922, in Churchill, Winston S., *The Aftermath* (London, 1929), pp. 324–5.

24   Hansard (House of Commons), *Debates*, 153 (12 April 1922), cols 517–8.

25   *Ibid.*, col. 522.

26   Churchill to Cope, 31 March 1922, in Hopkinson, *Green Against Green: The Irish Civil War*, p. 66.

27   Churchill to Collins, 5 April 1922, S.1322, NAI.

28   Macready, General Sir Nevil, *Annals of an Active Life*, Vol. 2 (London, 1924), p. 631.

29   Collins to Churchill, 5 April 1922, S.1322, NAI.

30   Churchill to Collins, 12 April 1922, *ibid.*

31   Churchill to Collins, 5 April 1922, *ibid.*

32   Churchill wrote on 4 April 1922, Gilbert, *Churchill*, 4, p. 703.

33   *Ibid.*, p. 705.

34   Churchill to Collins, 5 April 1922, S.1322, NAI.

35   Collins to Churchill, 6 April 1922, S.1322, NAI.

15 'DRIFT ABOUT IN RECRIMINATORY CORRESPONDENCE'

1   Minutes of the Provisional Government, 21 April 1922, NAI.

2   Collins to Craig, 22 April 1922, S.1801A, NAI.

3   Collins to Churchill, 25 April 1922, *ibid.*

4   Churchill to Collins, 25 April 1922, *ibid.*

5   Collins to Craig, 27 April 1922, *ibid.*

6   Craig to Collins, 28 April 1922, *ibid.*

7   Craig to Collins, 25 April 1922, *ibid.*

8   *Ibid.*

9   *Ibid.*

10   Macready to Churchill, 16 April 1922, in Gilbert, Martin, *Winston S. Churchill: World in Torment*, Vol. 4 (London, 1975), p. 710.

11   Churchill to Lloyd George, 17 April 1922, *ibid.*, p. 709.

12   Churchill to Lloyd George, 19 April 1922, *ibid.*

13   *Poblacht na h-Éireann*, 4 May 1922.

14   *Ibid.*

15   *The Freeman's Journal*, 1 May 1922.

16   De Valera, interview with John Steele, *Poblacht na h-Éireann*, 18 May 1922.

17   Churchill to Collins, 29 April 1922, in

Churchill, Winston S., *The Aftermath* (London, 1929), pp. 326–8.

18   *The Irish Times*, 7 April 1922.

19   *Ibid.*, 11 April 1922.

20   Collins letter to editor, *The Irish Times*, 27 April 1922.

21   *The Irish Times*, 27 April 1922.

22   Collins letter to *The Irish Times*, *The Freeman's Journal*, 28 April 1922.

23   Eoghan Harris, 'Scarred by Forced Exodus of Southern Protestants', *Sunday Independent*, 14 December 2008.

24   Churchill to Collins, 29 April 1922, in Churchill, *The Aftermath*, pp. 326–8.

25   Dáil Éireann, *Official Report: Debate on the Treaty between Great Britain and Ireland* (Dublin, 1922), S2 (28 April 1922), p. 332.

26   *The Freeman's Journal*, 29 April 1922.

16 'WE ARE FAST VERGING TO ANARCHY'

1   *Connaught Tribune*, 29 April 1922.

2   *Irish Independent*, 26 April 1922.

3   Dáil Éireann, *Official Report: Debate on the Treaty between Great Britain and Ireland* (Dublin, 1922), S2 (3 May 1922), p. 357.

4   Seán Ó Muirthile, 'Memoirs', MS 125, Mulcahy Papers, UCDA.

5   IRA Officers' Appeal, *Irish Independent*, 2 May 1922.

6   *Ibid.*

7   Dáil Éireann, *Debate on the Treaty*, S2 (3 May 1922), p. 360.

8   *The Freeman's Journal*, 2 May 1922.

9   Dáil Éireann, *Debate on the Treaty*, S2 (3 May 1922), p. 338.

10   *Ibid.*, p. 365.

11   *Irish Independent*, 2 May 1922.

12   *Ibid.*

13   Collins to Paddy Daly, 5 May 1922, in Coogan, Tim Pat, *Michael Collins: A Biography* (London, 1990), p. 325.

14   *Irish Independent*, 16 May 1922.

15   *The Irish Times*, 16 May 1922.

16   *Ibid.*

17   *Ibid.*

18   McNiffe, Liam, *A History of the Garda Síochána: A Social History of the Force, 1922–52* (Dublin, 1997), pp. 18–20.

17 The Election Pact

1   Dáil Éireann, *Official Report: Debate on the Treaty between Great Britain and Ireland* (Dublin, 1922), S2 (17 May 1922), p. 440.

2   *The Irish Times*, 16 May 1922.

3   Dáil Éireann, *Debate on the Treaty*, S2 (17 May 1922), p. 440.

4   Hopkinson, Michael, *Green Against Green: The Irish Civil War* (Dublin, 1988), pp. 96–7.

5   *Ibid.*, p. 96.

6   Ó Broin, Leon, *Michael Collins* (Dublin, 1980), p. 128.

7   Dáil Éireann, *Debate on the Treaty*, S2 (17 May 1922), p. 429.

8   Collins, memo of negotiations with de Valera, Mulcahy Papers, P7a/145, UCDA.

9   *Ibid.*

10   Churchill to A. Chamberlain, 13 May 1922, in Gilbert, Martin, *Winston S. Churchill: World in Torment*, Vol. 4 (London, 1975), pp. 714–15.

11   Churchill to Collins, 15 May 1922, in Churchill, Winston S., *The Aftermath* (London, 1929), p. 330.

12   Cabinet Minutes, 16 May 1922, CAB23/30, TNAGB.

13   Hopkinson, *Green Against Green*, pp. 97–8.

14   Collins, Memo of negotiations with de Valera, Mulcahy Papers, P7a/145, UCDA.

15   Dáil Éireann, *Debate on the Treaty*, S2 (19 May 1922), p. 478.

16   Seán T. O'Kelly to Collins, 15 May 1922, DE2/514, NAI.

17   Collins to O'Kelly, *ibid.*

18   Dáil Éireann, *Debate on the Treaty*, S2 (19 May 1922), p. 461.

19   Seán T. O'Kelly, 'Memoirs', p. 335, MS 27,707, NLI.

20   *The Times* quoted in the *Irish Independent*, 22 May 1922.

21   *Daily Herald* quoted in *The Freeman's Journal*, 22 May 1922.

22   *Daily News* quoted in *The Freeman's Journal*, 22 May 1922.

23   Dwyer, T. Ryle, *Big Fellow, Long Fellow: A Joint Biography of Collins and de Valera* (Dublin, 1998), p. 297.

24   Ó Muirthile, 'Memoirs', MS 125, Mulcahy Papers, UCDA.

25   O'Kelly, 'Memoirs', pp. 338–9, MS 27,707, NLI.

26   *Ibid.*, p. 339.

27   Ernest Blythe, WS 939, BMH.

28   *Ibid.*

29   *The Freeman's Journal*, 22 May 1922.

18 'Northern Rebellion'

1   Macready, report for week ending 29 April 1922, CAB24/13, TNAGB.

2   Minutes of meeting of 11 April 1922, S.1011, NAI.

3   3rd Northern Division Report, 27 July 1922, Mulcahy Papers, P7/B/287, UCDA.

4   North East Advisory Committee Meeting, Belfast, 15 May 1922, S.1011, NAI.

5   Cabinet Minutes, 16 May 1922, CAB23/30, TNAGB.

6   *Irish Independent*, 22 May 1922.

7   James J. McCoy, Report of 3rd Northern Division, 27 July 1922, Mulcahy Papers, P7/B/287, UCDA.

8   *Ibid.*

19 'I can't leave these people unprotected'

1   *The Freeman's Journal*, 23 May 1922.

2   Dwyer, T. Ryle, *Big Fellow, Long Fellow: A Joint Biography of Collins and de Valera* (Dublin, 1998), p. 299.

3   Mary MacSwiney to McGarrity, 29

April 1922, in Hopkinson, Michael, *Green Against Green: The Irish Civil War* (Dublin, 1988), p. 100.

4   *Ulster Herald*, 27 May 1922. Churchill in Hansard (House of Commons), *Debates*, 154 (22 May 1922), col. 800.

5   Churchill to Collins, 22 May 1922, in Coogan, Tim Pat, *Michael Collins: A Biography* (London, 1990), p. 325.

6   Collins, address to Civic Guard, Kildare, 26 May 1922, S.9524, NAI.

7   Churchill, Memo, 23 May 1922, CO739/5, TNAGB.

8   Wilson address at Liverpool Ulster Association, *The Irish Times*, 26 May 1922.

9   Hansard (House of Commons), *Debates*, 153 (10 May 1922), col. 2299.

10 *Ibid.*

11 *The Irish Times*, 24 May 1922.

12 *Ibid.*

13 Churchill to Craig, 24 May 1922, in Churchill, Winston S., *The Aftermath* (London, 1929), p. 332.

14 *Ibid.*

15 *The Irish Times*, 27 May 1922.

16 Towey, Thomas, 'The Reaction of the British Government to the 1922 Collins–de Valera Pact', *Irish Historical Studies*, 22 (March 1980), p. 73.

17 *Ibid.*

18 *Ibid*, p. 74.

19 Cabinet 30 (22), 30 May 1922, CAB23/30, TNAGB.

20 Collins to Kitty Kiernan, 28 May 1922, in Ó Broin, Leon, *In Great Haste: The Letters of Michael Collins and Kitty Kiernan* (Dublin, 1983), pp. 165–6.

21 Collins to Kitty Kiernan, 30 May 1922, *ibid.*, p. 166.

22 Cabinet 30 (22), 30 May 1922, TNAGB.

23 *Ibid.*

24 Jones, Thomas, *Whitehall Diary*. Vol. III: *Ireland, 1918–25* (London, 1971), p. 202.

25 *Ibid.*, p. 206.

26 *Ibid.*, p. 204.

27 Collins to Kitty Kiernan, 31 May 1922, in Ó Broin, *In Great Haste*, p. 167.

28 Collins to Kitty Kiernan, 28 May 1922, *ibid.*, p. 166.

20 'THIS GULF IS UNBRIDGEABLE'

1   Cabinet conclusions, Cabinet 30(22), 30 May 1922, CAB23/30, TNAGB.

2   *Ibid.*

3   *Ibid.*

4   Diary entry for 30 May 1922, Jones, Thomas, *Whitehall Diary*. Vol. III: *Ireland, 1918–25* (London, 1971), p. 203.

5   Churchill told Parliament on 31 May 1922, Hansard (House of Commons), *Debates*, 154, col. 2132.

6   Craig to Churchill, 24 May 1922, McMahon, Paul, *British Spies and Irish Rebels: British Intelligence and Ireland 1916–1945* (Woodbridge, 2008), p. 144.

7   Hansard (House of Commons), *Debates*, 154 (31 May 1922), cols. 2133–4.

8   *The Freeman's Journal*, 1 June 1922.

9   Hansard (House of Commons), *Debates*, 154 (31 May 1922), col. 2125.

10 *Ibid.*, col. 2129.

11 *Ibid.*, cols 2131–41.

12 *Ibid.*, cols 2129–33.

13 *Ibid.*, col. 2138.

14 *Ibid.*, col. 2148.

15 *Ibid.*, cols 2166–7.

16 *Ibid.*, col. 2139.

17 *Irish Independent*, 1 June 1922.

18 Diarmuid O'Hegarty to Churchill, *The Irish Times*, 1 June 1922.

19 Churchill, Winston S., *The Aftermath* (London, 1929), p. 336.

20 *The Times* (London), 1 June 1922.

21 *Westminster Gazette*, 1 June 1922.

22 *Ibid.*

23 Hankey, diary, 23 May 1920, in Roskill, Stephen, *Hankey: Man*

of Secrets. Volume II: *1919–1931* (London, 1972), p. 153.

24   Wilson, diary, 14 October 1920, in Callwell, C. E., *Field-Marshal Sir Henry Wilson: His Life and Diaries* (London, 1927), 2, p. 265.

25   Gilbert, Martin, *Winston S. Churchill: World in Torment*, Vol. 4 (London, 1975), pp. 725–6.

26   Diary entry for 2 June 1922, Jones, *Whitehall Diary*. Vol. III, p. 209.

27   Minutes of Provisional Government, 3 June 1922, NAI.

28   McMahon, *British Spies*, p. 145.

29   Instructions to Intelligence Officers, 6 June 1922, *ibid.*

21 'Worse than Armenian atrocities'

1   Cope to Churchill, 5 June 1922, CP 4017, CAB24/137, TNAGB.

2   Gilbert, Martin, *Winston S. Churchill: World in Torment*, Vol. 4 (London, 1975), p. 727.

3   Churchill to Collins, 6 June 1922, CAB24/137, TNAGB.

4   *Ibid.*

5   Diary entry for 7 June 1922, Jones, Thomas, *Whitehall Diary*. Vol. III: *Ireland, 1918–25* (London, 1971), p. 210.

6   Churchill to Lloyd George, 7 June 1922, in Gilbert, *Churchill*, 4, p. 728.

7   Lloyd George to Churchill, 8 June 1922, *ibid.*, pp. 729–30.

8   *Ibid.*

9   Macready, report for week ending 3 June 1922, CP 4022, CAB24/137, TNAGB.

10   Lloyd George to Churchill, 8 June 1922, in Gilbert, *Churchill*, 4, pp. 729–30.

11   *Ibid.*

12   *Ibid.*

13   Churchill to Lloyd George, 8 June 1922, in Churchill, Winston S., *The Aftermath* (London, 1929), p. 338.

14   Gilbert, *Churchill*, 4, p. 731.

15   Churchill, *The Aftermath*, pp. 338–9.

16   *The Freeman's Journal*, 10 June 1922.

17   *Ibid.*

18   Collins interview with Clyde A. Beales, *The Freeman's Journal*, 12 June 1922.

19   *Ibid.*

20   *Ibid.*

21   *Ibid.*

22   Collins, notes, undated, Collins Papers.

23   *The Freeman's Journal*, editorial, 12 June 1922.

24   Churchill, *The Aftermath*, p. 336.

22 'Collins might appoint a charwoman'

1   Churchill to Craig, 10 June 1922.

2   Hansard (House of Commons), *Debates*, 155 (14 June 1922), col. 363.

3   Bates to Craig, 15 June 1922, in Coogan, Tim Pat, *Michael Collins: A Biography* (London, 1990), p. 369.

4   Spender to Tallents, 29 June 1922, *ibid.*, p. 371.

5   Lynch, Robert, *The Northern IRA and the Early Years of Partition* (Oxford, 2006), p. 253.

6   Cabinet conclusions, Cabinet 31(22), 1 June 1922, CAB23/30, TNAGB.

7   Cabinet conclusions, Cabinet 32(22), 2 June 1922, CAB23/30, TNAGB.

8   *Ibid.*

9   *Ibid.*

10   Griffith to Lloyd George, 2 June 1922, CP 4014, CAB24/137, TNAGB.

11   De Valera to Griffith, 16 October 1921, DE2/304, NAI.

12   Jones, Thomas, *Whitehall Diary*. Vol. III: *Ireland, 1918–25* (London, 1971), p. 199.

13   *The Irish Times*, 12 June 1922.

14   *Nenagh Guardian*, 17 June 1922.

15   *Irish Independent* and *The Irish Times*, 12 June 1922.

16   *The Irish Times*, 13 June 1922.

17 *The Freeman's Journal*, 20 November 1922.
18 *Irish Independent*, 14 June 1922.

23 'YOU UNDERSTAND FULLY WHAT YOU HAVE TO DO'

1   *The Irish Times*, 15 June 1922.
2   *The Freeman's Journal*, 15 June 1922.
3   *The Irish Times*, 15 June 1922.
4   *Ibid.*
5   *The Freeman's Journal*, 16 June 1922.
6   *Irish Independent*, 19 June 1922.
7   Collins notes, Mulcahy Papers, P7/B/28, UCDA.
8   *Ibid.*
9   Fitzpatrick, David, *Harry Boland's Irish Revolution* (Cork, 2003), p. 301.
10 Boland, diary, *ibid.*, p. 299.
11 *The Irish Times*, 22 June 1922.
12 Macready, report dated 11 July 1922, CP 4101, CAB24/138, TNAGB.
13 MacEoin, Civil War Notes, MacEoin Papers, P151/1808, UCDA.
14 Macready, report for week ending 1 July 1922, CP 4085, CAB24/137, TNAGB.
15 Dwyer, T. Ryle, *Big Fellow, Long Fellow: A Joint Biography of Collins and de Valera* (Dublin, 1998), p. 306.

24 'THE SAFETY OF THE NATION IS THE FIRST LAW'

1   Lloyd George to Collins, 22 June 1922, Provisional Government Minutes, 23 June 1922, G1/2, NAI.
2   Hart, Peter, *The IRA at War, 1916–1923* (Oxford, 2004), p. 201.
3   Joseph Sweeney interview, O'Malley Papers, P17b/97, UCDA.
4   De Valera, Éamon, *Speeches and Statements by Éamon de Valera, 1917–1973*, ed. M. Moynihan (Dublin, 1980), pp. 105–6.
5   Lloyd George to Collins, 22 June 1922, Provisional Government Minutes, 23 June 1922, G1/2, NAI.

6   Macready, General Sir Nevil, *Annals of an Active Life*, Vol. 2 (London, 1924), pp. 653–4.
7   McMahon, Paul, *British Spies and Irish Rebels: British Intelligence and Ireland 1916–1945* (Woodbridge, 2008), p. 143.
8   Hansard (House of Commons), *Debates*, 155 (26 June 1922), col. 1712.
9   *Ibid.*
10 O'Connor, Frank, *The Big Fellow: Michael Collins and the Irish Revolution*, rev. edn (Dublin, 1965), p. 207.
11 Cope to Lionel Curtis, 27 June 1922, in Hopkinson, Michael, *Green Against Green: The Irish Civil War* (Dublin, 1988), p. 118.
12 Hansard (House of Commons), *Debates*, 155 (27 June 1922), cols 1822–3.
13 *Ibid.*, col. 1823.
14 Collins, statement to INS, *Irish Independent*, 29 June 1922.
15 *Ibid.*
16 Hugh Martin's report, *Weekly Freeman*, 1 July 1922.
17 Cuthbert, Jim, 'Beware of the Deal', *Scottish Left Review*, 46 (May–June 2008). This on-line review is available at http://www.scottishleftreview.org (accessed 23 February 2012).
18 Hansard (House of Commons), *Debates*, 156 (12 July 1922), col. 1210.
19 *Ibid.*, 156 (18 July 1922), col. 1882.
20 Churchill to Collins, 30 June 1922, in Forester, Margery, *Michael Collins: The Lost Leader* (London, 1971), p. 323.
21 De Valera to Cathal Ó Murchada, 13 September 1922, quoted in *The Freeman's Journal*, 16 October 1922.
22 De Valera, statement, 28 June 1922, in Dwyer, T. Ryle, *De Valera: The Man and the Myths* (Dublin, 1991), p. 113.
23 J. F. Homan, diary, 1 July 1922, NLI, in Young, Peter, 'Michael Collins a

Military Leader', in Gabriel Doherty and Dermot Keogh, eds, *Michael Collins and the Making of the Irish State* (Cork, 1998), pp. 86–7.

24   Homan, diary, 2 July 1922, *ibid.*, p. 87.

25   *Ibid.*, p. 88.

26   Collins, notebook, 1 July 1922, in Taylor, Rex, *Michael Collins* (London, 1958), p. 193.

25 'KEEP OPEN SOME AVENUE OR AVENUES TO PEACE'

1   *Irish Independent*, 1 July 1922.

2   Johnson to Diarmuid O'Hegarty, 1 July 1922, S.1332B, NAI.

3   Dwyer, T. Ryle, *Big Fellow, Long Fellow: A Joint Biography of Collins and de Valera* (Dublin, 1998), p. 311.

4   Collins interview with *Sunday Express*, 2 July 1922, *The Freeman's Journal*, 3 July 1922.

5   Erskine Childers to Molly Childers, 12 July 1922, Childers Papers, MS 7855, TCD.

6   Collins memo in letter to Thomas Gay, 24 July 1922, in Béaslaí, Piaras, *Michael Collins and the Making of a New Ireland*, Vol. 2 (Dublin, 1926), pp. 43–4.

7   Dwyer, *Big Fellow, Long Fellow*, p. 312.

8   Collins to John O'Kane, 17 July 1922, in Taylor, Rex, *Michael Collins* (London, 1958), p. 193.

9   Collins to Griffith, 14 July 1922, MacEoin Papers, P151/106, UCDA.

10   Provisional Government address to Collins, *Sunday Independent*, 16 July 1922.

11   Young, Peter, 'Michael Collins a Military Leader', in Gabriel Doherty and Dermot Keogh, eds, *Michael Collins and the Making of the Irish State* (Cork, 1998), pp. 89–90.

12   De Valera to Joe McGarrity, 10 September 1922, quoted in Cronin, Seán, *The McGarrity Papers* (Tralee, 1972),

p. 125. Other quotes from Collins, Stephen, *The Cosgrave Legacy* (Dublin, 1996), pp. 28–30.

13   Cosgrave to Collins, 14 July 1922, in Coogan, Tim Pat, *Michael Collins: A Biography* (London, 1990), p. 393.

14   Churchill, memo, 31 July 1922, CAB24/138, TNAGB.

15   Collins to Kathleen MacKenna, 18 July 1922, in Kathleen Napoli MacKenna Papers, MS 22,600, NLI.

16   Dwyer, T. Ryle, *Michael Collins: The Man Who Won the War* (Cork, 2008), pp. 98–100.

17   Collins to Eugene Gayer, 23 July 1922, Mary MacSwiney Papers, UCDA.

18   Collins to Thomas Gay, 24 July 1922, in Béaslaí, *Collins*, 2, p. 411.

19   Collins to Cosgrave, 25 July 1922, in Hopkinson, Michael, *Green Against Green: The Irish Civil War* (Dublin, 1988), pp. 139–40.

20   De Valera to Cathal Brugha, 6 July 1922, Mary MacSwiney Papers, UCDA.

21   Churchill, memo, 31 July 1922, CAB24/138, TNAGB.

22   Collins draft note for Provisional Government, 26 July 1922, Mulcahy Papers, P7/B/28, UCDA.

23   *Ibid.*

24   Collins to Mulcahy, 26 July 1922, Mulcahy Papers, P7a/57, UCDA.

25   Dwyer, *Big Fellow, Long Fellow*, p. 315.

26   Cosgrave to Collins, 27 July 1922, in Regan, John M., *The Irish Counter-Revolution, 1921–1936: Treatyite Politics and Settlement in Independent Ireland* (Dublin, 1999), p. 106.

27   Collins to Harry Boland, 28 July 1922, in Taylor, *Collins*, p. 194.

28   Collins to Government, 29 July 1922, in Regan, *Irish Counter-Revolution*, p. 106.

29   E. Blythe, book review, *The Irish Times*, 13 July 1966.

30 Collins to Kitty Kiernan, *circa* 2 August 1922, in Ó Broin, Leon, *In Great Haste: The Letters of Michael Collins and Kitty Kiernan* (Dublin, 1983), p. 210.
31 *Ibid.*
32 Kiernan to Collins, 4 August 1922, *ibid.*, p. 211.
33 Collins to Kiernan, 4 August 1922, *ibid.*, p. 212.

26 'DOGGING THE FORTUNES OF IRELAND'

1 Collins to Thomas Gay, 1 August 1922, in Béaslaí, Piaras, *Michael Collins and the Making of a New Ireland*, Vol. 2 (Dublin, 1926), p. 413.
2 Ó Cuill to Collins, 1 August 1922, quoted in *Sunday Independent*, 6 August 1922.
3 *Ibid.*
4 Collins to Ó Cuill, 4 August 1922, quoted in *The Irish Times*, 7 August 1922.
5 *Ibid.*
6 *Daily Mail*, 30 June 1922.
7 Cosgrave to Collins, 14 July 1922, in Coogan, Tim Pat, *Michael Collins: A Biography* (London, 1990), p. 382.
8 Mulcahy to Collins, 24 July 1922, *ibid.*
9 Collins to Churchill, 25 July 1922, in Dwyer, T. Ryle, *Big Fellow, Long Fellow: A Joint Biography of Collins and de Valera* (Dublin, 1998), p. 319.
10 Churchill to Collins, 31 July 1922, CAB43/2, TNAGB.
11 Coogan, *Collins*, p. 379.
12 *Ibid.*, p. 396.
13 Affidavit of Thomas A. Kelly, in Ryan, Meda, *The Day Michael Collins Was Shot* (Dublin, 1989), p. 35.
14 Coogan, *Collins*, p. 383.
15 'Ulster Month' refers to the one month given to withdraw from the Treaty which applied to all of Ireland; if it did withdraw the boundary commission
would be set up. Collins to Churchill, 9 August 1922, in Gilbert, Martin, *Winston S. Churchill: World in Torment*, Vol. 4 (London, 1975), p. 744.
16 Collins to Cosgrave, 5 August 1922, Mulcahy Papers, P7/B/28, UCDA.
17 Collins to Cosgrave, 6 August 1922, *ibid.*, P7/B/29.
18 Collins to Kitty Kiernan, 8 August 1922, in Ó Broin, Leon, *In Great Haste: The Letters of Michael Collins and Kitty Kiernan* (Dublin, 1983), p. 213.
19 Collins to McGrath, 9 August 1922, in Coogan, *Collins*, p. 398.
20 Collins to Cosgrave, 6 August 1922, Mulcahy Papers, P7/B/29, UCDA.
21 *The Freeman's Journal*, 14 August 1922.
22 *Ibid.*
23 *Ibid.*
24 *The Freeman's Journal*, 16 August 1922.
25 Béaslaí, *Collins*, 2, pp. 424–5.
26 Hayden Talbot interview, *Southern Star*, 26 August 1922.
27 *Ibid.*
28 For statement issued to press by Provisional Government on 'the surrender of Dublin Castle', see pp. 20–1 of this text.

27 'WHAT MATTER IF FOR IRELAND DEAR WE FALL'

1 G.B. Shaw, interview, *The Irish Times*, 21 August 1922.
2 Collins to Director of Publicity, 19 August 1922, Kathleen Napoli MacKenna Papers, MS 22,779, NLI.
3 Lynch-Robinson, Sir Christopher, *The Last of the R.M.s* (London, 1951), p. 170.
4 *Ibid.*, p. 171.
5 Quoted in *The Irish Times*, 24 August 1922.
6 *The Irish Times*, 21 August 1922.
7 *Ibid.*
8 Macready, report for week ending 19 August 1922, CAB24/138, TNAGB.

9   Coogan, Tim Pat, *Michael Collins: A Biography* (London, 1990), p. 385.

10   Brennan, Robert, *Allegiance* (Dublin, 1950), p. 352.

11   De Valera, diary, 13 August 1922, in Longford, Earl of, and Thomas P. O'Neill, *Éamon de Valera* (Dublin, 1970), p. 198.

12   Ryan, Meda, *The Day Michael Collins Was Shot* (Dublin, 1989), p. 61.

13   Dwyer, T. Ryle, *Big Fellow, Long Fellow: A Joint Biography of Collins and de Valera* (Dublin, 1998), p. 323.

14   Deasy, Liam, *Brother Against Brother* (Cork, 1982), pp. 76–7.

15   Collins, notebook, 21 August 1922, quoted in *Sunday Independent*, 10 May 1964.

16   Deasy, *Brother Against Brother*, pp. 77–8.

17   Dwyer, *Big Fellow, Long Fellow*, p. 325.

18   John Collins interview, *Sunday Independent*, 10 May 1964.

19   Dalton, interview, in Ó Broin, Leon, *Michael Collins* (Dublin, 1980), p. 143.

20   Dalton, interview, in Twohig, Patrick J., *The Dark Shadow of Béalnabláth* (Cork, 1991), p. 59.

21   *Ibid.*

22   Dalton, interview, in Ó Broin, *Collins*, p. 43.

23   Dalton, interview, in Twohig, *Dark Shadow*, p. 60.

24   *Ibid.*, p. 59.

25   *Ibid.*, p. 163.

26   Ryan, *The Day Michael Collins was Shot*, p. 110.

27   Emmet Dalton, interviewed by Cormac MacCathaigh, *Sunday Independent*, 23 August 1970.

28   *Ibid.*

28 'HANG UP YOUR BRIGHTEST COLOURS'

1   Emmet Dalton, interviewed by Cormac MacCathaigh, *Sunday Independent*, 23 August 1970.

2   Ryan, Meda, *The Day Michael Collins Was Shot* (Dublin, 1989), p. 113.

3   Mackay, James, *Michael Collins: A Life* (Edinburgh, 1996), p. 291.

4   Cronin, Seán, *The McGarrity Papers* (Tralee, 1972), p. 123.

5   Shaw to Hannie Collins, 25 August 1922, in Taylor, Rex, *Michael Collins* (London, 1958), pp. 209–10.

6   Aiken to Mulcahy, 27 August 1922, Mulcahy Papers, P7a/178, UCDA.

7   Stack to McGarrity, 27 August 1922, in Gaughan, J. Anthony, *Austin Stack: Portrait of a Separatist* (Tralee, 1977), p. 216.

8   Twohig, Patrick J., *The Dark Shadow of Béalnabláth* (Cork, 1991), p. 226.

9   Canon Jeremiah Cohalan, address in Bandon, 8 September 1927, *Irish Independent*, 15 September 1927.

10   Fr P. Tracy, PP, to *The Cork Examiner*, 14 September 1927.

11   Béaslaí, Piaras, *Michael Collins and the Making of a New Ireland*, Vol. 1 (Dublin, 1926), p. 80.

12   MacDowell, Vincent, *Michael Collins and the Brotherhood* (Dublin, 1997), p. 112.

13   Lee, Joe, *Ireland 1912–1985: Politics and Society* (Cambridge, 1989), p. 103.

14   MacEoin, Notes on the Treaty, MacEoin Papers, P151/1799, UCDA.

15   Chamberlain, memo, 8 March 1932, in Fanning, Ronan, *The Department of Finance* (Dublin, 1978), p. 277.

16   Dwyer, T. Ryle, *Behind the Green Curtain: Ireland's Phoney Neutrality During World War II* (Dublin and New York, 2009), p. 6.

17   For more on the role of Haughey and Captain Kelly in the Arms Crisis see Dwyer, T. Ryle, *Haughey's Forty Years of Controversy* (Cork, 2005), pp. 42–51.

Bibliography

Unpublished sources

Official records

Bureau of Military History (BMH)
National Archives of Ireland (NAI)
National Library of Ireland (NLI)
The National Archives (TNAGB), Kew, London
Trinity College, Dublin (TCD)
University College, Dublin, Archives (UCDA)

Private papers

Aiken, Frank, Papers, UCDA
Barton, Robert C., Papers, NAI
Béaslaí, Piaras, Papers, NLI
Blythe, Ernest, Papers, UCDA
Blythe, Ernest, Witness Statement, BMH
Childers, R. Erskine, Papers and Diaries, TCD
Collins, Michael, Papers then in possession of the late Liam Collins, Clonakilty,
    County Cork
de Valera, Éamon, Papers, UCDA
Devoy, John, Papers, NLI
Dolan, Joe, Witness Statement, BMH
Doyle, Fr Paddy, Witness Statement, BMH
Johnson, Thomas, Papers, NLI
MacEoin, Seán, Papers, UCDA
McGarrity, Joseph, Papers, NLI
MacSwiney, Mary, Papers, UCDA
Mulcahy, Richard, Papers, UCDA
Napoli, Kathleen (*née* McKenna), Papers, NLI
O'Malley, Ernie, Papers, UCDA
Stack, Austin, Papers, NLI and a private source

Published material

Newspapers

Belfast Telegraph
Connaught Telegraph
Connaught Tribune

Kerry Leader
Kildare Observer
Morning Post

Cork Examiner, The   Nenagh Guardian
Daily Mail   New York Times, The
Daily News   Poblacht na h-Éireann
Daily Telegraph   Southern Star
Evening Echo (Cork)   Sunday Independent
Freeman's Journal, The   Times (London), The
Gaelic-American   Ulster Herald
Irish Independent   Weekly Freeman
Irish Times, The   Westmeath Examiner
Irish Weekly Times   Westminster Gazette

Books and journal articles

Béaslaí, Piaras, Michael Collins and the Making of a New Ireland, 2 vols (Dublin, 1926)

Birkenhead, Frederick, 2nd Earl of, The Life of F. E. Smith, First Earl of Birkenhead (London, 1960)

Borgonovo, John, Military History of the Irish Civil War: The Battle for Cork (Cork, 2011)

Bowman, John, De Valera and the Ulster Question, 1917–1973 (Oxford, 1982)

Boyle, Andrew, The Riddle of Erskine Childers (London, 1977)

Brasier, Andrew and John Kelly, Harry Boland: A Man Divided (Dublin, 2000)

Brennan, Robert, Allegiance (Dublin, 1950)

Callanan, Frank, T. M. Healy (Cork, 1998)

Callwell, C. E., Field-Marshal Sir Henry Wilson: His Life and Diaries, 2 vols (London, 1927)

Canning, Paul, British Policy Towards Ireland 1921–1941 (Oxford, 1985)

Chamberlain, Austen, Down the Years (London, 1935)

Churchill, Winston S., The Aftermath (London, 1929)

Churchill, Winston S., Thoughts and Adventures (London, 1932)

Collins, Michael, Arguments for the Treaty (Dublin, 1922)

Collins, Michael, The Path to Freedom (Dublin, 1922; reprinted Cork, 2011)

Collins, Stephen, The Cosgrave Legacy (Dublin, 1996)

Colum, Padraig, Arthur Griffith (Dublin, 1959)

Coogan, Tim Pat, Michael Collins: A Biography (London, 1990)

Coogan, Tim Pat, De Valera: Long Fellow, Long Shadow (London, 1993)

Costello, Francis, ed., Michael Collins: In His Own Words (Dublin, 1997)

Cronin, Seán, The McGarrity Papers (Tralee, 1972)

Curran, Joseph M., The Birth of the Irish Free State, 1921–1923 (Alabama, 1980)

Cuthbert, Jim, 'Beware of the Deal', Scottish Left Review, 46 (May–June 2008). This on-line review is available at http://www.scottishleftreview.org (accessed 23 February 2012)

Dáil Éireann, Private Sessions of Second Dáil (Dublin, nd)

Dáil Éireann, Official Correspondence Relating to Peace Negotiations, June–September 1921 (Dublin, 1921)

Dáil Éireann, Official Report: Debate on the Treaty between Great Britain and Ireland (Dublin, 1922)

Deasy, Liam, *Brother Against Brother* (Cork, 1982)

de Valera, Éamon, *Speeches and Statements by Éamon de Valera, 1917–1973*, ed. M. Moynihan (Dublin, 1980)

de Valera, Terry, *A Memoir* (Dublin, 2004)

de Vere White, T., *Kevin O'Higgins* (Tralee, 1966)

Doherty, Gabriel and Dermot Keogh, *Michael Collins and the Making of the Irish State* (Cork, 1998)

Douglas, James G., *Memoirs of Senator James G. Douglas: Concerned Citizen*, ed. by J. Anthony Gaughan (Dublin, 1998)

Durney, James, *The Civil War in Kildare* (Cork, 2011)

Dwyer, T. Ryle, *Éamon de Valera* (Dublin, 1980)

Dwyer, T. Ryle, *De Valera's Darkest Hour: In Search of National Independence, 1919–1932* (Dublin and Cork, 1982)

Dwyer, T. Ryle, *De Valera: The Man and the Myths* (Dublin, 1991)

Dwyer, T. Ryle, *Big Fellow, Long Fellow: A Joint Biography of Collins and de Valera* (Dublin, 1998)

Dwyer, T. Ryle, *Tans, Terror and Troubles: Kerry's Real Fighting Story* (Cork, 2001)

Dwyer, T. Ryle, *Haughey's Forty Years of Controversy* (Cork, 2005)

Dwyer, T. Ryle, *The Squad and the Intelligence Operations of Michael Collins* (Cork, 2005)

Dwyer, T. Ryle, *'I Signed My Death Warrant': Michael Collins & the Treaty* (Cork, 2007)

Dwyer, T. Ryle, *Michael Collins: The Man Who Won the War* (Cork, 2008)

Dwyer, T. Ryle, *Behind the Green Curtain: Ireland's Phoney Neutrality During World War II* (Dublin and New York, 2009)

Fanning, Ronan, *The Department of Finance* (Dublin, 1978)

Figgis, Darrell, *Recollections of the Irish War* (London, 1927)

Fitzpatrick, David, *Harry Boland's Irish Revolution* (Cork, 2003)

Forester, Margery, *Michael Collins: The Lost Leader* (London, 1971)

Foy, Michael T., *Michael Collins' Intelligence War: The Struggle between the British and the IRA 1919–1921* (Stroud, Gloucestershire, 2006)

Gallagher, Frank, *The Anglo-Irish Treaty* (London, 1971)

Gaughan, J. Anthony, *Austin Stack: Portrait of a Separatist* (Tralee, 1977)

Gilbert, Martin, *Winston S. Churchill: World in Torment*, 4 vols (London, 1975)

Gillis, Liz, *Military History of the Irish Civil War: The Fall of Dublin* (Cork, 2011)

Girvin, Kevin, *Seán O'Hegarty: O/C 1st Cork Brigade Irish Republican Army* (Mill-street, 2007)

Griffith, Arthur, *Arguments for the Treaty* (Dublin, 1922)

Griffith, Kenneth and Timothy E. O'Grady, *Curious Journey: An Oral History of Ireland's Unfinished Revolution* (Cork, 1982)

Hansard (House of Commons), *Debates*, vols 149–56 (London, 1921–2)

Hansard (House of Lords), *Debates*, vol. 49 (London, 1922)

Hart, Peter, *The IRA at War, 1916–1923* (Oxford, 2004)

Hart, Peter, *Mick: The Real Michael Collins* (London, 2005)

Hayes, Michael, 'Dáil Éireann and the Irish Civil War', *Studies*, 58 (Spring 1969), pp. 1–24

Healy, T. M., *Letters and Leaders of My Day*, 2 vols (London, 1928)

Hopkinson, Michael, *Green Against Green: The Irish Civil War* (Dublin, 1988)

Hopkinson, Michael, 'The Craig–Collins Pacts of 1922', *Irish Historical Studies*, 27 (1990), pp. 145–58

Jones, Thomas, *Whitehall Diary*. Vol. III: *Ireland, 1918–25* (London, 1971)

Kee, Robert, *Ireland: A History* (London, 1981)

Lawlor, Pearse, *The Outrages, 1920–1922: The IRA and the Ulster Special Constabulary in the Border Campaign* (Cork, 2011)

Lee, Joe, *Ireland 1912–1985: Politics and Society* (Cambridge, 1989)

Liam, Cathal, *Fear not the Storm: The Story of Tom Cullen, an Irish Revolutionary* (Cincinnati, 2011)

Lloyd George, David, *Is it Peace?* (London, 1923)

Longford, Earl of, and Thomas P. O'Neill, *Éamon de Valera* (Dublin, 1970)

Lynch, Robert, *The Northern IRA and the Early Years of Partition* (Oxford, 2006)

Lynch-Robinson, Sir Christopher, *The Last of the R.M.s* (London, 1951)

Macardle, Dorothy, *The Irish Republic* (London, 1968)

MacBride, Seán, *That Day's Struggle: A Memoir, 1904–1951* (Dublin, 2005)

MacDowell, Vincent, *Michael Collins and the Brotherhood* (Dublin, 1997)

MacEoin, Uinseann, *Survivors* (Dublin, 1980)

Mackay, James, *Michael Collins: A Life* (Edinburgh, 1996)

MacManus, M. J., *Éamon de Valera* (Dublin, 1944)

Macready, General Sir Nevil, *Annals of an Active Life*, 2 vols (London, 1924)

Maher, Jim, *Harry Boland: A Biography* (Cork, 1998)

Makey, James, *Michael Collins: A Life* (Edinburgh and London, 1996)

McColgan, John, *British Policy and the Irish Administration, 1920–22* (London, 1983)

McCoole, Sinéad, *Hazel: A Life of Lady Lavery, 1880–1935* (Dublin, 1996)

McGarry, Fearghal, *Eoin O'Duffy: A Self-Made Hero* (Oxford, 2005)

McMahon, Paul, *British Spies and Irish Rebels: British Intelligence and Ireland 1916–1945* (Woodbridge, 2008)

McNiffe, Liam, *A History of the Garda Síochána: A Social History of the Force, 1922–52* (Dublin, 1997)

Neeson, Eoin, *The Civil War in Ireland, 1922–1923* (Cork, 1966)

Nicholson, Harold, *King George V* (London, 1952)

O'Brien, William, *Forth the Banners Go* (Dublin, 1969)

Ó Broin, Leon, *Revolutionary Underground: The Story of the Irish Republican Brotherhood, 1858–1924* (Dublin, 1976)

Ó Broin, Leon, *Michael Collins* (Dublin, 1980)

Ó Broin, Leon, *In Great Haste: The Letters of Michael Collins and Kitty Kiernan* (Dublin, 1983)

O'Callaghan, John, *Military History of the Irish Civil War: The Battle for Kilmallock* (Cork, 2011)

O'Connor, Batt, *With Michael Collins in the Fight for Irish Independence* (London, 1929)

O'Connor, Frank, *The Big Fellow: Michael Collins and the Irish Revolution*, rev. edn (Dublin, 1965)

Ó Cuinneagáin, Mícheal, *On the Arm of Time: Ireland 1916–1922* (Donegal, 1992)

Ó Duibhir, Liam, *Donegal & the Civil War: The Untold Story* (Cork, 2011)

O'Farrell, Padraic, *The Seán MacEoin Story* (Cork, 1981)

Official Correspondence Relating to the Peace Negotiations, see www.ucc.ie/celt/published/E900003-007/text001.html (accessed 23 February 2012)

O'Hegarty, P. S., *A History of Ireland under the Union, 1801–1922* (London, 1952)

O'Higgins, Kevin, *Civil War and the Events which Led to It* (Dublin, 1922)

O'Malley, Ernie, *The Singing Flame: A Memoir of the Civil War, 1922–24* (Dublin, 1978)

Ó Ruairc, Pádraig, *Military History of the Irish Civil War: The Battle for Limerick City* (Cork, 2010)

Osborne, Chrissy, *Michael Collins Himself* (Cork, 2003)

Pakenham, Frank, *Peace by Ordeal*, rev. edn (London, 1967)

Regan, John M., *The Irish Counter-Revolution, 1921–1936: Treatyite Politics and Settlement in Independent Ireland* (Dublin, 1999)

Riddell, Lord, *Intimate Diary of the Peace Conference and After, 1918–1923* (London, 1933)

Robinson, Sir Henry, *Memoirs: Wise and Otherwise* (London, 1923)

Roskill, Stephen, *Hankey: Man of Secrets*. Volume II: *1919–1931* (London, 1972)

Ryan, Meda, *The Day Michael Collins Was Shot* (Dublin, 1989)

Ryan, Meda, *Michael Collins and the Women in His Life* (Cork, 1996)

Salvidge, Stanley, *Salvidge of Liverpool* (London, 1934)

Shakespeare, Sir Geoffrey, *Let Candles Be Brought In* (London, 1949)

Stevenson, Frances, *Lloyd George: A Diary* (New York, 1971)

Sturgis, Mark, *The Last Days of Dublin Castle: The Diaries of Mark Sturgis*, ed. Michael Hopkinson (Dublin, 1999)

Talbot, Hayden, *Michael Collins' Own Story* (London, 1923)

Taylor, Rex, *Michael Collins* (London, 1958)

Taylor, Rex, *Assassination: The Death of Sir Henry Wilson and the Tragedy of Ireland* (London, 1961)

Towey, Thomas, 'The Reaction of the British Government to the 1922 Collins–de Valera Pact', *Irish Historical Studies*, 22 (March 1980), pp. 65–76

Twohig, Patrick J., *The Dark Shadow of Béalnabláth* (Cork, 1991)

Valiulis, Maryann Gialanella, *Portrait of a Revolutionary: General Richard Mulcahy and the Founding of the Irish Free State* (Dublin, 1992)

Winter, Ormonde, *Winter's Tale* (London, 1955)

Young, Peter, 'Michael Collins a Military Leader', in Gabriel Doherty and Dermot Keogh (eds), *Michael Collins and the Making of the Irish State* (Cork, 1998), pp. 81–91

Younger, Calton, *Ireland's Civil War* (London, 1968)

INDEX